D1241505

JAMES WHITE

Virgil Robinson

JAMES WHITE

Review and Herald Publishing Association
Washington, D.C. 20012

28629

rh

Credits: Photographs on p. 130, courtesy
of the General Conference Archives;
p. 147, Ellen G. White Estate

BOOKS BY VIRGIL E. ROBINSON

Cabin Boy to Advent Crusader

Hudson Taylor, Man of Faith

John Nevins Andrews, Flame for the Lord

The Judsons of Burma

Luther the Leader

Magnificent Missionary

Mighty Mary

Only in Africa

and others

DEDICATION

To the Adventist Church leaders around the world
who are building upon the foundations
laid by James White a century ago.

ABOUT THIS BOOK

At James White's death at the age of 60, a fellow editor and publisher, George Willard, of the Battle Creek *Journal,* a former Congressman representing the State of Michigan, wrote of his patriarchal character, his heroic mold, his logical clearness, and the power to infect others with his own zeal. Then he observed, "If executive ability to establish a sect and to give it form and stability; if the genius to shape and direct the destiny of great communities, be a mark of true greatness, Elder White is certainly entitled to the appellation."

Yet James White is little known today, except as one of the triumvirate of pioneers of the Seventh-day Adventist Church. Of the James and Ellen White team, the distaff member is now best known, for she was nearer to our time, having outlived her husband by 34 years, and because of her unique role as the Lord's messenger, with more than half a hundred books in current circulation.

Those with a good knowledge of Seventh-day Adventist history recognize the important place filled by James White—apostle, author, executive, and driving power in the development of the church. Nearer the time of his active service, such books as *Life Incidents in Connection With the Great Advent Movement* (1868) and *Life Sketches of Elder James White and His Wife, Ellen G. White* (1880) acquainted Adventists with his vision, drive, and his large contribution to the founding and upbuilding of the church. But these books have been long out of print.

To provide an interesting, accurate, and enlightening account of the life of James White, Virgil Robinson was asked to dig into the early records and write this volume. He began this project when his retirement from active educational work allowed him time for the months of research required for the task. Available to him were rich sources of the Ellen G. White Estate offices; the vault at the General Conference headquarters, stocked with the full file of the *Review and Herald*, the leading journal founded by James White and, for thirty years, directly or indirectly edited by him; other journals of his founding; the files of James and Ellen White correspondence and correspondence from leading Adventist workers; the W. C. White papers; et cetera. Also available to him were the archives of the General Conference.

Robinson, well known in Adventist circles, carries credentials as a teacher of history, both church and secular. By paternity he is the great-grandson of James and Ellen White on his mother's side, and on his father's side, the great-grandson of William Farnsworth, one of the very first Seventh-day Adventists.

This well-written account, constructed from the documents of the time of James White, makes that noble, yet very human, man live. May the knowledge of his dedication, his vision, his sacrifice, and his innate confidence in the triumph of the church, inspire the generation who must carry to its conclusion the work he, under the leadings of God's Spirit, began so well.

Arthur L. White, Secretary
ELLEN G. WHITE ESTATE

CONTENTS

Chapter One

SON OF MAINE

DEACON John White had much for which to be thankful that sunny August morning. His wife had just been safely delivered of a son, their fifth child. A fixed believer in the promises of Scripture, the deacon agreed fully with the psalmist when he observed: "Children are an heritage of the Lord," and, "Happy is the man that hath his quiver full of them" (Ps. 127:3, 5).

But even while looking over his hillside farm and meditating pridefully on his expanding household, he must have had a nagging worry about how he could possibly provide for them all. At the time this latest baby was born the good deacon had already lived on the farm for 15 years. On that land one could toil and sweat, plowing the thin soil over the rock so near the surface, year after year, always finding that the rewards were too small in proportion to the amount of energy expended.

It was just as well that the deacon had no way of knowing that eventually there would be a total of nine children. Besides the tiny newborn, there would later be added to the family young Benjamin, the adventurous one, doomed to be killed by Indians as he was returning from a gold-seeking expedition to the far West; Anna and Nathaniel, neither of whom would live to be 30; and a last-born, Joseph, who would be carried to the family burial ground at the age of 3, felled by one of the childhood diseases so prevalent in the early 1800's. Of the entire family, only Joseph would find a final resting place in the family plot near White's Pond in the township of Palmyra, Maine.[1]

But the present was cheerful. When the deacon entered his house he saw around the breakfast table the smiling faces of Mary, John, Elizabeth, and Samuel—his and Betsy's children. From the bedroom came a small wail, indicating that the newest arrival was

already making his wants known.*

When breakfast was finished Mary asked, "What are you going to name the baby, Father?"

"We'll call him James Springer," answered the deacon. "Fetch the Bible, John. We'll write his name in it now."

John went to the parlor and returned with the Sacred Book, which he handed to his father. The deacon turned to the family register. There were the names of the parents with the date of their wedding, followed by the listing of the children, each with his birth date. In the first blank space Deacon John wrote, "James Springer White, August 4, 1821."

A Sunday or two later the family walked proudly into the sanctuary of the Christian church. Betsy White carried Baby James in her arms, as they all filed into the pew the deacon had rented. Twelve-year-old John thought his father looked very fine—the deacon wore Sunday-best clothes, which were adorned with the heirloom pair of silver knee buckles that had been handed down by generations of John White's family. Young John thought, Someday they will be mine.

Perhaps during the church service the father reminisced a bit. He may have remembered how he had moved to Palmyra when he was 21 years old, and soon afterward bought his farm, on which only twenty acres of forest had been cleared.

A devout Christian, Father John first joined the local Congregational church. An earnest seeker for truth, as well as a Bible student, he established the first Sunday school in the entire State of Maine.[2] When he became convinced that immersion was the only proper form of baptism he joined the Baptist Church and remained a member for ten years, after which he again changed his religious affiliation, joining the Christian Church, where he now served as a deacon.[3]

We can be sure that, except on Sunday, everyone was kept busy on the farm, and each child was expected to do his share of the work. The girls no doubt helped their mother with the numerous household tasks essential in New England homes a century and a half ago. The boys slept in a room directly over their father's bed-

---

* Occasionally in this book, conversation and descriptive material of a minor nature have been supplied to add human interest. However, in each case the material comports with known facts.—THE EDITORS.

The house at Palmyra, Maine, in which James White was born, August 4, 1821.

room. Even in winter, long before daylight, it was the duty of the boys to take care of the animals.

We can imagine Father White going to the foot of the stairs and calling out vigorously, "Time to get up, boys." If he heard no movement he would probably pound on the low ceiling, shouting at the same time, "Boys, boys, let me hear your feet on the floor." They were wise to heed that request; for father's word was law, and woe betide the child who forgot or ignored that fact.

Work on the farm was seasonal, but the deacon was determined that his sons should be kept busy the whole year. The problem was, What could he find for them to do, especially during the long winter evenings? He solved the problem by learning the shoemaker's trade himself, then teaching it to each of his boys. The boots and shoes they made were sturdy, and there was never any trouble selling them.[4]

But the children were doubtless allowed some time for wholesome recreation. In winter there probably was skating on White's Pond, and sleigh rides over the glistening snow, ranging far over the white, sparkling roadways. There were also merry times in the farmhouse. On the cold, dark winter evenings we can imagine the family gathering around a roaring fire, roasting chestnuts, or cracking nuts while Father White told stories of the long ago. Sometimes, perhaps, he would read to them from Washington Irving's or James Fenimore Cooper's latest books.

In contrast to his sturdy brothers and sisters, Baby James was a sickly child. Betsy White often wondered whether he would live to reach manhood. Before he was 3 he fell ill with what doctors called worm fever, which resulted in severe fits. After weeks of sickness he recovered, but his eyes remained badly crossed. This condition continued for many years.

"I am reported to have been . . . a feeble, nervous, partially-blind boy," wrote James in later years, recalling his childhood. When he was 7 he went with his brothers and sisters to the local school, hoping that somehow he might learn to read. It was hard enough for the best student in those days. Many years later John, James's elder brother, described the school of those long-ago years:

"How different now the opportunities for an education to those we found in the old Palmyra schoolhouse a half century ago.

Every winter we would get over in old Webster as far as booby—
then go home and work it all out of body and brain. And next
winter, repeat the farce." [5]

All efforts made by James White to learn to read were fruit-
less. The letters ran together, making word recognition impossible. It seemed he would be forced to accept the bleak prospect that
he would probably have to go through life as an illiterate.

Though James's mental growth was hindered, his physical development was remarkable. He became his father's right-hand
man on the farm. By the time he was 18 years old he was six feet
tall and exceptionally strong physically.

Then, in his late teens, something akin to a miracle happened
to James. His eyes became normal, and he found the letters of the
alphabet clear and understandable. With determination he enrolled as a student in the local academy at St. Albans. When this
19-year-old six-footer presented himself to the teacher he was told
he would have to take his place among the beginning pupils. Many
of his friends laughed at him and advised him to stick to farming
for the rest of his life. But, like a thirsty animal suddenly discover-
ing a spring of water in a desert, James threw himself into his
studies. The school term was only twelve weeks long. So devot-
edly did the young man apply himself to his studies that when the
term closed, the schoolmaster handed him a certificate stating that
the bearer was qualified to teach the common branches. With this
in hand he secured a position and taught school the following winter. He soon discovered it was necessary for him to study long
hours each day to keep ahead of his pupils, but nothing daunted
him.

Deacon White, though sorry to lose James's help on the farm,
did what he could to aid his son in obtaining an education. When
James was ready to resume his studies his father gave him a suit of
clothing, three dollars for his tuition, and a ration of bread—
enough to last a week. Each Monday for three months James
walked five miles to the academy, returning home the following
Saturday evening to get his weekly supply of bread.

Determined to gain his education independent of parental aid,
James began looking for employment when school closed. Hearing
of an opening at a sawmill on the Penobscot River, he walked the
forty miles and was hired by the mill owners.

2

The work was new to him. Shortly after starting, he cut his ankle severely and was forced to quit work for a while. This cost him several weeks' wages and also resulted in crippling his foot, so that for many years he walked with a limp. At the end of that summer, with thirty dollars he had managed to save at the sawmill, he returned home, collected his books and clothing, and enrolled at the Methodist school at Reedfield.

During the three months he spent at this school his diet consisted of corn-meal pudding, which he cooked himself, and raw apples. He studied so faithfully that, when the term was over, the headmaster told him that with one more semester of schooling he could qualify to enter college. James returned home, delighted with this prospect and determined that nothing should interfere with his plan to gain a college education.

What James did not know was that his school days were over. The twelve weeks he had spent in primary school and the twenty-nine weeks he had spent in various higher schools of learning were all the formal education he would ever enjoy. That winter he taught a large school and saved his money, hoping with the money to further his education.

At the age of 15, James had been baptized and had joined the Christian Church, of which his parents were members. But his religious experience had been formal. As he plunged into his schoolwork as scholar and teacher, he laid aside the cross and fixed his heart on worldly goals. James was never wicked. He never swore, used liquor or tobacco, or committed any criminal acts. There was just no time, he thought, for religious things in his life.

James had not been long at home when his mother brought up a subject that was to interest many people profoundly in the early 1840's.

"Do you know, James," she said, "that Brother Oakes from Boston has been holding meetings in the schoolhouse, proving from the Bible that Jesus will return to earth about 1843? Many people in this neighborhood believe that what he says is true, and they have been converted." [6]

James frowned. He had heard of this doctrine and rejected it as wild and fanciful.

"Do you mean he is a Millerite?"

"I suppose you might call him that," his mother replied, "although his teachings come from the Bible, and not from any man."

"But, Mother," James protested, "William Miller is simply a fanatic on this subject. He claims to know more than Jesus Himself, who said He did not know the day nor the hour of His return."

But the young student was soon to discover that his mother was more than a match for him. She had the answer to every objection he advanced. To please her, James attended the meetings to see for himself whether the message was based on Scripture. Night after night, as he listened to powerful sermons and heard the testimonies of his school friends, he became convinced that God was leading in the Advent movement. Thus James was brought face to face with some weighty decisions. The conviction that it was his duty to help warn the world of impending destruction swept over him.

But this feeling brought him unhappiness. What would happen to his former ambitions? Was he to give up all plans to gain an education and amount to something in the world? [7]

Painful as it was, the conviction that it was his duty to help warn the world of Christ's soon return continued to strengthen. If He was coming in three years, nothing else was really of much importance. James was gripped by the impression that it was his duty to return to the community where he had taught the previous winter, visit and pray with his former pupils, and thus bear witness for Christ.

The struggle was severe. At first he felt it was an impossible call. He wept and prayed, begging the Lord to remove the burden. He thought of his unsatisfied thirst for an education. He tramped the fields, hoping that the impression might pass. But the conviction became stronger than ever. Visit your scholars! Visit your scholars!

There he stood, under the open sky. As the thought of all his former hopes and plans swept over him, he decided that the sacrifice would be too great. Stamping his foot on the ground, he looked up and almost shouted his answer.

"I will not go!"

Five minutes later he was back in his room, packing his books and clothing, getting ready to leave for Newport Academy. He borrowed one of his father's horses, packed a few necessities in saddlebags, mounted, and rode out of the yard. James White had set his course. He was going to get an education, and nothing could turn him from his goal. [8]

So he thought! [8]

---

[1] James White, *Life Incidents* (Battle Creek, Mich.; 1868), pp. 9-19. Much of the material in this chapter is based on the first part of *Life Incidents*.

[2] James White, "Sabbath-Schools," in *The Review and Herald*, Aug. 22, 1878, p. 68.

[3] *Life Incidents*, pp. 10, 11.

[4] Letter written by James White's nephew, son of Samuel White (Boston, Massachusetts), July 28, 1927.

[5] John White letter, Battle Creek, June 26, 1878.

[6] *Life Incidents*, p. 15.

[7] William C. White, "Sketches and Memories of James and Ellen White," in *The Review and Herald*, Feb. 28, 1935, p. 9.

[8] *Life Incidents*, pp. 18, 19.

Chapter Two

HEAVEN'S HORSEMAN

JAMES was accompanied to Newport Academy by a local minister, an Elder Bridges, who also happened to be going there. As they rode along on their horses, it seemed to James that the minister could talk about only one thing—preaching. That was the last subject James wanted to discuss,[1] so he was greatly relieved when they arrived at the academy, and he no longer had to listen.

At the academy James rented a room and started right in with his studies, hoping in this way to drive away the prickings of the Holy Spirit on his heart. But this did no good. Although he read the assigned lessons, he found it impossible to concentrate on them.

This will never do, James decided. I'll have to go visit those students, then return and carry on as before.

As he set out for Troy that spring day, his feelings underwent a transformation. The peace of God flooded his heart. He raised his eyes to heaven and praised God.

The following day he reached the vicinity of Troy and stopped at the home of some of his former pupils. He knocked on the door, not knowing just what he was going to say. The woman of the house opened it and recognized James.

"It's the schoolmaster!" she exclaimed. "Do step inside."

James, determined to waste no words, came directly to the point.

"May I have the privilege of praying with you and your family?"

"Oh, yes, of course," said the woman, tears gathering in her eyes. "But wait, you must pray with our neighbors also. They must share the blessing." She turned to her children.

"Thomas, go up the road, and Millie, you go the other way.

21

Tell everyone you meet that the schoolmaster has returned and wishes to pray with us."

The children ran off on their errand. Within thirty minutes, twenty-five persons were present. Wondering how many were already Christians, James decided to find out. Not one was. He talked with them earnestly about what it means to follow Jesus and get ready for His soon coming. Then they prayed together, and James said good-by as he went on to look up more of his pupils.

Within a few days he had found them all and prayed with each. Having performed this duty, he returned to the academy. But he still found it impossible to settle down to his studies. It seemed as if the command "Go and preach" was sounding ever louder in his soul.

This burden stayed with him for several weeks. But to surrender his hope of getting an education and turn to preaching seemed more than he could bear. He decided to make a trial of his ability by announcing a meeting in the Troy townhouse. The room was crowded when he stood up to preach. He felt embarrassed and inadequate. After struggling with words for about twenty minutes he abruptly sat down.

Alone in the woods he spent several hours trying to discover the reasons for his failure. The fact remained that he was still longing for the worldly success while at the same time working for God. When he finally renounced all for Christ, his heart was flooded with peace and freedom. James White had put his hand to the plow and was never to let go or turn back.

In October, 1842, James attended a meeting that the Adventists held in their big tent in Exeter, Maine. When James White left the tent he was more certain than ever that Jesus would return to earth within a year after April, 1843, and that he must do his part in warning the world of its coming doom. He invested his small savings in books and a copy of the big lithographical prophetic chart.

Deacon John offered his son the use of one of his horses. An Elder Polley provided the young man with a much-battered saddle and part of a bridle that James managed to stitch together.

James began his ministry by holding meetings in the town of Palmyra. The Lord blessed his efforts, but the young preacher felt that results were meager.

A friend who was teaching school in Burnham had just suffered the loss of an eye. He asked James to substitute for him for a week. James agreed. As soon as he reached Burnham he announced a series of evening meetings in the schoolhouse.

The place was crowded when the evangelist stood up to speak. He dwelt on the subject of Christ's soon return and the importance of preparing for that great event. In his concluding sermon he invited sinners to come forward and find salvation. Sixty pressed to the front, where James talked and prayed with them.

Feeling unprepared to minister to the people further, James remembered his older brother, Samuel, who had already been a minister for five years, and wrote inviting him to come and help. Samuel responded; he spent six weeks among the people, baptized the believers, and organized a church. James was happy to see the first fruits of his work for God.

About that time an Advent believer suggested that James follow the Kennebec River as far as Brunswick, preaching in each community along the way. No Adventist preacher had visited that area.

So on a January morning, in 1843, James White mounted his horse and rode away on a preaching tour among total strangers, his light clothing giving him scant protection from the cold.

Arriving in the vicinity of Augusta, the capital of Maine, James found shelter with a humble Christian. A short time later he was invited to speak at a nearby schoolhouse not far from the Kennebec River. The place was packed, with people standing at every window and door. James preached with power.

The next night a group of rowdies tried to frighten him from the pulpit. One man threw a spike, which struck him on the head, then fell onto his Bible. James put it into his pocket.

When James had finished preaching, a noted Universalist editor, invited in to refute the message, asked James to request the people to wait to hear a rebuttal. James stated he had no further claims on the audience. They could do as they wished. Only about twenty-five persons remained. This angered his opponent.

The house was crowded for the next evening's meeting. All around the building a mob stood ready for action against the young preacher.

As James made his way toward the pulpit he was warned that

his meeting would be broken up because of his lack of cooperation the previous night.

"If that is the will of God," James replied, "let it be so."

Not daring to kneel for prayer because of the angry mob, James stood by the pulpit and prayed with his eyes open. Then, as he launched into his subject, snowballs, thrown through the open windows, began to spatter on the walls behind him. The wild screaming of the mob made it almost impossible for anyone to hear the speaker.

James closed his Bible and in a loud voice launched into a graphic description of the day of judgment.

"Repent and be converted," he urged, "that your sins may be blotted out. Turn to Christ and get ready for His coming, or in a little time from this you will call on rocks and mountains to fall on you. You scoff now, but you will pray then."

The shouting abated somewhat. James reached into his pocket and took out the nail hurled at him the previous evening. Holding it up, he said, "Some poor sinner cast this spike at me last evening. God pity him. The worst wish I have for him is that he is at this moment as happy as I am.

"The hands of Jesus were nailed to a cruel cross," he went on. "Why should His followers expect better treatment?" He stretched out his hands against the wall in the position of one nailed to a cross.

"Hark! Hark!" cried many voices. The young James went on to speak of the love of Christ. He urged sinners to accept salvation and prepare for His soon return. When an invitation to stand was made for those who would believe on Christ and follow Him, nearly one hundred rose to their feet. The meeting had lasted almost two hours.

James closed with prayer, then picked up his books and chart and left the schoolhouse. The rioters outside opened a path. One man stepped up, locked arms with him, and steered him through the crowd. Then James realized that the man was gone. He wondered whether he had been in contact with an angel of God.

The meetings in this schoolhouse continued for another three or four evenings, and were accompanied by a reformation in the area. James went on to make appointments in other schoolhouses farther down the river. He usually remained only two nights in a place. He was indeed a pilgrim and a stranger, and could not tarry long.

At a place called Bowdoinham Ridge, James found that two ministers had begun to conduct at least two meetings a day in the church. He was invited to become the speaker, and encouraging results followed. The last day he was in town he spoke morning and afternoon, with the last meeting ending as the sun was setting in the wintry sky.

"Don't you think you should spend the night here with us?" one of the ministers asked. "It's getting dark and colder."

"I'd like to," replied the evangelist, "but I have a meeting at Lisbon Plains, and I must hurry on my way."

They brought his horse, and James, damp with perspiration, mounted and rode off into the gloom of that cold February night. As he traveled, his clothing nearly froze on his body. Although the distance was only sixteen miles, it seemed much farther to the chilled horseman. As he galloped past many a lighted farmhouse the temptation to stop and find warmth and food must have been strong. But he knew people were waiting for him, and he could not disappoint them.

At the door of the meetinghouse James dismounted and tossed the reins to a man standing nearby.

"Please take care of my horse," he said, then stepped into the church just in time to hear the pastor say to the people, "I'm sorry to have to announce that we are disappointed. The speaker we expected to hear this evening has not come." The minister reached out his hands. "Please rise for the benediction," he said.

But before the congregation could get to their feet, James cried out, "Hold! I am here!"

"Good," said the minister; and the people, having waited nearly an hour, prepared to listen. After apologizing for the delay, James plunged into his subject. For a few minutes his teeth chattered so violently that some of his words were cut short. But he soon warmed up, and then spoke with freedom.

After dismissing the meeting James went to get his horse. He found it tied to a fence, exposed to the cutting wind, trembling in the cold, without even a blanket thrown over it. James indignantly realized it had stood there for an hour and a half while he was preaching.

The next morning he found the animal very sick. It never did fully recover from the effects of that exposure. James learned from that unfortunate experience always to give directions to the person caring for his horse.

James arrived at a place called Litchfield Plains, where he had a speaking appointment, to find the building packed with almost a thousand people. Every seat was taken, the aisles were filled, and people had even crowded onto the platform.

Pushing his way down the crowded aisle, he mounted the steps to the pulpit. To quiet the people, he launched into one of the sweet Advent hymns so popular at the time.

> "You will see your Lord a coming,
> You will see your Lord a coming,
> You will see your Lord a coming,
>   In a few more days.
>
>   While a band of music,
>   While a band of music,
>   While a band of music,
> Shall be chanting through the air." [2]

When James White incorporated this song in the earliest Adventist hymnal he omitted the first verse, for obvious reasons.

These simple words had a remarkable effect on that large congregation. The sweet melody struck home to their hearts as they sat almost breathless, listening to all eight stanzas. This was not the first nor last time that James White would begin a service singing to his audience.

On April 2 James headed for home. The snow on the road was still very deep. Often he had to dismount and plunge into the drifts to relieve the horse as it struggled through the piled-up snow.

On the fifth of April, James White rode his poor broken-down horse into the yard of his home in Palmyra. He had been gone for four months. It was later reported at the next church conference that during those four months a thousand souls had joined the church as a result of the work of 22-year-old James White!

A few days after his arrival in Palmyra, James White was ordained as a minister of the Christian Church. During most of the summer months of 1843 he held no evening meetings. But he was invited to speak at local churches on Sundays, and was pleased when these services resulted in baptisms. According to the Advent leaders, Christ would come during the twelve-month period beginning in April, 1843, and this was the good news that James White proclaimed to towns and cities in many parts of Maine.

---

[1] This chapter is based on *Life Sketches of Elder James White, and His Wife, Ellen G. White* (Battle Creek, Mich., 1888), pp. 18-23, 48-55, 67-79.

[2] *Life Incidents*, p. 94.

Chapter Three

TARRY BUT A NIGHT

URING the spring of 1843 James White was far less active as a preacher than he had been during the previous winter. Most people were busy on their farms, and could attend meetings only on Sundays. James took advantage of this lull. Wishing to learn all he could from the Adventist leaders, he went to Portland, Maine, and spent some time there. He found warm fellowship with many firm believers in the near Advent. These true friends welcomed him into their homes. They had heard of his fruitful campaign of the previous winter.

While attending one of the Adventist meetings in Portland, James was deeply impressed as he listened to the testimony of a 16-year-old girl. He may have been introduced to her at the time, but, if so, the occasion apparently made little impression on her.

Back at his parents' home in Palmyra, James determined to become financially independent. Since he had worked on his father's farm, he decided to earn some money mowing hay. Offering his services to a prosperous farmer, he was handed a scythe and sent into the field. Engaged to cut hay for this same farmer was a group of rough, irreligious young men. Recognizing James as the youthful preacher from Palmyra, and fiercely resenting his presence, they plotted to make things so hard for him he would quit. Their plan was to place him at the head of the line, intending to crowd in behind him and run him out of the field.

So, professing great respect for him as a minister, they invited him to lead them across the field. James accepted the position and began energetically, cutting a wide swath. The others took narrower ones.

Soon the plotters found the distance between them and their leader becoming greater. They simply couldn't keep up with him.

Little did they know that with every swing of the scythe James was sending up a prayer to heaven for physical strength. Back across the field they came, the others falling ever farther behind James. At the end of the second time across, James paused to rest under a tree.

Exhausted, the others came up one by one, laid down their scythes, and sat on the grass. Their leader walked up to James, placed his hands on his hips and asked a question:

"White, do you mean to kill yourself and us? We thought you were a minister and wouldn't know how to handle a scythe, but we must give you credit for being far ahead of us and the best mower we ever saw. You have taken no beer nor liquor, and the sun is hot. We give up." [1]

That fall, word went out that an important conference of Christian ministers would be held in the town of Knox, Maine. Deacon John, now an ardent Adventist, decided to attend. With James and two of his daughters, Mary and Elizabeth, Father White set out for the conference. Running into a heavy shower in the late afternoon, they drove their team and carriage into the yard of a hotel, where they put up for the night.

The Whites were a musical family. Deacon John had at one time been a teacher of voice. James and his sisters were first-class singers. To pass the time at the hotel, the four began singing some of the old, stirring revival hymns, as well as the newer popular songs of the Advent. The landlord, his family, and many guests crowded into the room where the visitors were singing, and listened to the music.

The next morning, when the time came to leave, Father White asked the landlord for the bill.

"There is no bill for you," the man replied with a smile.

"How do you figure that out?" asked the deacon.

"Your singing last evening more than paid for your room and supper. Anytime you come along this way again, just stop in and we'll put you up in exchange for a similar concert." [2]

As winter drew on, opportunities for preaching increased for James and for his fellow Advent preachers. Doors began opening for them on every side. James found particular satisfaction in returning to settlements where he had labored the previous winter, finding his converts and helping to strengthen their faith.

Not all of the ministers of the Christian Church joined in proclaiming the Advent message. One man felt that the work was against the best interests of the church and opposed White continually. One day James met this man on the road. As they passed, the minister expressed surprise at seeing White again.

"Mr. White," he exclaimed, "are you still in the land of the living?"

"No, sir," came the quick retort, "I am in the land of the dying, but at the soon coming of the Lord I hope to go to the land of the living." [3]

The winter wore on, and 1843 gave place to 1844. James White, along with thousands of others, believed this was the year that would bring the Saviour to earth to take His waiting saints to glory. The believers thought they had endured their last winter on earth. The Jewish year ended on March 21, but March 22 came and went, and there was no sign of the Son of man. Unbelievers mocked the Adventists and asked sarcastically, "Why haven't you gone to heaven?"

A verse from the book of Habakkuk brought the sorrowing ones much comfort. "Though it tarry, wait for it; because it will surely come, it will not tarry" (chap. 2:3). They also remembered the parable of the ten virgins and of how the bridegroom had tarried. William Miller and his companions studied the Bible as never before. Rechecking their figures, they found no errors of computation. All they could do was to watch and pray and be ready. [4]

It was during this "tarrying time," as they called it, that James was invited to go to West Gardiner, a small settlement some twenty miles from Palmyra. Ten or twelve children there had heard him preach the previous winter and had been convicted and converted. Now they requested baptism. James White lost no time in responding to this invitation. All his life he loved children, and would go out of his way to help and encourage them.

Arriving at West Gardiner, he talked first with the parents of the candidates, many of whom were opposed and felt the children should wait. Several who were not parents were very scornful.

"What kind of experience does Mr. White suppose those babies can have?" asked a Baptist minister.

Elder White first called for a meeting of the parents and children. He placed the children on the front row of seats in the church while the adults remained in the rear. After a discourse by him, the children stood one by one and told why they loved Jesus and wanted to follow Him in baptism. James asked them a few questions, which they answered simply but clearly.

"If there is anyone present who opposes my baptizing these children, let him now stand," said Elder White. No one moved. So, leading the procession out of the church, James walked to a nearby lake, where he immersed the young candidates in the cool water. As the children walked out onto the shore they greeted their parents and friends with smiles of joy. James always felt that this was one of the most beautiful baptismal services he ever conducted.[5]

Spring gave way to summer, and still there was no sign of Christ's coming. Toward the close of July, James read a notice in an Adventist paper stating that there would be an important meeting of Adventist leaders and laity in the town of Exeter, New Hampshire, in August. Although it meant a journey of nearly two hundred miles, James decided to attend. He arranged to join a group leaving from Portland.

The meeting opened on August 12 and lasted five days. At first there seemed to be no new light. Adventist leaders simply took turns speaking to the people.

One afternoon Joseph Bates was preaching, exhorting the believers to hold fast their confidence. As might be expected for a retired sea captain, he compared the Advent movement to a ship at sea, blown a bit off course perhaps, delayed by contrary winds, but sure to reach the harbor at last.

As he was speaking, the attention of the audience was attracted by a man on a horse, riding up to the tent. Quickly tying his panting horse, the man entered the tent, sat down beside a woman, and whispered something to her. It was Samuel Snow. When he had finished his whispering, the woman stood up and addressed Elder Bates, telling him it was too late for worn-out preaching; that a man had just arrived with new light. She urged Bates to let Snow speak. He agreed and invited Snow into the desk, where he expounded "new light." The cleansing of the sanctuary, Snow declared, would take place on the Jewish Day of Atonement, which would fall on October 22 of that year.

It was new light indeed. Joseph Bates accepted it, and so did James White. When that five-day meeting ended, and the wagons had rolled away to their respective destinations, the granite hills of New Hampshire rang with the shout, "Behold the Bridegroom cometh, go ye out to meet Him. . . . Get ready! Get ready!"[6]

James White returned to Maine to proclaim this Midnight Cry in his area. And how little time he had; only about ten weeks remained. As October 22 drew nearer, James White's labors became more fervent.[7]

At last the great day arrived. We are not told where the White family spent it, but probably they waited for their Lord at their home on the farm, near Palmyra. All up and down the Atlantic Coast thousands of believers watched the sky. The sun sank into the west, clocks ticked off the hours, and finally midnight came, and beyond. The day had passed, and they were disappointed again.

James White wondered what he should do next. He had made no other plans for his life than to proclaim the coming of Jesus as expounded by Miller and other Adventist preachers and supported, as they believed, by the prophecies of Daniel and Revelation.

A few days after the Disappointment he made a trip to Portland, where Joshua Himes was meeting with many of the leaders from all parts of Maine. When Elder Himes told them that they should prepare for another long, hard winter, it seemed more than James could endure. He wrote that he "left the place of meeting and wept like a child."[8]

The scoffing of unbelievers was hard to bear. One of them met James White on the morning after the sad day. Laughingly the man pointed his finger at the disappointed youthful preacher and asked scornfully, "Well, you didn't go up yesterday, did you?"

James had a quick reply.

"And if I had gone up, *where would you have gone?*"

It was a sobering thought. The sneer left the skeptic's face.

---

[1] Ellen White manuscript 19, 1885.

[2] *Life Incidents*, p. 105.

[3] *Ibid.*, p. 108.

[4] *Ibid.*

[5] *Ibid.*, pp. 110-112.

[6] Francis D. Nichol, *The Midnight Cry* (Washington, D.C.: Review and Herald Pub. Assn., © 1944), pp. 214, 215.

[7] Arthur Spalding, *Origin and History of Seventh-day Adventists* (Washington, D.C.: Review and Herald Pub. Assn., © 1961), vol. 1, pp. 92-94.

[8] *Life Incidents*, p. 182.

Chapter Four

CROWN AND REJOICING

ISAPPOINTMENT and dismay spread through the Adventist ranks when Christ did not come on October 22, 1844, as had been expected. To James White and the Millerite leaders it was evident that a mistake had been made. Later, they were to discover that the error had not been in the date fixed, but rather in the nature of the event that took place on that memorable day.

After the Disappointment, James remained on the farm, waiting, wondering, studying. He busied himself helping his father and his brothers, reaping what harvest there was and preparing for the "hard winter" Elder Himes had warned them was surely coming—a winter they had never expected to experience.

As winter closed in and the evenings grew longer James had more time to spend in reviewing his experience as a participant in the Advent movement. There was one major question for him to ponder. Had the movement come from God? As he thought back over the events of previous years he called to mind the Spirit-filled meetings held and the love and fellowship that had drawn the Adventists together. He had seen the Spirit of God working on the hearts of men. Could all that have been devil inspired or man inspired? "Impossible!" declared James White.

He was willing to wait, to study, to pray, but not to cast away his confidence. Had not the book of Hebrews spoken of something resembling their experience? "Ye have need of patience. . . . For yet a little while, and he that shall come will come, and will not tarry" (Heb. 10:36, 37).

Waiting never came easy to the impulsive young preacher. It was not his nature. As early as March, 1843, he had written a note that had appeared in the *Signs of the Times:* "Most of the preachers were silent on the subject of Christ's immediate coming.

3

Some of them tell the people they are willing to wait for a time to decide the question. *Brethren, I cannot wait.* God forbid that I should fold my arms in lazy-lock while sinners are sinking to eternal night."[1]

Now, on the farm, he was searching for fresh light that would help explain why Christ had not come as expected.

Among the ranks of Adventist believers, every wind of doctrine now began to blow. In some places fanaticism flourished, and no part of New England produced a greater supply of counterfeit religion than did the State of Maine. James did what he could, wherever he could, to put out the fires of fanaticism. The people needed help and a unified leadership.

Sometime during that winter James heard that Ellen Harmon, living in Portland, Maine, had seen in vision the travels of God's people to the Holy City. Miss Harmon, only 17 at the time, was a Christian girl, and the fruit of her testimony was good.

James remembered this young woman whose testimony he had heard in Portland a year before.[2] He had been surprised to note how small and delicate she appeared. Ellen had suffered much physically, but her Christian experience burned bright.

One day early in 1845 James White learned that a sleigh he had lent a friend, Brother Jordan, of Poland, Maine, was being returned. The sleigh would be taken to Orrington, where James was to get it. On the day appointed, James walked the twenty miles from Palmyra to Orrington. At Orrington, James learned that Jordan had brought his sister and Ellen Harmon with him. That evening Ellen spoke to a group meeting in a home. What James saw and heard convinced him that she was God's chosen messenger; it was a conviction that was to strengthen during the years to come. He talked with her of her experience. She had heard of the thousand converts he had won in a few short weeks. Apparently, as she looked at this stalwart, six-foot-tall man, and listened to him talk, she was attracted by his warm personality and evident sincerity.

Perhaps James remembered some of the mobs he had encountered the previous year, and wondered how this frail, innocent, timid girl would be treated as she continued traveling and speaking. She needed a stronger protector than a woman could provide. Since it was winter and not much could be done on the farm, why shouldn't he travel with Ellen and Jordan's sister, organize Ellen's meetings, and see that no harm came to the two girls? He offered his horse, sleigh, and services to Ellen, which she was happy to accept. So the three set out on a tour of Adventist companies in eastern Maine. Notices were sent ahead, and meetings were held on appointed dates. Sometimes Ellen's testimony was accepted. At other places fanatics rejected her words of reproof, and carried on as before.

Thus the winter months passed. With the arrival of spring, melting snows made it impossible for them to continue to travel by sleigh.

One day Ellen received a letter from her mother that dismayed her. "Come home, Ellen, my daughter," Mrs. Harmon had written. "False reports are being circulated about you. You should not be traveling all over the countryside like this. It is not fitting and proper for one of your age." [3]

Charges made against her and James were, of course, completely false. Never had the two gone anywhere without some other adult accompanying them. But Ellen highly respected her mother and felt it was best to comply with her wishes.

James decided to escort Ellen and the Jordans, who had been traveling with them, down the Penobscot River to Belfast, where they could board the steamer for Portland.

James found two friends to help him, and they borrowed a boat for the twenty-mile trip to Belfast. It was a beautiful spring day, and the current helped carry them along. At Belfast they parted, with Ellen and her companions on board the steamer, and James White and his friends on the wharf. No doubt James wondered when he would see Ellen again.

The twenty-mile journey back up the river was not so easy, for the men had to row against the swift current. Late in the day the tired trio completed the trip and pulled their boat up to the landing at Orrington. A group of rough-looking men were standing nearby, studying the boat and its passengers.

"Where is Miss Harmon?" one of them shouted.

"She's gone to Portland."

"All right, let them have it, men."

The rowdies made a rush at James and his friends. One man had a horsewhip, which he laid again and again across James's back. When the mob had beaten the men, they dragged them to the jail and threw them into it for the night. In the morning the three were let out and permitted to return home, though suffering from wounds and bruises.[4]

The next time James and Ellen met was at the home of Stockbridge Howland, in Topsham, Maine. Howland was a staunch Adventist. So bravely did he defend his home as a citadel of truth that in later years James White referred to it as "Fort Howland."[5]

At the time James and Ellen were there, Howland's daughter, Frances, was very sick with rheumatic fever. The family physician came regularly, doing what he could to relieve her pain. One morning, as Frances lay in one of the upstairs bedrooms, a large group downstairs was praying for her. After the prayers one of the brethren cried out, "Is there a sister here who has the faith to go and take her by the hand, and bid her arise in the name of the Lord?"

Before he had finished speaking a Sister Curtis was on her way up the stairs. In the name of the Lord she bade the sick girl, "Arise, and be made whole." Life-giving power flowed through the girl's frame. She arose, dressed, and joined the family downstairs.

At the worship hour the next morning, as James was reading a portion of the fifth chapter of James, the doctor came into the house and went upstairs to visit his patient, only to find her gone. Alarmed, he hurriedly descended the stairs and stepped into the kitchen, where the family was sitting around the table. Seeing Frances sitting with them, he exclaimed in astonishment: "So Frances is better!"

"Yes, the Lord has healed her," was the reply.

James White continued reading from the Bible: "Is any sick among you? Let him call for the elders of the church; and let them pray over him." A puzzled look came over the doctor's face as he left without saying another word.[6]

Feeling that God had called her to bear her testimony to the Advent people in New Hampshire, Ellen prepared to go. Three or four others accompanied her, one of whom was James. Ellen found him an efficient help in arranging her meetings. She appreciated it when he sometimes spoke to the people.

The weeks passed, with James and Ellen going from company to company, encouraging the weak, rebuking fanatics, and assuring believers that God had not forgotten them. Traveling together in this ministry, the two discovered in time that they shared many beliefs and ideals. Time and time again Ellen found in James a strong protector; he, in turn, became more and more convinced that her visions were of God, and that a supernatural power worked through her.

When word came that fanaticism was flourishing in Paris, Maine, they went there. While in Paris they stayed with a family named Stowell, who observed the seventh-day Sabbath.

One morning a man drove into the Stowell yard and asked to see Ellen Harmon. Ellen went out, greeted the stranger, and asked him what he wanted. He pointed to his expensive carriage and offered to take her in it wherever she wanted to go—Maine, New Hampshire, Vermont, Massachusetts, or anywhere.

Ellen politely declined his invitation.

"The Lord has told me I must do this," said the man.

Ellen replied that that wasn't so. She had special orders. The Lord had shown her she could safely trust Elder James White.[7]

At this time Ellen did not expect ever to marry. Adventists felt that the coming of the Lord was so near that it would be better not to enter into this relationship. James White and a number of others, on the basis of the "fourth watch," believed that the Lord's coming would be delayed for just one year and looked for the Advent in the autumn of 1845. (See Matt. 14:25.)

On September 20, 1845, he wrote to Brother Jacobs: "Do we *know* what watch the Lord is coming? Certainly. Three have passed, and there is but four. All who see this light will receive a certainty that before the 10th day of the 7th month, 1845, our King will come, and we will watch, and like Noah, know the day. . . . Awake! Awake! Awake! ye heralds of the Jubilee, and tell the scattered flock, The morning cometh."[8]

But Ellen Harmon, who was at this time visiting friends in Massachusetts, wrote that she had been shown in vision this date would pass and Christ would not come as they expected.[9]

James and Ellen took up their travels again during the winter of 1845 and were always accompanied by a chaperone. Their messages continued to comfort the people of God.

Soon, perhaps inevitably, the old ugly rumors began spreading again. We are not told in just what manner they came to the attention of James White, but he was told the situation was becoming serious. He talked to Ellen, pointing out that something had come up, and it would be necessary for him to leave her free to travel with someone else. He was an ordained minister, and she was a worker for God. Both must guard their reputations.

Ellen was dismayed. She had come to lean so heavily upon him that the thought of permanent separation was painful, and the idea of someone else traveling with her was no less disturbing to him. After allowing the implications of his announcement to sink in, he pointed out that there was another solution to the problem. They could get married. He was willing if she was.

"Ellen," he said, "let's accept the situation. You need me, and I need you. What about it?"

"We must do nothing rash, James," she replied. "We must beware of injuring our testimony or making any move that could prevent our doing acceptable work for God. We must do God's will. Let's pray about it."

They agreed to spend much time in prayer over the matter. When they met again, they decided that they should marry.[10]

This was not an easy decision to make. With others James had maintained that because Christ would soon come, Adventists should not marry. In fact, he had written a letter to a couple planning to get married, accusing them of denying their faith by so doing. Now he was planning for his own marriage.[11] Indeed, there were some who were dismayed.

As soon as James returned to Portland he published the banns* for their forthcoming marriage. Had the Harmons still been members of the Methodist Church, James and Ellen would probably have had a church wedding. But the Adventists in Portland had no church of their own. So on Monday, August 30, 1846, James White and Ellen Harmon were married by Charles Harding, a justice of the peace for the city of Portland.

There was no honeymoon. A century ago people who earned their bread by the toil of their hands seldom had time or money for such enjoyable, but not always essential, pleasures. Certainly, the newlyweds could not afford one, for they did not have much of this world's goods. Whatever James had earned he had donated to the

---

* A public notice of a proposed marriage so that any person knowing of impediments to the marriage might make them known.

Advent cause or spent traveling from place to place.

How did James and Ellen feel about each other?

Wrote James White in later years, "She has been my crown of rejoicing." [12]

Ellen declared long after, "Although he is dead, I feel that he is the best man that ever trod shoe leather." [13]

---

[1] Ellen G. White Estate Document File, 718.

[2] Margaret Rossiter Thiele, *By Saddle and Sleigh* (Washington, D.C.: Review and Herald Pub. Assn., 1965), p. 102.

[3] *Ibid.*, p. 106.

[4] *Ellen G. White, Her Friends and Fellow-Workers*, p. 13, "Interview" with James White; cf. James White letter to Brother Jacobs, Sept. 6, 1845.

[5] James White, "The Cause," in *The Review and Herald*, Oct. 27, 1863.

[6] Ellen G. White, *Life Sketches* (Mountain View, Calif.: Pacific Press Pub. Assn., 1915), pp. 74, 75.

[7] Document File, 733 C.

[8] James White letter to Brother Jacobs, Sept. 20, 1845.

[9] James White, in *A Word to the Little Flock*, p. 22.

[10] *By Saddle and Sleigh*, p. 128; also Document File 733 C.

[11] James White letter to Brother Jacobs, published in *Day Star*, Oct. 11, 1845.

[12] *Life Sketches* (1888), p. 125.

[13] Document File, 733 C. Interview.

Chapter Five

NO PERMANENT RESTING PLACE

I N THE spring of 1846, before their marriage, James and Ellen had visited Joseph Bates at his home in Fairhaven, Massachusetts. Elder Bates was at that time 54 years old. Ellen was still a teen-ager and James only 25. While visiting in the Bates home, Ellen told him of what she had seen in vision.

"I am a doubting Thomas," he said. "I do not believe in visions." But he never questioned her sincerity.

If Joseph Bates was not prepared to accept Ellen's messages as from Heaven, neither were his visitors prepared to accept his practice of observing the seventh day as the Sabbath of God.[1] To their way of thinking, Elder Bates made a mistake in emphasizing the Sabbath commandment more than the other nine.

In August of this same year James visited Fairhaven again. Just about that time Bates's pamphlet dealing with the Sabbath doctrine came from the press. He gave a copy to James, asking him to read it and to give the matter prayerful study. This James promised to do, and he returned to Portland, where a few days later he was married.

After their marriage the Whites looked up every text in the pamphlet and by the time they had completed their examination were convinced that the seventh day was God's true Sabbath. They immediately began to keep it, much to the surprise of Father and Mother Harmon, in whose house they were living. When James and Ellen took their stand on the Sabbath there were about 50 Sabbathkeepers in all New England—25 in Maine, and about the same number outside the State.

Some members of James's family were shocked by his religious ideas regarding not only the Sabbath but other matters. His brother John, writing to James's sister Anna, took him to task for accepting and promulgating the doctrines of William Miller and heaped scorn on the Adventist leader's teachings.

"I deeply regret that Brother James has fallen into the snare of the devil and Mr. Miller. [Miller] started out by soaring into the regions of speculation. Spun in fancie's flight, his cobweb system of divinity, and then returned to the Bible, determined to find a basis on which to rest it. Suddenly . . . he turns mathematician and introduces lines and diagrams into his system . . . drew a fancy piece and then went out into the crowd to find a face to suit it. So he, after forming in his sickly imagination a system, comes to the Bible and science to torture them for an original."

The early Adventists, insisting as they did that the door of mercy had been closed to certain classes of people, stirred the indignation of John's wife, who waxed poetic on the subject:

"O! what a cruel work has Satan wrought
Upon the brain of our dear brother James.
The door of mercy shut to sinful man?
Not yet! Thank God; for Christ is pleading still
Before His Father's throne; with wounded hands
And feet and side, and temples pierced there
With sword and thorns; saying, 'Father, spare them.
I have bled, and groaned, and sweat, and died.'
Not yet! Oh, no! My soul prays God not yet
Has pity ceased to flow for fallen man.
But from the rocky heights of Calvary
I see its crimson tide of mercy flow
To wash away the guilty stain of sin." [2]

For a time James and Ellen were the only Sabbathkeepers in Gorham. But Robert and Eunice Harmon were sincere Christians, ever seeking to know and do the will of God. They too studied the tract by Bates, and by August, 1848, James was able to write to friends that the Harmons "are with us in the faith." [3]

Joseph Bates was thankful when word reached him that the Whites were keeping the Sabbath. Bates had known James during the stirring times when both were preaching the Advent message, and saw in James indications that he would be a strong leader in the work of God.

About this time Ellen was rebaptized. She had been baptized as a girl of 14 when she joined the Methodist Church. Would it not be fitting for her to be baptized into the ranks of Sabbathkeepers?

We have no record of the time or place where James baptized her, or who was present to witness the rite. But James, in the only record of this experience, wrote that immediately as he raised her out of the water, she was taken off in vision.[4]

At that time the believers were few and widely scattered, and it was only as money came in that James and Ellen could travel among them, bearing a message of hope, cheer, and sometimes reproof. There was a small group in Washington, New Hampshire. Another company worshiped with Joseph Bates in Fairhaven, while still another cluster met with Hiram Edson in western New York. With a few from around Boston, there may have been as many as a hundred Sabbathkeeping Adventists in 1847.

That November the Whites attended a meeting of Sabbathkeepers in the home of Stockbridge Howland in Topsham, Maine. It was there that Ellen received her vision of the open heavens, and Joseph Bates once and for all was convinced that her visions were valid.

Shortly after returning to Gorham, Ellen was taken suddenly and violently ill. So severe was her pain that she begged those praying for her to cease, that she might find relief in death. Day after day the pain continued. Hearing of her illness, Brother and Sister Nichols sent their son Henry from Dorchester to Gorham to unite his prayers with those of the distraught husband and parents. While they prayed, the power of the Spirit came upon Henry. Placing his hand on her head, he commanded Ellen to be well. The disease instantly left her.[5]

Early in 1847 James and his wife traveled to Boston by ship. A severe storm developed, and for a time it seemed as if the boat would sink. However, God's hand protected His servants, and they arrived safely in port.[6]

They spent seven weeks visiting the scattered believers in Massachusetts before returning to Gorham in the middle of March. Except for Ellen's illness, they had enjoyed good health during the winter.[7]

Besides James and Ellen White there were no Sabbathkeepers in Gorham in 1847. However, there were believers in Topsham, thirty miles away, and the Whites frequently went there to spend the Sabbath. James wrote a description of the group at Topsham to Mrs. Leonard Hastings. "Here is a strong band of 13 bold soldiers in this place, in union and in the spirit and power of the truth and love of Christ."[8]

James's willingness to work hard for his wages enabled him to find employment. He succeeded in earning $25 in six weeks. But he did not have enough money to spread the message of truth very far. No doubt he made good use of Joseph Bates's pamphlet on the Sabbath.

Hearing that Elder Bates had printed a description of one of Ellen's early visions, James wrote and asked him to send a thousand copies. This Bates did, with a bill for $7.50. James was forced to borrow money to pay for this printing, trusting God to impress someone to send the necessary means. The money came, and the loan was repaid.[9]

During the summer of 1847 Ellen did little traveling, but busied herself at home, helping her mother and preparing for the arrival of her first child. On August 26 James and Ellen became the proud parents of a baby boy. James named his son Henry Nichols White, after his friend in Dorchester. Less than a week later James, visiting at "Fort Howland" in Topsham, announced Henry's birth. He had no idea then that Henry was going to live for five years in this hospitable home while Ellen and he traveled from place to place as God directed.[10]

Since work opportunities were more numerous around Topsham and Brunswick than in the neighborhood of Gorham, James decided to move his family to that area. The Howlands invited James and Ellen to move into their large house, offering them furnished rooms on the second floor in which to set up housekeeping. In October they moved there. The trip from Gorham to Topsham was approximately thirty-five miles.

If there was one thing James White abhorred more than debt, it was the feeling that he was dependent upon the labors of others for the support of his family. He first found work hauling stone for the railroad being built between Portland and Brunswick. The work was hard. Many times the handling of the stones abraded his finger tips until the blood oozed from them. But the most discouraging aspect of this job was that he found it almost impossible to collect even the small amount of money due him. He soon began looking for an employer from whom he could be sure of collecting his pay.

James White hauled stone from this railway cut between Portland and Brunswick, Maine, when the cut was made.

A short time later James went into the woods with his ax and began cutting wood.[11] In spite of a continual pain in his side, he continued this work from morning till night, earning approximately fifty cents a day. He refused to become discouraged. Each morning he and Ellen knelt and prayed for strength for that day's work, and each evening they gave thanks that this request had been granted.

One stormy morning the Whites found themselves with no food. James pulled on his boots. "I'm going to see my employer. He owes me several dollars, and perhaps I can collect some from him."

"I wish you wouldn't go out in such a storm," said Ellen soberly, looking at little streams of water trickling down the windowpanes.

"I can't help it," replied James, putting on his overcoat. "There's no way to stop the rain," he went on, trying to be cheerful.

44

More than two hours passed before James returned. Wearily he shook water out of his hat brim and stamped his feet to warm them. Then he climbed the stairs, entered the room, and laid down his bag of provisions. He had walked six miles. On his way he had passed through the town of Brunswick on the south side of the Kennebec River. He was well known in that area, having often lectured there during the time the Second Coming was being preached. Suddenly the picture of her husband carrying provisions in a cloth sack over his shoulder through the town in the rain struck Ellen with overwhelming force.

The floodgates of her tears were unleashed, and she wept a long time. At last she fainted. James and Brother Howland knelt beside her and pleaded with God to give her relief. Their prayers were answered, and when Ellen recovered, she expressed regret at allowing feelings of discouragement to overwhelm her.[12]

Though the Whites had a good home, it was a long, hard winter. The Howlands willingly shared everything with them. But they also had invested most of their means in the Advent cause and were dependent upon their current income for food and clothing.

About that time Ellen had a vision in which she was shown that it was their duty not to settle down but to go from place to place for the salvation of others.

"You mean we must leave our home here and go traveling?" James asked in surprise. "That means we will have to take our small baby with us on steamers, stagecoaches, and rattling trains! How can we do such a thing?"

"James, I'm only telling you what the Lord showed me. You know that this winter we have not been prospered. I saw that the Lord was stirring up our nest so we wouldn't settle down in comfort and thus fail to do His work."

Together they discussed their problem. Seldom did they receive much help to pay travel expenses. They had no money themselves. And carrying a small child around from place to place, at all hours, and not always under comfortable circumstances, made leaving their home seem impossible at the time.

Not long after this, little Henry became very ill. No remedy seemed to help. James and Ellen wondered, Since they had made their baby an excuse for not engaging in God's service, was He going to take him from them, thus removing that excuse?

It was a sobering thought. They talked the matter over and decided they must obey by taking little Henry and going wherever God's providence should lead them.[13]

Some time later James received a letter from a Brother E. L. H. Chamberlain, who lived in Middletown, Connecticut, inviting them to attend a conference of all the believers in that part of the State the following month. James and Ellen talked it over and decided the call was from God. They wrote back that they would come if they could find the money for fares.

James collected ten dollars that his employer owed him. Ellen used five to purchase some essential clothing. (Their second five dollars would take them to Dorchester, near Boston.)[14] Then she set to work to patch what was worth patching of the others. Humorously, she pointed out that she had to patch some of the patches on her husband's overcoat. "I doubt if anyone will be able to guess the original color," she laughed.

The Whites took Henry with them to Dorchester, where they visited their friends, the Nicholses. As they were leaving to continue their journey to Connecticut, Mrs. Nichols handed James five dollars. At the railway station they bought tickets costing $4.50, saw their trunk loaded onto the baggage car, and boarded the train.

At the Middletown station they claimed their trunk. Not willing to spend their last fifty cents for a conveyance to take them to the home of believers, James tossed the trunk onto a pile of lumber. Then they walked, carrying Henry, in to the center of town. A few inquiries enabled them to find Chamberlain, who took the weary travelers and their trunk to his home. Albert Belden, a relative of Ellen's, sent his two-horse wagon to Middletown to carry the Whites and the few believers in Middletown the eight miles to Rocky Hill.

"Do you have a room large enough to hold the people who will come?" James asked Belden as they visited together.

"My large unfinished room should be big enough for all who come," Belden answered.

The next day, Friday, other Sabbathkeeping Adventists arrived, along with some who had not yet decided to keep the Sabbath. In all, about fifty attended.

During the meeting, which lasted through Sunday afternoon,

Elder Bates, who had joined the group the day before, presented the commandments clearly and convincingly. "The word had effect to establish those already in the truth, and to awaken those not fully decided," James wrote to Brother Howland.[15]

That year, 1848, was destined to be one of great importance in the history of Adventism. The meeting at Rocky Hill was the first of a series of six "Sabbath conferences" (so called because they were held by "friends of the Sabbath") that would be held before the end of the year.

The "little flock" was growing. James White exclaimed, "Praise the Lord!"

---

[1] A. W. Spalding, *Origin and History*, vol. 1, p. 127.

[2] John and Anna White letter, June, 1846, Document File, 701.

[3] James White letter to a "Dear Brother and Sister," Aug. 26, 1848.

[4] *Life Incidents* (1868), p. 273.

[5] *Life Sketches* (1888), p. 239.

[6] *Ibid.*, pp. 240, 241.

[7] James White letter to S. Howland, March 14, 1847.

[8] ———— letter to Sister Hastings, Aug. 22, 1847.

[9] ———— letter to Sister Hastings, May 21, 1847.

[10] Arthur Spalding, *Footprints of the Pioneers* (Washington, D.C.: Review and Herald Pub. Assn., 1947), p. 85.

[11] *Life Sketches* (1888), p. 242.

[12] *Ibid.*, pp. 242, 243.

[13] *Ibid.*

[14] *Life Sketches* (1915), p. 107.

[15] *Ibid.*, p. 108.

Chapter Six

LAYING THE FOUNDATIONS

RETURNING from the Middletown post office one morning, Albert Belden went to the upstairs room where James and Ellen White were living and handed them a letter. It was from Hiram Edson, who was the first to receive light on the sanctuary and the reasons for the disappointment of 1844.

"What does he say?" asked Ellen, as James glanced over the letter.

"There are plans to hold a meeting of all the believers. It will be held in Volney, in western New York, sometime this summer. Brother Edson invites us to meet with them."

"I think we ought to go," said Ellen decisively. "Don't you?"

"Yes, we must go if at all possible. But he points out in his letter that the brethren are poor, and will be able to do little to help pay our expenses."

"That is a problem, but I think the Lord will show us what to do," said Ellen encouragingly.

James did not sit at home and wait for pennies to fall from heaven to help him get on with the Lord's work. He, with two brethren, George W. Holt and John Belden, contracted to mow one hundred acres of hay, for which they would be paid $87.50.[1]

It was hot work, and to swing the heavy scythe took almost more energy than James possessed. Many times he knelt and prayed for strength to continue.

One day he wrote in a letter to his friend Stockbridge Howland: "It is rainy today, so that I do not mow, or I should not write. . . . God gives me strength to labor hard all day. . . . Praise the Lord! I hope to get a few dollars here to use in the cause of God."[2]

This last sentence is significant. All his life James White would be searching for and finding ways to get dollars with which to advance the work of God on earth.

After five weeks in the hayfield James received forty dollars. With this he and Ellen purchased some new clothing. The remainder was used to pay their fare to the meetings in Volney and return. When they took the boat for New York City, little eleven-month-old Henry was left at Middletown with a friend, Miss Clarissa Bonfoey. This was the first time Ellen White and her baby were apart for even a single night.[3] But it was not to be the last.

Standing on the Brooklyn pier in New York, they saw a boat, the *Bay State*, sailing in from Fairhaven. There on deck stood Joseph Bates. "We were very glad to see the old Pilgrim once more," wrote James.

The group that met them on the way to the Volney meetings got together and looked over their respective resources. Bates and Chamberlain each had two dollars, and James had a dollar and a half, making a total of five dollars and fifty cents. Fares were low on the river boats and barges, and they were all able to get to Volney using this small amount.[4]

While in New York they were entertained by a Brother D. Moody. From there they sailed up the Hudson to Albany. Next, they changed to a canal boat, traveled over most of the famous Erie Canal, and disembarked near Volney, where they were met and escorted to David Arnold's home.

There were between 35 and 40 persons present at this second Sabbath conference, which was held in David Arnold's barn.[5] James was distressed to discover that the brethren were disagreeing on nearly every point of doctrine. Each had pet theories to which he clung and which he tried to force upon everyone else.

Hoping to quiet the disharmonious spirit of the conference, someone suggested that the Lord's Supper be celebrated. Most of those present agreed, but Arnold promptly raised an objection— "The Lord's Supper took the place of the Jewish passover, so it should be celebrated only once a year," he insisted. This is not the time for it.

"Not so," another protested. "The early church members broke bread daily."

The discordance among the group caused a heavy burden to rest upon Ellen White. During the conference the Lord gave her a vision revealing the various errors of those present. Many of them

4

were seeing the Lord's servant in vision for the first time. The Spirit of God entered powerfully into the assembly, and when Ellen came out of vision and clearly pointed out the true teachings of the Bible, her message was believed to be from God. The meeting closed triumphantly.[6] James was seeing that the Spirit of Prophecy, as manifested through his wife, could prove to be a great unifying factor among the believers.

Shortly afterward the third conference was held in Hiram Edson's barn. Edson lived some 60 miles east of Volney, near Port Gibson, New York. Again there were differences of opinion in interpreting points of doctrine. Again the testimony of the Lord's servant brought peace and unity.

The Whites, Joseph Bates, and H. S. Gurney, an evangelistic singer, were now ready to return to New England. On the way, they hoped to spend a Sabbath visiting believers in the vicinity of New York City. At Port Gibson they expected to catch a fast canal boat for the city. Unfortunately, it had already left, so they decided to travel on a slower freight boat until the next fast boat, known as a packet boat, came along. Then they hoped to transfer to it.

After a time they spotted the packet overtaking them. Evidently the captain did not realize what was desired, for he never slowed down. As the packet came alongside, James and Ellen sprang and landed safely on its deck.

Bates tried to follow James's example, but his foot caught on the edge of the boat, and he fell into the canal. Seeing his predicament, the pilot of the packet immediately stopped the boat and

Elder Bates was pulled on board, dripping wet. Because of this accident, plans to go to New York were temporarily abandoned. A Brother Harris and his wife lived in the next town so the three left the boat there and went to the Harris home, where Elder Bates's clothing was dried and made presentable.[7]

After spending several days with believers along their route, the Whites, Gurney, and Bates, now at Brooklyn, planned to catch a boat for Middletown, Connecticut. It was now Thursday afternoon and failure to catch the boat would involve traveling on the Sabbath. The Whites were staying at the Moody home and, before they left, it was suggested that the group pray together. Not realizing the urgency of the Whites' need to catch the boat, some prayed lengthy prayers so that, when the prayer session was finished, very little time remained before the boat was to leave.

Grasping James's arm, Ellen ran with him toward the pier, which was about a mile away.

Meanwhile, Bates and Gurney, already on the boat, were trying to persuade the captain to wait just a little longer. Five minutes passed, and the impatient captain would wait no more.

Finally, just as the gangplank was being removed, the Whites, panting from exertion, raced down the pier. Springing on the plank, they managed to get aboard the boat.[8]

Arriving at Rocky Hill, Connecticut, the Whites attended a Sabbath conference held there early in September. This was the fourth conference of 1848.[9]

Throughout the trip Ellen had been longing to see her baby, Henry. Now, back at Middletown, her first thought was of him. She found him sick, and his condition continued to worsen; it was felt by some that he would not live long. But God heard the earnest prayers that were offered daily, and after a time the child began to mend.

In October James and Ellen set out for Maine, taking Henry with them. At Topsham they were happy to meet their old friends, the Howlands, again. And at Topsham the fifth Sabbath conference was held, October 20-22, during which the great foundation truths that had been established at the previous conferences were reviewed and built upon. In order to spread the truths unfolded at the conferences it was felt that a paper should be published and sent everywhere.

The third Bible conference, attended by James and Ellen White, was held in Hiram Edson's barn, near Port Gibson, New York.

The home of Stockbridge Howland, Topsham, Maine, where the Whites first set up housekeeping, and where their son Henry lived for five years.

Another general meeting was called to meet in Dorchester, Massachusetts, in mid-November.

"How can we take little Henry with us?" the Whites asked themselves. "Winter is coming, and travel is difficult for anyone at this season."

After laying their problems before the Lord they reached two decisions. First, they would go to Dorchester. Second, they would leave little Henry in the care of the Howland family, where he could live an undisturbed life and be brought up properly.

The time came for the heartsore parents to leave Topsham. Sadly they kissed their little boy, now fifteen months old, and placed him in the arms of Sister Howland. The sad little face he wore when they left him haunted them for days. But they knew they were walking in the path of duty and could leave their own future, as well as that of the child, in the hands of God.[10]

A number of leaders had gathered for study at Dorchester. As at the previous conference in Topsham, one of the subjects discussed was how the wonderful truths they had studied could be brought to the attention of the scattered Adventists. Joseph Bates's 48-page pamphlet about the Sabbath had been instrumental in bringing a number of honesthearted families into what they were already beginning to call "the truth."

"I have wanted to print our message for some time," James White had declared at Topsham. "But before we can do so, we must have money. I certainly have none with which to launch such an enterprise." The others present had no money to spare, either. And no one knew how the problem was to be solved.[11]

Before the Dorchester conference ended, Ellen White was given a most important vision. When it was finished she spoke to her husband, relaying instruction that he knew had come directly from Heaven:

"I have a message for you. You must begin to print a little paper and send it out to the people. Let it be small at first; but as the people read, they will send you means with which to print, and it will be a success from the first. From this small beginning it was shown to me to be like streams of light that went clear round the world."[12]

But *how, when, where,* was the paper to be printed? and *with what?* James White began searching for the answers.

----

[1] *Life Sketches* (1915), p. 109.

[2] *Ibid.*

[3] *Life Sketches* (1888), pp. 246, 247.

[4] James White letter to Brother and Sister Hastings, Aug. 26, 1848.

[5] *Life Sketches* (1888), pp. 247, 248.

[6] *Ibid.*, p. 248.

[7] *Ibid.*, p. 249.

[8] *Ibid.*, pp. 252, 253.

[9] Arthur L. White, *Ellen G. White, Messenger to the Remnant* (Ellen G. White Publications), pp. 38, 39.

[10] *Life Sketches* (1888), p. 255.

[11] *Origin and History of Seventh-day Adventists*, vol. 1, p. 194.

[12] *Life Sketches* (1915), p. 125.

Chapter Seven

THIS SMALL BEGINNING

JAMES and Ellen White spent most of the 1848-1849 winter in Maine. It was only natural that they would spend as much time as possible with their friends, the Howlands, since this gave them an opportunity to be with their little son, Henry. Also James and Stockbridge were firm friends. Mr. Howland was a well-known builder in the area, and his influence among the businessmen of Topsham must have made it easier for him to help the young minister find employment.

One cold morning during family worship Ellen was given a vision. When it was over she said to her husband, "The Lord has shown me that it is our duty to go to Dartmouth, Massachusetts."

"Were you shown why we should go there?" James asked. "Travel is not easy at this time of the year."

"No, I don't know just why we are needed. We will surely find out after we get there."

After breakfast James walked to the post office to pick up the morning mail. When he returned he entered the house, ascended the stairs, and went into the room where Ellen was working. He was waving a letter in his hand.

"Here's the answer, Ellen," he told her. "This letter explains why we must go to Dartmouth."

"What does it say, James? Who is it from?"

"It's from Philip Collins. He says his son Gilbert is very sick and he begs us to come and pray for the boy."

"Why doesn't he call for Joseph Bates? He is a man of prayer and faith, and he doesn't live far away!"

"I shouldn't be surprised if Elder Bates is away. He travels constantly, you know."

So James and Ellen packed their small trunk and took the train for Dartmouth. Brother Collins was relieved when they arrived at his home. He led them to his son's room, where the boy lay apparently at death's door. He had wasted away almost to a skeleton.

"Nine weeks ago he came down with whooping cough," the father explained. "His mother and I fear that now he may be going into consumption."

With the parents of the sick boy, the Whites knelt by the bed of the apparently dying youth. As they prayed, the power of God flooded the room. James White rose from his knees, picked up the young lad in his arms, lifted him heavenward, and exclaimed as he walked to and fro in the room, "You will not die, but live!"

The Whites spent eight days visiting believers in the area before they turned their steps again toward the Collins home. The boy was at the gate to meet them. His cough was gone, and he had already gained four pounds in weight.[1]

"Praise the Lord," exclaimed James White, as he and Ellen hurried into the house to greet the joyful parents.

While the Whites were still in the area they received a request from the Hastings family in New Ipswich, New Hampshire, asking them to come, for there was serious trouble in their home. Laying this request before the Lord, James and Ellen were impressed they should go.

At New Ipswich they found that the eight-week-old Hastings child was crying continually while it was awake. Mrs. Hastings, nearly frantic, found it impossible to get any rest, and she and her husband were at their wits' end.

Elder White anointed the little one, and he and Ellen prayed that it might find rest. Soon the baby's crying stopped. Its difficulty did not return.[2] A few days later James and Ellen were again on their way back to Topsham, where they remained the rest of the winter.

When spring came the Whites received letters from friends in both Connecticut and New York, urging them to work in those States. Uncertain about what to do, they finally decided to go to Utica, New York, so they wrote a letter accepting the invitation.

But before James could mail the letter Ellen began to experience a feeling of distress, as though something was wrong. At this James burned the letter they had written and prayed that his wife's burden might be removed.

Returning from the post office the next morning, James brought

another letter, which was to change their plans. This one was from Albert Belden, in whose home they had stayed for a few weeks the previous summer. Not only were they warmly invited to return to Rocky Hill but Belden had actually sent them money for transportation.[3] So in the spring of 1849 James and Ellen traveled again to Rocky Hill, Connecticut. It is probable that they occupied the same large unfurnished chamber in Belden's house in which the Sabbath conference had been held the previous year.

The Whites had few possessions to set up housekeeping, but this problem was solved by Miss Clarissa Bonfoey, the guardian of little Henry while his parents had attended the previous year's Sabbath conferences. Her mother had recently died, leaving her a houseful of furniture. She was willing that the Whites use this if she could live with them. She would help with the housework, and thus free Ellen for work and travel with her husband.[4]

Now James began to feel deeply impressed that he must begin publishing the "little paper" about which his wife had received instructions in vision the previous November.[5]

Determining to follow his impressions, James felt God's blessing upon him. But then he was weighed down with perplexity when he thought of the fact that he was totally without money for such a venture. And those who could afford to help were not willing. Finally, discouraged, he said to Ellen, "I'm going to find a field of hay to mow. At least I will be able to earn something to help pay for the printing." He headed for the door.

As he was going out, a crushing burden fell upon Ellen and she fainted. Returning to her side, James knelt and began praying earnestly. Soon he could see she was in vision. He knew there was nothing to fear. Ellen would be strengthened. After the vision was over Ellen said, "James, the vision dealt with you and your work. You did right last year, mowing grass to earn money to attend the conferences. But it is not God's plan that you do so again. You must step out by faith. You must begin to write, write, write! If you go into the hayfield, you will be stricken with sickness."[6]

James accepted the message, although he still couldn't see just how everything was going to work out. He acted by faith, and wrote. *Present Truth* would be the name of his paper, James decided. He penned the words "It is through the truth that souls are sanctified, and made ready to enter the everlasting kingdom. Obedience

The instructions to James White that he must write began today's stream of Adventist literature. Below: The Belden home where the first *Present Truth* was written.

to the truth will kill us to this world, that we may be made alive, by faith in Jesus." [7]

James went to visit Charles Pelton, a printer in Middletown, eight miles from Rocky Hill, and asked him whether he would be willing to print an eight-page paper. The conversation probably went something like this:

Pelton: "Printing is my business. I don't see why I shouldn't print for you just as I do for everyone else."

James: "Perhaps there is a little difference in my case. You see, I have no money. But I expect to receive some soon after the papers go out."

Mr. Pelton undoubtedly eyed his customer warily. He had probably never met anyone who talked like this.

"You look like an honest man. What's your occupation?"

"I'm a minister of the gospel."

"I've met a few crooked preachers in my time, but I don't think you are one of them. I'll take the risk. Bring your material and we'll set it up and print it."

"Thank you, Mr. Pelton. I'll be back later."

With a light heart James White walked the eight miles back to Rocky Hill. The way was open. He would put God to the test, stepping out, as Ellen had said, depending wholly on the "naked promises of God."

James had taken the first step. The *Present Truth* would be published.

---

[1] *Life Sketches* (1888), pp. 255, 256.
[2] *Ibid.*, p. 257.
[3] *Life Sketches* (1915), p. 123, footnote.
[4] *Footprints of the Pioneers*, p. 106.
[5] *Ibid.*, p. 125.
[6] *Ibid.*, pp. 125, 126.
[7] James White, *Present Truth* (Middletown, Conn.: 1849), vol. 1, No. 1, p. 1.

Chapter Eight

THE LITTLE PAPER

A SOLITARY figure trudges along the dusty road connecting Rocky Hill with Middletown. The man is James White, "that dauntless man of God," on his way to the printer. In his pocket is something very precious—material for the first issue of the paper, *Present Truth*.[1]

James was to make that trip on foot many times. After the material for each paper was typeset at Charles Pelton's print shop he would go from Rocky Hill to Middletown to indicate any changes necessary before it was printed.

In late July James drove up to the Belden home in Belden's horse and buggy, which he had borrowed for the occasion, with one thousand copies of the eight-page *Present Truth*.

The first edition of that little paper was off the press!

The papers were laid out on the floor and the little group in the house, with many prayers and tears, called down Heaven's blessing on the leaflets and prayed that the Holy Spirit would speak through those papers to the readers, guiding them into the truth. James and Ellen, Clarissa Bonfoey, and perhaps some of the Beldens, folded and addressed the papers. It was a time-consuming task to address the papers by hand, but for the workers it was a joyful task.

The following morning James placed the papers ready for mailing in his old carpetbag and took them to the Middletown post office.[2]

A few days later, on July 28, a second son was born to James and Ellen White. They named him James Edson—James, after his father, and Edson, perhaps after Hiram Edson, the pioneer farmer-preacher of western New York.

James received a hearty response from the readers of the papers.

The first *Present Truth* came from the press in Middletown, Connecticut, in the room above the A.O.H. sign.

They wanted to see *Present Truth* continued. The flock was hungry, and this was spiritual food for their souls. The first number was quickly followed by three others. Readers generously sent in money so that the work might go on. James was thus able to pay Mr. Pelton the cost of printing the first four numbers, reported to be $64.50. Realizing that he and Ellen might soon be called on to travel again, he wrote constantly, often far into the night. His articles dealt with such subjects as the advent of Christ, the judgment, the three angels' messages, and similar topics.

When baby Edson was six weeks old his parents traveled to Maine, taking him with them. Assumedly, they made their headquarters at the Howland home, where their 2-year-old Henry was staying.

Shortly after James and Ellen arrived at Topsham, Ellen told James they were needed in Paris, Maine. The Lord had shown her

60

that serious trouble was there. So with Stockbridge Howland they journeyed the 60 miles to Paris.

Paris was the home of the Stevens, the Stowell, and the Edward Andrews families—all stalwart and strong in the faith. It was also plagued by some of the wildest fanatics in New England, and Elder and Mrs. White were directed to go to Paris to check this spirit. One fanatic was F. T. Howland (no relation of Stockbridge), who tried to break up a meeting the Whites held with the Paris group.

As Stockbridge Howland rose from prayer the Spirit of God rested upon him. Pointing his finger at F. T. Howland, he said in a voice of authority, "You have torn the hearts of God's children and made them bleed. Leave this house, or God will smite you." The fanatic leaped to his feet, grabbed his hat, and fled.

A spirit of reformation and revival swept over the company. Heartfelt confessions were made, and long-standing differences vanished. Twenty-year-old John Nevins Andrews exclaimed with deep emotion, "I would exchange a thousand errors for one truth."[3]

John Andrews always dated his conversion from that meeting in Paris, held on September 14, 1849. The believers, who had ceased holding meetings of any kind for more than a year, now began anew to meet regularly.

From Paris, the Whites hastened to Gorham, for they had learned that Ellen's mother had injured her foot severely. In answer to prayer, Mrs. Harmon was healed.

There is no clear record of the travels of James and Ellen White during the fall of 1849. But it is known that they traveled widely, visiting the scattered believers in New England and New York.

As Ellen White had predicted, money began to come in to meet the expense of printing the paper. And although there were discouraging moments connected with it, and the going was slow at first, it was a success from the beginning. Letters began to come from new families who were accepting the message the paper presented. Many were earnest Christian people of good judgment, whose lives served as a testimony to their faith. Lights began springing up all over New England. How long would it be before that light would circle the earth as Ellen White had predicted?

That autumn of 1849 the Whites were invited to labor for a while in New York State. Much work had been done in Massachusetts and Connecticut, but now the work was opening up in the north, especially in Vermont and New York.

November found them in Volney, New York, where they attended a conference. After visiting other places they decided that for the present their work was in New York State, so resolved to make their home in Oswego, which was a rapidly growing center of Adventist influence. They rented a house, borrowed furniture from some believers, and James began to write and publish.

. No doubt James was glad to be finished with the time-consuming and wearisome task of walking the sixteen-mile round trip from Rocky Hill to Middletown to carry on the work of issuing the *Present Truth.* And he was probably pleased with not having to tramp through the deep snow that would fall during the coming winter.

Clarissa Bonfoey apparently moved with the Whites to Oswego, and little Edson was left in her care while his parents traveled. Henry was still with the Howlands in Maine.

Two months passed after the publishing of the fourth number of *Present Truth* before another was printed. When he first published the paper, James expected to issue only a few numbers. Now it was becoming evident that it should be continued beyond that.

One thing James was firmly decided upon. No longer would he and his wife be the only major contributors to the paper. He had written to Joseph Bates and other workers, inviting them to furnish him with articles for the paper. In the fifth number James also invited subscribers to write in concerning their experiences or thoughts on some Bible topic. Each paper also contained an invitation to readers to send a contribution to help meet the expenses of getting out *Present Truth.*

On both points James met with disappointment. The quick response with funds that came after his appeal in Number 1 was not repeated. For two months there had been no paper, and interest had fallen off. Nor was he very successful in securing articles for it.

James received his most crushing disappointment in a letter written by Joseph Bates. Bates wrote that he felt a paper should not be published.[4] Bates no doubt believed it was better to prepare a tract or pamphlet dealing with some vital truth, print 2,000 or 3,000 copies, carry them into the field, and scatter them everywhere.

Bates's attitude was too much for Elder White. The oldest and most influential Sabbathkeeping minister felt he was on the wrong track! In a letter James wrote shortly afterward he announced he was giving up the paper "forever." [5]

His "forever" lasted a very short time. Ellen was given a vision and shown many things in regard to the paper.

"I saw that God did not want James to stop yet, but he must *write, write, write, write,* and speed the message and let it go."

With fresh courage, James White picked up his heavy burden. [6] For the remainder of that winter of 1849-1850, and into the spring of 1850, *Present Truth* came regularly from the Oswego press until Number 10 had appeared. Individuals began writing for the paper, and as new converts were made they sent James money to meet printing costs. He was solidly committed to the publishing work. From then on, for the most part, the name of James White would fly from the masthead of denominational periodicals, but this never prevented his traveling freely from place to place, visiting churches and, later, attending camp meetings. He loved public work, and no one could ever accuse him of burying himself in an editorial office.

How was he able to do so much writing in addition to his preaching and administrative duties? In later years he was to describe how for long periods of time he wrote his editorials between the hours of 8:00 P.M. and midnight. This was not done so he could travel for pleasure. Field trips were not reserved for spring and summer. Some of his most difficult, as well as fruitful, trips were taken in the dead of winter. With Ellen by his side, he braved hardships and defied storms. Nothing would prevent him from visiting and bringing comfort and instruction to the scattered flock.

On May 15, 1850, James and Ellen set out from Oswego on a trip. Their first stop was at Topsham, Maine, where they fellowshiped with the Howlands and once again saw little Henry, now nearing the age of 3. From there they paid a short visit to North Paris, where they found some of the members discouraged. The meetings James and Ellen held there did much to strengthen that company's faith in God.

From Paris they went down to Dorchester, where they enjoyed visiting with the Nichols family before going to Fairhaven. Did they find Joseph Bates at his home? The record is silent, but prob-

ably he was away. However, it is known that this was the year
when Prudence Bates, Joseph's devoted wife, began to keep the
Sabbath after she had resisted the teachings of her husband for four
years.[7] Did this visit by the Whites have any part in bringing
about the happy change? We do not know.

James and Ellen now journeyed up across Massachusetts, entered New Hampshire, and visited the bereaved family of Leonard
Hastings at New Ipswich.

Six weeks before their arrival Mrs. Hastings had begun a letter to a brother and sister, entreating them to respond to God's
truth, a letter she never completed. Interrupted, perhaps by some
household duty or by sickness, she never picked up her pen again.
Two days later she was dead from what could be called acute ap-
pendicitis. There was no known cure in her time.

Ellen and James met the bereaved father and motherless children, and shed tears of sympathy with them. Ellen had been
strongly attached to Elvira Hastings. When news of her sudden
death came, Ellen had found it difficult to be reconciled to the
tragedy.[8]

The Hastings children had been drifting from God and were
losing their religious faith. We may be certain that James and
Ellen used the sad experience they were passing through to talk to
them of their souls' salvation. Before they left, James had the
privilege of baptizing four of the Hastings children. James felt
sure that the mother's death had made the children think seriously,
and had helped to turn their steps heavenward.[9]

Only a few more stops, and the travelers would be back home
again with their little boy. Crossing the frontier into Canada East,
now known as Quebec, they arrived at Melbourne. There they
found an active company of some twenty believers. Then they
hurried back to Sutton and Irasburg, Vermont. At this latter place
there were children awaiting baptism, much to the joy of their
devoted parents and the young traveling minister who would ad-
minister the rite.

It was not far to Waitsfield, Vermont, and from there to Hamilton, New York, where they spent a profitable weekend. James
found eleven persons waiting for baptism. One more day on the
train, and they were safely home again.

How did Ellen and James travel? Part of the way by train. But where churches were close together friends drove them from one appointment to another by horse and carriage, or by sleigh in winter. To reach points not on the railway they may have used stagecoaches, still quite common in 1850.

Railway trains were crude affairs; coaches were made of wood and had stoves in them. The roadbeds were rough. Since they carried no nonsmoking cars, it was impossible to avoid inhaling tobacco smoke. Stations were inadequate.

In a letter, written some years later, Ellen described how they sometimes left smoke-filled waiting rooms and stood in the bitterly cold air outside rather than breathe warm, polluted air. Certainly they were not traveling for pleasure in those days.[10]

The tenth number of *Present Truth* was published in Oswego in May, 1850. While on the trip just described James was thinking of a different type of publication, which he hoped would win many converts. His plan was encouraged by his wife, who wrote, "The Lord showed me that he, James, must take the testimonies that the leading Adventists published in 1844 and republish them and make *them* ashamed. He is now doing that work."[11] On July 21 he wrote to Leonard Hastings from Hamilton about his plans. He would publish a new paper, which he would call the *Advent Review*. (This is not to be confused with the *Review and Herald*, which was launched later in the year.)[12]

For material for this new paper, James went to back numbers of Advent papers printed by leaders of the 1844 movement and reprinted some of their articles. He would show that the large majority of Sundaykeeping Adventists had forsaken the pillars of faith once so widely proclaimed.[13]

Meanwhile, James had moved his family from Oswego to Centerport, not far from Auburn, New York, where he found another printer. Brother Harris, of Centerport, kindly offered part of his house to the Whites. Three years had passed since James and Ellen, accompanied by Elder Bates, had first knocked on the door of that home. It was there that Bates had dried out his clothes after falling into the Erie Canal.

In Centerport troubles began descending thick and fast on the Whites. After breakfast one morning James and Ellen drove one of their visitors, Elder S. W. Rhodes, two miles to Port Byron, where he boarded a boat. When they returned, Mrs. Harris met them at the door with the alarming words, "Your babe is struck with death!" The parents rushed into the bedroom and found it was true. Only prayer could save his life. James longed for the presence of another minister and decided to get one.

Leaving little James Edson in his mother's arms, he rode as fast as possible along the towpath of the canal. After he had gone five miles he overtook the line boat and persuaded Elder Rhodes to return with him to the bedside of the sick child.

We may be sure that all the way back to Centerport both men were praying that they might not be too late. At the house they hurried into the sickroom, where Elder Rhodes anointed the little fellow and prayed for him. The child opened his eyes and recognized his parents. From that hour he began to get better.[14]

Then another danger threatened. James was attacked by cholera, the scourge that took so many lives before a remedy for it was discovered. Ellen, with Sisters Harris and Bonfoey and Ellen's sister, Sarah, knelt by the bedside of the sick man, and their prayers ascended to God, pleading that He would display His healing power.

They were heard. Color came back to his face, and joy showed from his countenance. Later, he had another attack, but then his sickness retreated and he continued to improve.[15]

In August Numbers one and two of the *Advent Review* appeared, followed by three and four in September. For this paper, James did little writing. Practically all its content included articles previously written by Miller, Himes, Bliss, Litchfield, and other Advent leaders.

Three thousand copies of each edition of the paper were printed[16] and went far and wide. The results were thrilling. But though they contained material on which all Adventists had at one time united, they did not present the particular truths cherished by the Sabbathkeeping Adventists. James now prepared to issue a purely missionary church paper, one that could be used to carry "the light," as they called present truth, to people everywhere.

The hour had struck for the birth of James White's third paper, *The Second Advent Review and Sabbath Herald.*[17]

This periodical would enjoy a long and useful life.

---

[1] *Footprints of the Pioneers,* p. 107.
[2] *Ibid.,* pp. 107, 108.

3 *Life Sketches* (1888), pp. 260, 261.
4 *Origin and History of Seventh-day Adventists*, vol. 1, p. 200.
5 *Ibid.*, p. 201.
6 *Life Sketches* (1888), p. 265.
7 Virgil E. Robinson, *Cabin Boy to Advent Crusader* (Nashville, Tenn.: Southern Pub. Assn., 1960), p. 124.
8 *Life Sketches* (1888), p. 257.
9 *Ibid.*, p. 258.
10 Ellen G. White letter to Edson and Emma W. 16a, 1870.
11 Ellen G. White letter 8, to Arabella Hastings, Aug. 4, 1850.
12 James White letter to Leonard Hastings, July 21, 1850.
13 *Origin and History*, vol. 1, p. 202.
14 *Life Sketches* (1888), pp. 272, 273.
15 *Ibid.*, pp. 274, 275.
16 James White letter to H. L. Hastings, July 21, 1850.
17 *Origin and History*, vol. 1, pp. 202, 203.

Chapter Nine

PARIS HILL

A GENERAL gathering of workers took place at Paris Hill in November, 1850, during which it was decided that a new paper should be published.[1] James found that the paper could be economically printed at a local printing establishment, the G. L. Mellen Company. He had already taken rooms with the Edward Andrews family, where they would be only two blocks from the print shop. It was at Paris Hill that James published the last issue of *Present Truth* while gathering material for the new paper he had in mind, which he finally would name *The Advent Review and Sabbath Herald*.

Before leaving Auburn for Paris, the Whites made the hard decision that it would be best to separate from their two-year-old son, Edson, thus freeing them for labor among the churches. Clarissa Bonfoey took the child to the hospitable home of Ira Abbey in North Brookfield, New York.[2]

John Andrews soon became attracted to James White. With the encouragement of the older man, he began preaching in surrounding towns and villages. The accession of this aggressive, scholarly young man represented, as James White wrote, "no small reinforcement."

Before the end of November, James gave Mr. Mellen the material for the first number of *The Second Advent Review and Sabbath Herald*, which came off the press before the month ended. The word *second* was soon abandoned. Since 1850 the name has been shortened still more, until today it is known simply as the *Review and Herald*, or the *Review*.

All during that busy winter at Paris Hill, James White kept up a continual correspondence with leading brethren scattered throughout New England and New York. He also had proof

In the Paris, Maine, print shop, which also housed the post office, the *Review and Herald* had its beginnings.

sheets to read, correct, and return to the printer. Between November and June, 1851, thirteen numbers of the *Review* were printed in Paris Hill and sent out into the field.

The paper carried no subscription price. Those who were too poor to pay could receive it free. Others were invited to send in whatever sums of money they could spare, and a few made generous donations for the struggling paper. Each issue listed the names of those who were assisting, with the amount they gave. Even as small a sum as twenty-five cents was acknowledged.

It was particularly gratifying to James White that after the position Joseph Bates had taken in regard to the regular publication of a paper, the first number contained an article by the sea captain.

One day a letter of invitation came for the Whites to attend a general meeting at Waterbury, Vermont, January 18 and 19, 1851.

The question was not whether to go, but how. Since James had lent his only horse to John Andrews and another brother so that they could visit believers in Canada East and northern Vermont, he and Ellen decided to use public transportation.[3] They first went by train south to Boston, then west to New Ipswich for a visit with the Hastings family. From New Ipswich they went to Washington, New Hampshire, forty miles away, by private conveyance.

Continuing north, a fifteen-mile ride brought them to the home of Stephen Smith, a member whom they knew to be entangled with spiritualism. Hoping that he might be strengthened and straightened out at the coming conference, James gave him five dollars to help him buy a horse and sleigh to make the journey. They agreed to ride with him to Waterbury, the place of meeting. On the way they stopped to see Elder Joseph Baker. Discouraged and troubled by poor health, Elder Baker had decided not to attend. Out came another five dollars from the generous pocket of Elder White, and Baker went by train.

The Whites and their driver then pushed northward for three days in order to arrive at Waterbury in time for the meeting. They rode in an open sleigh, without even a buffalo robe to keep them warm. After the trip it took them quite awhile to thaw out!

There were members at the meeting who needed more than thawing out. Rumors had been circulating that the Whites had a better horse than necessary and were living easy lives off money James received from believers—money intended for the support of the paper. In particular, a Brother N. A. H. had been giving expression to such sentiments. When news of what was being said reached the ears of James White, he was both dismayed and disheartened.

Thinking back only seven or eight months, James remembered how he had found this man poor and in need of encouragement. Taking twenty dollars from his pocket—money donated by friends of the cause to use wherever it was most needed—he gave this to N. A. H. And he had gone further than that. He had taken his own coat off his back and put it on that brother! After this, he had influenced the brethren to buy N. A. H. a horse and carriage.

At the close of the Waterbury meetings a collection was taken up to help meet the expenses of attendants who had traveled long distances and spent considerable to get there. But none of the money thus collected was given to the Whites, who had probably come the farthest of any. Somewhat disheartened by such an attitude, James and Ellen White retraced their steps through Massachusetts and Maine until they were once again at Paris.[4]

Rumors concerning the Whites' personal finances continued to spread. One believer in Massachusetts wrote a long letter to James, reproving him for his extravagant way of living. Naturally, the question arose in his mind, What's the use? How could men who professed to love the Lord and believe the Bible treat him so cruelly?

Completely discouraged, he sat down and wrote a short note to appear on the back of the next issue of the *Review*. He then put on his hat and headed for the door. Before going out he turned to Ellen.

"Wife, it is no use trying to struggle on any longer. These things are crushing me, and will soon carry me to the grave. . . . I have written a note for the paper stating that I shall publish no more." [5] As he stepped across the threshold Ellen fainted. He hurried to her side. In answer to his prayer, she recovered.

The following morning while praying at family worship Ellen White had a vision. Specific instruction was given in regard to the paper. It was not to be discontinued, for that was just what Satan wanted. If James would continue to publish, the Lord would uphold him.

This was the sixth and last time that James White proposed to stop printing and was kept from doing so by the testimony of his wife. From this time on, nothing could separate James from the publishing work.

But if Elder White received some critical letters that tended to crush his spirit he also received some that had the opposite effect. If he had his detractors, he likewise had loyal supporters who loved him and were not afraid to tell him so.

In a communication submitted to the *Review and Herald*, Elder S. W. Rhodes wrote these cheering words to his associate: "Be of good cheer, my dear tried brother, and in Jesus' name, turn the battle to the gate. . . . I mean to go to heaven with you. I love you more and more." Another brother by the name of Laughhead wrote, "My dear brother, be strong for the Lord is with us, and we shall soon receive the reward if we faint not." [6]

Also, from Massachusetts came a letter from the man who had been so critical. In an entirely new tone, he expressed heartfelt sorrow for having so misjudged his brother. So moving was his confession that James and Ellen wept when they read it. But even the writing of this letter did not entirely satisfy the brother. He traveled all the way to Paris to see the Whites and once again confessed his error. He told them he had been influenced by a false friend.

The Whites had suffered severely physically as well as emotionally on that winter tour through New England. Later, Ellen wrote that it was years before James recovered fully from the effects of that long exposure, and then only in answer to prayer.[7]

James and Ellen were compelled to travel by stagecoach, which was often wearying and inconvenient. During a visit to the church at Sutton, Vermont, some of the laity decided it was their duty to provide a good horse and carriage for the use of these spiritual leaders. Word was sent out inviting Sabbathkeeping Adventists who had horses to sell to bring them to a certain crossroads on a specified day, when James and his wife could make their choice.

The evening before they went to look at the horses, Ellen was instructed by the Lord not to take the first horse presented, a high-spirited sorrel, nor the second, an iron-gray horse, but to take the third, a well-built, dappled chestnut horse.

The next morning they went to the appointed place. There were the three horses she had seen the night before. Of course, they chose the chestnut horse. For many years this faithful horse took the Whites over long distances. Over good roads and bad, he carried them safely through all kinds of weather. His new owners were also given money with which to buy a new carriage.[8]

Dollars for the *Review* continued to come in, and the paper went out to an ever-widening circle of readers. As Andrews, Bates, Edson, Rhodes, and a dozen other preachers traveled far and wide they continually met persons interested in Bible truth. The names and addresses were sent to James White, and he made sure that these individuals received the paper.

Occasionally James received letters that especially touched his heart. One came from J. B. Sweet, a fisherman living in Connecticut:

"I should be glad, dear brother, to have your paper continued, but my limited means will not admit of it at present, and to ask it gratis is more than I can do. If you can do me the kindness to continue the paper, as soon as the means is in my hand you shall have it."[9]

Needless to say, his paper was not discontinued.

James felt concerned regarding those who were in a position to help support the paper but made no move to do so. He often wondered whether they should continue to get the *Review* free, while others were paying for it. He wrote about this problem in the *Review and Herald:*

"We do not speak of want [of means]. If this was any other than the cause of God, we then might have to urge appeal after appeal for help, as is done in other papers. More than a score of brethren have said to us, 'If you need means, just let me know it and you shall have it.' But shall we call on such free hearted brethren while three-fourths of those who read the *Review and Herald* have done nothing to support it? We think we should not." [10] Is it right that a few self-sacrificing souls should bear the whole expense, and share the whole blessing?

After mulling the problem over, however, James White decided to continue to send the paper gratis to anyone indicating a desire to have it, since, he decided, they were the very ones who needed it most.

---

[1] *Origin and History*, vol. 1, p. 202.
[2] *Life Sketches* (1888), p. 277.
[3] *Ibid.*, p. 278.
[4] *Ibid.*, pp. 278-280.
[5] *Ibid.*, pp. 280, 281.
[6] *Review and Herald*, Dec. 23, 1851.
[7] *Life Sketches* (1888), p. 282.
[8] *Review and Herald*, April 25, 1935.
[9] *Ibid.*, Vol. I, January, 1851.
[10] *Ibid.*, Vol. I, No. 7, March, 1851.

Chapter Ten

SARATOGA SPRINGS

THE first volume of the *Review and Herald,* which contained only thirteen numbers, was printed in Paris, Maine, over a period of seven months. During that time many invitations came to James White to attend meetings and conferences, but while he was away publication of the paper was suspended. At the time, there was no assistant editor to remain near the printing office and substitute for him. True, there was a publishing committee, but most of the time its members were out in the fields far away preaching.

Through the columns of the *Review,* Elder White called for a general meeting to convene at the home of Jesse Thompson near Ballston Spa, in eastern New York. Mr. Thompson was a lawyer and farmer of some means, who cheerfully made substantial donations to the work. A number of workers attended. The meetings were held in Thompson's barn from June 25 to July 1, 1851, and a wide range of subjects was discussed, with the publishing work receiving its share of attention. No doubt James asked whether the paper should be printed in a more central location; converts were coming in more rapidly in New York State than in New England. He may also have asked whether the paper should be published weekly. The believers were widely scattered, and the *Review* helped tie them together. Workers found it convenient to announce in the columns of the *Review* dates and places for general meetings.

James also may have pointed out his need for help in the office. Calls were continually coming in requesting Ellen and James to visit churches. It was difficult for them to answer these calls and at the same time keep the paper going regularly.

Deciding that Saratoga Springs, a few miles from Thompson's home, would be a good place to live and print the *Review,* James and Ellen moved from Paris Hill. For several weeks they lived in

SECOND ADVENT REVIEW,
AND SABBATH HERALD.

" HERE IS THE PATIENCE OF THE SAINTS; HERE ARE THEY THAT KEEP THE COMMANDMENTS OF GOD AND THE FAITH OF JESUS."

VOL. I.   PARIS, ME., NOVEMBER, 1850.   No. 1.

JOSEPH BATES, S. W. RHODES, J. N. ANDREWS, and
JAMES WHITE, Publishing Committee.
G. L. MELLEN & CO., Printers.

TERMS—Gratis, except the reader desires to aid in its publication.
☞ All communications, orders, and remittances, for the Review and Herald,
should be addressed to JAMES WHITE, Paris, Me., (Post paid.)

When was the Sabbath Instituted?

Some have contended that the Sabbath was not instituted until the law was given to Moses at Mount Sinai. But there are serious difficulties in the way of this belief. In the second chapter of Genesis, after having given an account of the creation, the sacred historian says: "On the seventh day God ended his work which he had made: and he rested on the seventh day from all his work which he had made. And God blessed the seventh day and sanctified it; because that in it he had rested from all his work which God created and made." Now, if any part of this narrative is to be construed literally, the whole of it must be; and if we may not venture to deny or explain away the account which Moses has given of the creation, then we may not deny or explain away this unequivocal statement respecting the original institution of the Sabbath in Paradise. The blessing and sanctifying of the seventh day is mentioned in connection with the first seventh day in the order of time, and it is so mentioned as most forcibly to impress the reader that the Sabbath was then instituted. God's resting on the day is given as the reason for its sanctification; and it cannot be supposed that this reason existed two thousand five hundred years before the institution. We conclude, therefore, that the Sabbath was enjoined immediately after the close of the work of creation.

This opinion is corroborated by some facts recorded in the Scriptures. There are frequent and early notices of reckoning by sevens. Noah observed a period of seven days in sending the raven and dove from the ark; the term week is used in the contract between Jacob and Laban; Joseph mourned seven days for his father; and Job and his friends observed the term of seven days.

Nor is it in the sacred volume or among the Jews alone that such facts are found. Nearly all the nations of antiquity were acquainted with the weekly division of time. The Assyrians, Egyptians, Indians, Arabians, and, in a word, all the nations of the East, have in all ages made use of a week of seven days.— And we find that these nations not only divided time thus, but that they regarded as holy the very day which had been sanctified as a Sabbath, although they had forsaken the true worship of God. Homer, Hesiod, and Callimachus, say, " The seventh day is holy." Theophilus of Antioch says, respecting the seventh day, "The day which all mankind celebrate." Josephus asserts that, " no city of Greeks or barbarians can be found, which does not acknowledge a seventh day's rest from labor." And Philo says, that "the Sabbath was a festival not peculiar to any one people or country, but so common to all mankind, that it might be called a public and general feast of the nativity of the world." These authors, who lived in different ages and were of different nations, cannot be supposed to have written thus in order to please the Jews, who were generally despised and persecuted; and this universal reverence for the seventh day cannot be accounted for upon any other supposition than that the Sabbath was instituted at the close of creation, and handed down by tradition to all the descendants of Adam.

If additional proof of this early institution of the Sabbath is needed, it may be drawn from the manner in which it was revived in the wilderness. Before the children of Israel came to Mount Sinai we find them voluntarily making provision for the Sabbath, by gathering on the sixth day a double portion of manna. "And all the rulers came and told Moses. And he said unto them, this is that which the Lord hath said; to-morrow is the rest of the holy Sabbath unto the Lord." "And it came to pass, that there went out some of the people on the seventh day to gather, and they found none. And the Lord said unto Moses, how long refuse ye to keep my commandments and my laws? See, for that the Lord hath given you the Sabbath, therefore he giveth you, on the sixth day, the bread of two days."— The rebuke, how long refuse ye to keep my commandments and my laws? implies the previous appointment of the Sabbath; and the positive assertion, the Lord hath given you the Sabbath, ought to settle the question in any mind disposed to understand the sacred historian.

What day of the week do the Scriptures designate as the Sabbath?

To this question, it might be supposed that every person who has any acquaintance with the subject would readily reply— The seventh. We are aware, however, that efforts are made to render this a difficult point to determine. We shall, therefore, make a few remarks upon it.

It is plainly recorded that the Creator, after laboring the first six days, in which he completed the work of creation, rested the following day, which was the seventh in the order of creation. This particular day God therefore sanctified and blessed. "And God blessed the seventh day." When the law was given at Mount Sinai, the observance of the seventh day was commanded; and the manner in which the fourth commandment is expressed, shows beyond a doubt, that one particular and definite day was known to Israel by this name. Consequently, they needed no instruction as to what day was intended. This is observable in Ex. xvi, 22, where the sixth and seventh days of the week are mentioned by their ordinal names, as a subject with which the people were familiarly acquainted. In this place, also, the seventh day is declared to be the Sabbath. There can be no reasonable doubt but that the day which in the time of Moses was known as the seventh day, was the same in its weekly succession with that which is called the seventh day in Gen. ii, 3. If the seventh day mentioned in the fourth commandment was not the same day of the week mentioned in Gen. ii, 3, as some profess to think, it must be perfectly inexplicable, that no intimation is given in the history of those events that another seventh day was intended than the one mentioned in the institution of the Sabbath, especially since both are recorded in the same appellation in a direct series of events. But what removes all obscurity from the subject is, that God has positively declared that the day which he commanded to be observed in Ex. xx, is the same on which he rested at the close of the creation. " Remember the Sabbath day to keep it holy." " The seventh day is the Sabbath of the Lord thy God." " For in six days the Lord made heaven and earth, the sea and all that in them is, and rested on the seventh day: wherefore the Lord blessed the Sabbath day and hallowed it." This language is definite; and while it assures us that the day here commanded to be observed is the same in its weekly returns with the day on which God rested, it assures us against any derangement of the week, or loss of time which might have been produced in the long lapse of time from the creation, by the general apostasy from the true worship of God. Had the true Sabbath been lost, it was certainly restored; and the day then known as the seventh day received the divine sanction. The same remark is applicable to the subject during the succeeding history of the Jewish nation. Had the weekly Sabbath fallen into total neglect, and the day of its regular recurrence been forgotten, our Lord Jesus Christ, by giving his divine example in favor of the day known by the Jewish nation as the proper seventh day of the decalogue, has settled the question conclusively, down to that time: so that the day known in the New Testament as the Sabbath, was the seventh day in regular succession from the creation of the world. A perfect uniformity among all the nations in the known world, as to the days of the

the Thompson home while James moved his supplies. Then they
found a house to rent in Saratoga Springs.[1]

Having a home of their own, even a rented one, was most
gratifying to James and Ellen White. At last they could get part
of their long-scattered family together. They sent to Rocky Hill,
directing Clarissa Bonfoey, who had returned there from New
York, to join them with little Edson.[2] (Henry remained with the
Howlands at Topsham, Maine.) At the same time, Ellen's sister,
Sarah Harmon, came up with her fiancé, Stephen Belden. On
August 5, 1851, James White married them.[3]

Records are brief concerning the Whites' nine-month stay in
Saratoga Springs. It is not certain whether they had a large enough
house to take in the newly married couple, as well as Miss Bonfoey,
but considering their "open door" policy, they probably did.

Sarah and Stephen were to remain with the Whites for a number of years. Sarah especially was a great blessing to Ellen. She took
over the housework, and this enabled Ellen to spend more time writing out testimonies for individuals. Stephen was an all-round
mechanic. He also took charge of the business of the *Review and
Herald.*

On Sarah and Stephen's wedding day Volume II, Number 1,
of the *Review and Herald* came from the press in Saratoga Springs.
The little group of workers were soon busy folding and addressing
these papers.

More help was to come. One morning shortly after the paper
had resumed publication James received a letter from a Miss A. R.
Smith, with a nine-stanza poem enclosed. At the time she wrote,
Miss Smith was living near Boston. James liked the poem and filed
it with other material for the September 16 issue of the paper.[4] But
first he took the letter and poem to Ellen, asking her to listen as he
read it. The letter began very modestly: "It is with much reluctance that I send you these verses on a subject which a few weeks
since were so foreign to my thoughts."

"It is evident," remarked James, "that she has not long been a
Sabbathkeeper. Now listen to the first verse of her poem:

> 'Fear not little flock,
> For Christ is our Rock;
> The promise stands sure,
> The kingdom He'll give, to the same that endure.' "

Ellen liked the poem also. "You know," James said, "I could use someone with a talent like that for writing. Why shouldn't this Miss Smith join our company of workers?"

Later, when James was talking with Joseph Bates he asked what he knew of Miss Smith. Bates gave a favorable report, so James sent a letter to Miss Smith inviting her to come to Saratoga and work as an editorial assistant on the *Review and Herald*.

The answer came promptly, but it brought disappointment to Elder White. Annie said she would like to accept his offer, but her physical condition made it impossible for her to be of service. For months her eyes had given constant pain, and there were times when she could read nothing.

James White pondered the problem. Then he wrote her a letter suggesting that she come anyway. They would pray together. Was it not true, he asked, that God can do for us what we cannot do for ourselves?

There is no indication that Annie had ever met James White prior to this time. But she had heard of him, had read some issues of the *Review and Herald*, and knew that he was a man of God. Her faith responded to his appeal. She packed her things and traveled from Boston to Saratoga Springs. In answer to the prayers of faith her eye trouble disappeared, and for the next three years she played an important role in getting the *Review and Herald* published regularly. Other poems from her pen were printed. Several of them have become hymns.[5]

With Sarah Belden looking after the house, Ellen had time to compile the visions she had written out, going back to her first vision in Portland, seven years before. James helped her arrange these and had them printed in a 64-page pamphlet under the title *A Sketch of the Christian Experience and Views of Ellen G. White.*[6] A notice appeared in the *Review and Herald* announcing that this booklet would be ready in a few days. Of the $100 it cost to print it, $38 had already been received. James hoped that those interested would supply the balance. This was the first Ellen G. White book ever published. There would be many more to follow.

The *Review and Herald* continued to operate on a free-gift basis. On page 1 of each issue the terms were outlined on which it could be obtained: "It is expected that all the friends of the cause will aid in its publication, as the Lord hath prospered them."

With additional help in the office, James and Ellen were released from some of the cares that had oppressed them. In the
November 25 issue, White reported about an "Eastern Tour" of
churches in various parts of New England. He had been away from
the office from October 23 to November 18.[7]

Hearing of the blessings that the Whites had brought to the
churches in the East, those in New York State asked for a similar
visit. So, leaving Saratoga Springs in January, the Whites braved
the winter storms and traveled from one church to another. They
had hoped to spend some time with the company at Camden, New
York. But a violent storm blanketed the country with heavy snow
on that particular Sabbath, and very few members living at a distance were able to attend. However, they came back to Saratoga
Springs with light hearts, rejoicing in the progress of the work,
but worn in body. James began to wonder how much longer he
could stand up under the strain. He wrote to his friend Stockbridge
Howland:

"We are unusually well, all but myself. I cannot long endure
the labors of traveling and the care of publishing. Wednesday night
we worked until two o'clock in the morning, folding and wrapping
Number 12 of the *Review and Herald,* then I retired and coughed
till daylight. Pray for me. The cause is prospering gloriously. Perhaps the Lord will not have need of me longer, and will let me rest
in the grave. I hope to be free from the paper. I have stood by it in
extreme adversity; and now when its friends are many, I feel free to
leave it, if someone can be found who will take it."[8]

During this summer Samuel Rhodes made a suggestion that
James thought extremely practical and proceeded to implement.
Each church or company was invited to appoint one of its members
to be the local "agent" to handle church publications. It would be
his duty to see that papers were received, old addresses corrected
when people moved, and so on. He would also collect funds so the
publishing work might continue to grow.[9]

For months James White had been thinking of how the publishing work might be placed on a more satisfactory foundation,
as well as of other problems and needs connected with the spreading
of the Advent message. He got in touch with Jesse Thompson and
broached the idea of a conference of all the workers who could come
to Ballston Spa. Thompson was cordial to the idea, and offered the

use of his twenty-one-room house to those coming to the conference.

So, under the heading "Conference," there appeared in the *Review and Herald* of March 2, 1852, notice of a conference to be held at the house of Jesse Thompson, two miles from Ballston Spa. It would begin at 10:00 A.M. on Friday, March 12, and continue for several days.

On that chilly March morning there gathered in the large parlor of Jesse Thompson's spacious house the leaders of the work. Among others there were James and Ellen White, Joseph Bates, J. N. Andrews, Hiram Edson, Frederick Wheeler, Samuel W. Rhodes, Washington Morse, Joseph Baker, as well as their kindly host, Jesse Thompson.

For James White the publishing work was probably the subject that loomed largest. What could be done to strengthen it? He had seen the papers going out to all parts of the field. Reports were coming back, telling of many converts brought into the church through reading the straight truths found in the publications. He was convinced that this was one of God's chosen methods for calling out His remnant ones.

"Brethren," we can imagine him asking earnestly during the afternoon devoted to that subject, "why should we not own and operate our own press? Think of the hundreds of dollars profit that we pour into the hands of the commercial presses. Do you feel it is right to have those presses turning out our literature on the Sabbath day?"

The brethren listened carefully. Where, they asked, would he find a staff qualified to operate printing presses, set type, and bind books? James pointed out that the work of operating a hand press was very simple. That was the only kind of press they could afford at present. As for pressmen, he was in touch with one who might be persuaded to help them and also train some apprentices.

Other questions followed. "What would it cost to move the office from here, secure printing equipment, and set up in some other city?"

"I think about $600 would be needed," [10] James replied. He went on to say that it would require faith, without which nothing could be done. He pointed out that three years earlier the believers in New York State had numbered only about twenty. Now there were almost a thousand believers.

So it was voted to move the publishing work to Rochester, a thriving city some three hundred miles west of Saratoga Springs, and buy printing equipment they could operate. To meet the cost, James said he would place an appeal in the next issue of the *Review and Herald,* inviting the believers to give as God had prospered them. The same paper would carry a notice that there would be no further issues of the paper until the new office and plant had been set up in Rochester.[11]

In the meantime money had to be found to purchase a hand press so the work could be started soon. He knew the money would come in, although it might be several weeks before they had enough. James White, the "man who could not wait," canvassed the workers present and took their pledges. Then Hiram Edson made them a proposition. He had recently sold one of his farms, and would be willing to advance $600 to get things moving immediately. His offer was gladly accepted.

The Peripatetic Press, as Spalding so aptly described it, was on the move again.

---

[1] *Life Sketches* (1888), p. 282.
[2] *Ibid.* (1915), p. 141.
[3] *Review and Herald,* May 23, 1935.
[4] *Ibid.,* Sept. 16, 1851.
[5] *SDA Encyclopedia,* "Smith, Annie," p. 1200.
[6] *Ibid.,* p. 1407.
[7] *Review and Herald,* Nov. 25, 1851.
[8] *Life Sketches* (1915), p. 141.
[9] *Review and Herald,* Aug. 19, 1851.
[10] *Ibid.,* May 6, 1852.
[11] *Ibid.,* March 23, 1852.

Chapter Eleven

THE PUBLISHING WORK
MOVES WEST

THE move to Rochester, New York, was made in April, 1852. To the publishing work, this move brought different problems than were faced previously. Because a press without a skilled man to operate it would be of little use, James White began looking for a pressman. During his months in Saratoga Springs he had become acquainted with young Luman Masten, who worked in the printing office where James had his printing done. Luman was a pleasant young man, about 22 years old, and was living with his widowed mother.

Mrs. Masten was a staunch Methodist, but Luman, while of a religious turn of mind, did not profess any religion. When James White invited Luman to go to Rochester and act as foreman of his printing establishment, he consented. He also promised to train some apprentices in the printing trade, while overseeing the presswork.[1]

It was a simple matter for the Whites to pack their few personal belongings, along with back numbers of the *Review* and other printed materials, preparatory to moving to Rochester. Unfortunately they had no money to pay for the transportation of their goods, so they had to get a loan.

A Washington hand press had been purchased in New York with the money lent by Hiram Edson. Along with a quantity of type, the press was shipped to Rochester. Meanwhile, James had gone to Rochester to find a place where he might settle his continually growing publishing family that would soon be arriving.

James found a large house for rent on Mount Hope Road, out beyond the city limits. As he walked through the house and noticed its many empty rooms, he decided to take it, particularly after he learned he could rent it for only $175 a year. The invitation

he had published on the back page of the *Review*, asking believers to send money to help meet the cost of moving the publishing work to Rochester and securing the necessary printing equipment and supplies, took time to bring results. It was obvious that he and his co-workers would have to practice the most rigid economy if the new enterprise was to remain solvent.

By ones and twos the various members of James White's "family" arrived. Since the house was vacant, their most urgent need was for some furniture. In a letter to their friends the Howlands, at Topsham, Maine, Ellen described how James went to town to pick up the cheapest furniture he could find. One day he came home with six chairs, no two of them alike. He had paid a dollar for the lot. Then he found two bedsteads at twenty-five cents each, plus four more chairs costing sixty-two cents. Since there was no table and no money left to buy one, they set up two barrels, laid a board between them and ate their meals in style.[2]

The spacious back yard where little Edson could play safely, was a feature particularly appreciated by Ellen White, and by Charlie the horse, who had been brought along.

The press from New York was slow in arriving. Having announced the hope of publishing the first paper from Rochester by the first of May, James was determined to get it started. So the first issue was printed on a commercial press in Rochester, and was dated May 6, 1852. Finally their own press arrived and was set up in the house on Mount Hope Road, and they were in business.

Money began to come in and soon James White was able to report that the press was free of debt. The total cost of the press and equipment was $652.93. The brethren had sent in $655.84, so there was a surplus of $2.91.[3]

As more and more young people gravitated to the Review and Herald printing office, it was necessary after four months to move the press out of the house. James White searched the town again and finally found a building on South St. Paul's Street.[4] The hand press, type, paper supplies, and ink were moved into quarters on the third floor of this building.

The center established by James White in Rochester in the spring of 1852 could be called a self-supporting organization today. While he might be cast in the patriarchal mold, James was no long-bearded patriarch. When he moved his flock to Rochester, he

Rochester, New York, painted near the place where the Whites lived a few years before they moved to that city.

was only 31 and his wife, Ellen, 25. One of James's great strengths was his ability to gather about him young people whom he inspired with his own enthusiasm for the cause of God and a willingness to make any sacrifice necessary to advance it.

There was a great need for the group to practice economy, not from choice, but of necessity. Only one member of the company of workers received a regular salary, Luman Masten, the press foreman. Some of the brethren in the field kept telling Elder White to call on them when he was in particular need of money, but he hesitated to do this. What money he received came principally from subscribers to the church paper, now offered at two dollars per year but supplied free to the poor who were unable to subscribe. Sometimes substantial amounts of cash arrived; at other times, scarcely any.

It was not easy for the cook, Jennie Frazier, to adequately feed the growing family within her limited budget. She found that potatoes were too expensive, so she substituted turnips. Instead of butter, they used sauce on their bread. Even more important was her discovery that dollar for dollar, few foods would go further than beans to assuage the pangs of hunger. Therefore, beans appeared so often on the table that Uriah Smith remarked one day that he didn't mind eating beans 365 days of a year, but when it came to making them a regular article of diet, he would have to object! [5]

By the time the printing equipment was set up and the household settled, it was time for spring planting. A man was hired to plow the garden, which was near the house. As the plowing progressed, many small, but good, potatoes were turned up that had not been harvested the previous autumn. The winter being mild, the potatoes had not frozen.

While the plowing was being done, a scene something like this took place in the White home. James White was busy writing when the door opened and Luman Masten entered. Elder White noticed that Masten was quite indignant. Jerking off his printer's apron he held it out to Elder White. "I quit!"

James, surprised, asked him the reason for such hasty action. In reply, Luman stepped to the window and pointed to the potato patch. There James saw his wife with a tin pail, following the plowman and picking up the potatoes.

"I shall not work for a firm where the wife of the proprietor has to go into the field to pick up potatoes," he said firmly.

Ellen herself explained to him that she felt it her duty to economize and gather up the fragments that nothing be lost. This satisfied him and he returned to his duties in the pressroom.[6] To the day of his death, which came only a few years later, he remained a worker in the Review office.

But the problem of hard times continued. There were endless calls for money for food, clothing, rent, paper, ink, and a hundred other necessities. In earlier days James had gone into the hayfield to earn money, but he could scarcely do that in Rochester. So to supplement what the believers sent, he found another source of income. James White, as a money-producing side line, sold certain articles. He became an agent for charts and stationery, Bibles, Bible dictionaries, Bible concordances, atlases, and medical books, which he sold at the Review office.

Years later, when he saw ministers and workers tempted to enter into trade while preaching the gospel, he was to deplore the example he had set during those hard years in Rochester. By 1867, when he wrote his apology, workers were supported by the church and received regular wages. "I should have been supported in my calling," he wrote in the *Review*, "and had nothing to do with selling books." [7]

James White had no intention of sitting forever behind a desk, editing papers and pamphlets.[8] As early as March 2, 1852, while still residing in Saratoga Springs, he penned a desire to turn over to a committee the publishing work he had built up.[9] This would set him free to preach the gospel. He had heard the Macedonian call, and he longed to bring men and women, young people and children, to Christ. But the publishing committee members did not assume responsibility for the struggling paper, and the final responsibility for its support remained in the hands of James White.

He felt a special burden to keep the believers encouraged and forward looking. He set before them in glowing terms his hope for a glorious future. His spirit shines forth in the following letter:

"I have no ambition to be an editor. No. God forbid. I only ask the precious privilege to feed, if possible, my poor brethren—the 'outcasts'. . . . Jesus is coming to gather the poor outcast *home*, HOME, HOME. . . . That bright New Earth, that golden city, is all to me. I want to see an immortal saint, and more than all, that dear Jesus. Oh, what a happy meeting when salvation is completed, and tribulation ended. Many a time has my poor wife wept, and wept, to find herself here in this dark world after viewing the beauty, order, and holiness of Heaven." [10]

He carried a particular burden for his fellow workers. His exhortation to them has a Pauline ring to it:

"Preaching brethren, go out leaning on the arm of your Master. Have faith! *faith!!* FAITH!!!! a little more FAITH! Without it you can do nothing. Don't go out to give light to others, while you are enveloped in darkness yourselves. Enter into the solemn work of God, and never rest satisfied unless you feel the responsibility of your calling, and the worth of precious souls. Don't get in the way of the church. O may God help us as a church to be as a city set on a hill." [11]

It is difficult today to realize the isolation of many Adventists in those pioneer times. Communications were extremely limited. Some believers wrote to the Review, mentioning that they lived thirty, forty, or fifty miles from the nearest Adventist. For these isolated members, the *Review* proved an invaluable source of news concerning the progress of "the cause of God," to use a favorite expression of the pioneers.

And workers were few. Ministers could not settle down to pastor one church. They roamed from State to State, preaching the message to all who would listen. Under the heading of APPOINTMENTS in the *Review,* these ministers would announce time and place of general meetings they planned to hold. Believers came in from many miles away, frequently sleeping in barns for lack of better accommodations. During his lifetime of service, James White ministered to hundreds of such assemblies.

The summer of 1852 brought great anxiety and sadness to the people of Rochester. Cholera raged through the city, and many persons died.

Meanwhile, James had a great longing to be preaching the gospel and strengthening the brethren. Particularly was his heart touched as he thought of the many believers scattered through New York and the New England States. Many invitations had come for the Whites to visit companies in many places. He decided to pay them a visit. He and Ellen would travel by carriage, and faithful old Charlie would provide the horsepower. Little Edson had just turned 3 and would go with them. Henry, now a lad of 5, was still with the Howlands in Topsham. James and Ellen hoped to see their little boy on this trip.

James published in advance a list of the various places he hoped to visit on what he came to call his "Eastern Tour." Then, just a few days before he and Ellen were to leave Rochester, Edson became ill with the dreaded cholera. Desperately anxious, Ellen and James went to the Lord in prayer for the little boy. The Great Physician heard their intercession, rebuked the disease, and a change for the better immediately took place. As one of the sisters continued to pray, Edson spoke up: "They need not pray anymore, for the Lord has healed me." The disease was halted in its progress, but he remained very weak and could eat nothing.

Meanwhile, the day was fast approaching when the Whites should leave on their eastern tour. But how could they leave Edson in such a critical condition? It seemed equally impossible to take him with them. Unless the child should show rapid improvement, they could not go. They prayed earnestly about it.

"If we are to go, Lord," they pled, "let him indicate feelings of hunger."

The next day, about noon, Edson asked his mother for some food. Their prayer had been answered. That same afternoon they set out on the first stage of a journey by carriage that may have been two-thousand miles long.[12]

---

[1] *Review and Herald*, "Sketches and Memories," June 13, 1935.
[2] *Life Sketches* (1915), p. 142.
[3] *Origin and History*, vol. 1, pp. 205, 206.
[4] *Review and Herald*, Oct. 14, 1852.
[5] *Ibid.*, June 13, 1935.
[6] *Ibid.*
[7] *Ibid.*, March 26, 1867.
[8] James White letter to Bro. Bowles, Oct. 17, 1849.
[9] *Review and Herald*, March 2, 1852.
[10] James White letter to Bro. Bowles, Nov. 8, 1849.
[11] *Review and Herald*, Oct. 4, 1853.
[12] *Life Sketches* (1915), p. 144.

Chapter Twelve

ROCHESTER

IT WAS late one afternoon in early August. James helped his wife with their little son into the carriage, got in himself, clucked to the horse and drove out of the yard. Thus they began their long journey. Just before dark they stopped at the home of one of the believers. They had traveled twenty miles that day. Though weary, there was no rest for Ellen. Edson was fretful and, it seemed, he could sleep only in his mother's arms. James also found it difficult to get any sleep. Whenever he awakened he would hear the rocking chair going backwards and forwards.

In the morning they faced the question again—should they go on, or return to Rochester?

"If you go on, you will surely bury your child by the road," warned the family with whom they had been staying. But Ellen felt that if they returned to Rochester, Edson would not survive, so they decided to drive on. Though worn out from lack of sleep and fearful lest she doze off and let Edson fall, Ellen tied him to her waist, and both she and the child slept as they drove along. They had a hundred-mile journey to make before they would reach their first appointment.[1]

They held well-attended meetings in a grove at Boyleston before continuing on to Potsdam, where they stayed at the hospitable home of John Byington. Meetings were held at Potsdam the following day; then they pushed on to Norfolk, where they held meetings for three days. Then it was on toward the east, visiting such widely separated places as Boston, Portland, and Bangor.

Wherever they went the Whites received a warm welcome. Scores of new believers crowded into schoolhouses and meetinghouses to see and hear for the first time the leaders of the work. Where believers were few they met in private homes. They listened eagerly to Elder White's powerful sermons and heard his wife's exhortations. They purchased books, tracts, hymnbooks, and copies of the church paper, which James carried with him.

Edson's health, as well as that of his parents, improved steadily on the journey. This seems to have been the experience of James White during much of his life. Whereas he suffered greatly from various ailments when tied to the editor's desk, he frequently revived and improved steadily in health when traveling to widely scattered appointments, or when standing behind the sacred desk ministering to God's people.

At Palmyra, Maine, James had the privilege of a pleasant visit with his parents, who were feeling the weight of their years. Deacon John and Betsy did not seem to have "the spirit and sweetness" of the blessed hope he had hoped to find in them. He prayed that their outlook would change in that respect, and that they would accept the Sabbath.

Back home once more, James was eager to catch up on office news. Walking around the house he greeted many "old hands," as well as some new workers who had joined the staff during his absence. He was particularly eager to see Annie Smith, who had cared for the paper during its editor's long absence.

"How is the paid-up subscription list of the *Review and Herald?*" he asked her.

"Going up steadily. We're printing more than 2,000 copies each fortnight."

"Excellent! What about the new paper I started before leaving, the *Youth's Instructor?*"

"New subscriptions coming in every day."

James had started this new paper because he always had a soft heart for children; for some time he had been thinking about their particular needs. He realized that the *Review and Herald* articles were beyond the comprehension of the younger ones. So, in the *Review* of July 8, some six weeks before setting out on his eastern tour, he placed a notice headed, "A Paper for Children":

"We design publishing a small monthly paper, containing matter for the benefit of the young." After inviting adults to supply suitable materials, he continued: "The paper will cost, including postage, only about three cents a month. Many little boys and girls spend enough for candies and toys, that are of no real value, to

THE YOUTH'S INSTRUCTOR.

VOL. I   ROCHESTER, AUGUST, 1852.   No. 1.

AN ADDRESS

TO THOSE WHO ARE INTERESTED IN THE YOUTH'S INSTRUCTOR.

WE are happy to send you the first number of this little paper. For some time we have been impressed that we had a more special work to do for the youth, but have not been able to commence it until the present time. We now cheerfully engage in this work, praying the Lord to help; and we feel sure of success.

The young, at this day, are exposed to many evils and dangers, and they must have right instruction to enable them to know how to shun them. And although the world never was so full of books and papers as at the present time, yet they need not bestow much labor on their children. This is a grievous error, sufficient to call down the frown of Heaven. We do not say that parents should bestow labor on their children that can be of no real benefit to them, which would only lead them into the spirit of the world; but we do say, that no pains should be spared to impart to them right instruction, calculated to elevate the mind, and guide in the way to the kingdom of God.

As we have seen children growing up at this corrupt age of the world, without an experimental knowledge of the religion of Christ, yet tender, and

The first *Youth's Instructor.* This paper was launched by James White as a monthly in August, 1852.

pay for five or six such papers. We mean that the children that cannot pay for it, who wish to read it, shall have it free, and we have no doubt but many of the children will deny themselves of toys, so as to pay for their own, and some poor little boy's or girl's paper." [2]

In a later note concerning the *Youth's Instructor,* James pointed out that he would use "sensible matter" in the paper. To him the most valuable part of each issue would be the Sabbath school lessons. In these lessons, Bible stories and fundamental doctrines of the Bible would be presented in a way that would interest and benefit young readers.

While on trips, James kept the new paper in mind. Frequently, when he and Ellen stopped for lunch by the roadside, he would take out pencil and paper and write. Using the top of the lunch box for a table he would write articles for the children's paper. While he was writing Charlie was eating oats, grass, or ripe apples, which was his lunch.

While the Whites were in the East, Luman Masten was stricken with cholera. Knowing that those attacked by this disease had less than a 50-50 chance of survival, the believers at Rochester were greatly alarmed for his life. The loss of the pressman would be serious indeed, for the apprentices had not yet had time to master the printing trade.

When James arrived back at the office Luman told him his experience. In his association with the Adventists Luman became convinced by their life and teachings that they had the truth. But pride did not permit him to follow his convictions. When he became ill from cholera, the fear of death terrified him. On what he thought was his deathbed he promised the Lord that if he were healed he would keep all the commandments and serve Him faithfully. The Lord healed him, and he kept his promise.[3]

Meanwhile, the Rochester group toiled on. James White had an enthusiastic and loyal band. Let us now ask him to introduce his large family. We can imagine the young folks gathered on the front steps of the large house. The year is 1853. James speaks:

"Well, you know me. I am 32, and my wife, Ellen, is 26. Here are our children, Henry, 6, and Edson, 4. Standing there with them is Clarissa Bonfoey. She has taken faithful care of Edson. She is 32. Next to her is Annie Smith, aged 25. She fills my place when I am away and is indispensable all the time. Her brother, Uriah, 21, is a budding author who helps with any kind of work that needs to be done. Then we have several young folks who are learning the printing business from Mr. Masten. George Amadon is 21, and Oswald Stowell is 25. Fletcher Byington is 20 and Warren Bacheler is 14. Jennie Frazier is our cook. We sample her product three times a day. Next is Luman Masten, our printer, who is 24. Here are two hard-working folks who came with us from Saratoga Springs, Stephen and Sarah Belden, aged 24 and 20, respectively. Stephen helps me with the business angle of the work, while Sarah, Ellen's sister, takes care of the household with its continual round of cleaning, mending, washing, and sewing.

"Finally, we have two new additions. These are Nathaniel and Anna White, my brother and sister. Nathaniel is 22, and Anna, 25."

"Elder White," we exclaim, "you do have a large family!"

"That's true, but these aren't quite all. John Loughborough and his wife live here in Rochester. When he isn't out preaching,

he comes around and gives us a hand in the pressroom. He is 21.
John Andrews, one of our competent writers, also drops by at times
for a rest. But most of the time he's in the field preaching also. He
is 24."

"But these are such *young* people, Elder White!" we exclaim.
"True," James laughs. "That's why we accomplish so much.
Only three of us are over 30. Our average age is only 23, and that
isn't counting the children!"

We shake our heads in bewilderment as the workers return to
their duties.

Fortunately, there was no time when every one of these workers
lived in the big house on Mount Hope Road at once. But, coming
and going, every one of them did live there at one time or another.

The work was hard, but no one shirked. They did not work an
eight-hour day. Orders for tracts, pamphlets, hymnbooks, and
charts were continually being received from the field. The *Review*
was printed on the cumbersome Washington hand press and it took
three days. The stitching, trimming, and addressing were all done
in the large house.

They had no cutter. John Loughborough would punch holes
for the sewing, then pass the pages over to George Amadon who
stitched them together. Then they went to Uriah Smith who, with
his penknife, trimmed the edges.

Describing this process years later Uriah remarked, "We blis-
tered our hands in the operation, and often the tracts in form were
not half so true and square as the doctrines they taught." [4]

The amount of work for the press was proportionate to the success of the "messengers" in the field. State after State was entered
by Adventist preachers, who traveled from town to town. It was not
unusual for a couple of ministers to spend a month in one place,
baptize sixty converts, and then move on.

To complete the task of indoctrinating the new converts, James
White sent them copies of the *Review and Herald,* pamphlets,
tracts, and whatever was available. As orders came in, everyone was
kept busy, from Elder White down to Warren Bacheler and Fletcher
Byington, who were known by the title of "printer's devils." [5] It
was often two and three o'clock in the morning before the workers
left the press and walked through the silent town to the house on
Mount Hope Road.

Meanwhile, James continued to repeat his conviction that the time was near when they should issue the *Review* as a weekly. He carefully explained several times how the paper was financed. Those who could do so were invited to send liberal donations so that those who could not afford the *Review* might have it free.

Elder White received scores of letters every week. Some contained articles for the *Review and Herald*. Other correspondents complained that they were not receiving their paper regularly. Some were general letters to be printed in the *Review*. Every letter was acknowledged in one way or another. If not published, it might be listed on the back page under the heading of "letters."

To James White, time was a precious commodity. When a letter dealt with some routine item, he answered it briefly on the back page of the *Review*. In the March 31, 1853, issue, for instance, the following notices appeared, each representing a letter James did not have time to write:

J. W. Stewart	"We have sent the *Review* regularly to John Stewart. . . . [address] If this is wrong, please inform us."
F. Wheeler	"A box of books was sent by express the 21st."
H. Lyon	"Does S. Van Horn wish the *Review?* You did not state."
W. S. Ingraham	"We sent your books to Elmira. Were they received?"
P. Gibson	"The money was receipted in No. 17 which we sent."

Of all the unifying factors at work in the Adventist Church during the formative years of the 1850's, the *Review and Herald* was probably the most important. Through its columns, members of the Adventist family were able to keep in touch with one another.

That was just the way James White wanted it to be.

---

1 *Life Sketches* (1888), pp. 291, 292.
2 *Review and Herald*, July 8, 1852.
3 *Ibid.*, Sept. 30, 1852.
4 Uriah Smith, in *General Conference Bulletin,* Oct. 29, 1889.
5 Ellen G. White letter 7 to Br. and Sr. Smith, Aug. 24, 1853.
6 *Review and Herald*, June 9, 1853.

Chapter Thirteen

SORROWS AND JOYS

ENERGETICALLY, James paced up and down the Rochester railway station platform to keep warm. He was waiting for the afternoon train from Albany that early winter day in 1852. A cold wind blowing from the north and a light snow falling made it uncomfortable outside the waiting room. But that room was blue with tobacco smoke. Ever mindful of the necessity to protect his lungs, James preferred the fresh, if cold, air outside.

After a time the train pulled into the station. James hurried alongside the train, scanning the faces of the passengers alighting. Then he saw his brother and sister, Nathaniel and Anna, descending the steps of a coach. Nathaniel had been staying in Boston and had come to Rochester hoping to regain his health in the less rigorous climate of New York. Anna had come to care for him and help lift some of the burdens from Ellen's shoulders.

James was shocked to note how much his brother had failed in health since visiting him in Boston a few weeks previously. Nathaniel's flushed cheeks and hollow cough pointed toward tuberculosis and an early grave. James greeted the two cordially, then led them to the waiting sleigh and drove them through the gathering dusk to the big house on Mount Hope Road.

In spite of good food and loving care, Nathaniel grew weaker. Anna did all she could for him, carrying him his meals and helping to feed him as he lay propped up in bed. Nathaniel died calmly, peacefully, on May 6, 1853,[1] only a few days after Uriah Smith joined the Rochester company. He was laid to rest in the Mount Hope Cemetery, Rochester.

The circumstances of Uriah Smith's connecting with the paper were similar to those that brought his sister, Annie, to Rochester. As we saw earlier, it was through a poem sent to the *Review* that

94

James White first learned of Annie Smith. Some two years later he
received a poem written by her brother, Uriah.

"The Warning Voice of Time and Prophecy," James read as
he looked over the poem. He recalled Annie's first contribution.
Some of her poems had already been set to music and were being
sung by Adventists. One such poem had appeared in the *Review*
several months before,[2] which was destined to be her most popular
hymn, and has been sung ever since. This is believed to be a bio-
graphical poem, the first stanza referring to Joseph Bates, the second to James White, and the third to J. N. Andrews, perhaps.[3]
Here is the stanza some have said refers to James White:

> "And one I saw, with sword and shield,
> Who boldly braved the world's cold frown,
> And fought, unyielding, on the field,
> To win an everlasting crown.
> Though worn with toil, oppressed by foes,
> No murmur from his heart arose;
> I asked what buoyed his spirits up,
> 'O, this,' said he, 'the blessed hope.' "

There was no danger of Uriah's poem ever being set to music!
It was 35,000 words long. Later, James ran it as a series in five issues of the *Review*.[4]

James showed the poem to Annie. "Do you think he would
come and join our staff if I invited him?" he asked.

"I think he would. Six months ago he took his stand and resolved to keep the Sabbath. Since then his ambitions have changed."

James promptly wrote to Uriah. In reply, the young man said
he would be glad to work on the *Review and Herald*. So Uriah arrived at the office while his poem was being run in the paper. For
the next 28 years he and James White were to be closely associated
in the publishing work.

Nathaniel's death was a severe blow to James and Ellen. James
may have wondered whether he too was marked for a consumptive's
grave, for at the time his own health was a cause for concern.

Meanwhile, the *Review and Herald* had already published appointments for him to meet with believers in New York and Michigan. He asked himself whether it was wise to take the risk and go.
He and Ellen both pondered the question, "Must we be driven from

the work by bodily infirmities? Would Satan be permitted to exercise his power upon us?" [5]

They decided to carry out their plans and walk out by faith. God honored their trust. It seemed that every hour they traveled, they became stronger. Not one appointment was missed on that long itinerary.

Meanwhile, invitations continued to pile up on Elder White's desk, calling for him to hold services in churches near and far. He found it very difficult to turn down these requests, particularly when he knew of the conditions in the churches that needed correcting. In those days of loose organization, or none at all, Ellen White's testimony often served to point out grave dangers threatening the little companies and helped to draw the believers together.

During the spring of 1853, shortly after Nathaniel's death, James and Ellen made a trip to meet appointments in New York State and Michigan.

One of the churches they were to visit was at Jackson, Michigan. The Jackson church, the first Seventh-day Adventist church in that State, had been raised up by Elder Bates. The group there consisted of several extremely warmhearted, generous Christians, always willing to come to the aid of Elder White when he was in need of money to carry on the work.

It was well that James and Ellen visited Jackson, for they were needed there to straighten out a very confused situation. Ellen was given a vision regarding the wrong course of two men, H. S. Case and C. P. Russell who were influencing some of the members. She plainly showed the two men their wrong. Except for Case and Russell, and a few others, the group drew together in unity. [6] But these two men openly rejected reproof and shortly afterward withdrew from the church. They began to print a paper, ironically called the *Messenger of Truth*. Their work was to tear down what James and Ellen White were seeking to build up. Into their paper went every word of malicious scandal they heard or could invent, and Elder and Mrs. White were the prime targets for their attacks.

Copies of the *Messenger* were sent to James White, with the hope that the Adventist leader would respond in kind. This James declined to do. Like Nehemiah of old, he was too busy building Zion to come down and argue with these opponents. Many years later, however, James White was to meet some of the charges fabricated by Case and Russell.

During their trip to Michigan, the Whites visited the Adventist groups at Tyrone, Sylvan, Bedford, and Vergennes. At Bedford James started to preach, but became faint and was forced to sit down. He requested Elder Loughborough to preach for him. As Loughborough began, James went outside into the fresh air and lay down under a tree.

A Brother Kelsey came out to help the sick man. James asked whether he had a horse he might borrow. Kelsey said he did, and brought the animal to him. The minister mounted and rode away to the home a mile and a half down the road where he and Ellen were staying.[7] He rested during the remainder of the day while Loughborough preached the sermon and conducted a baptism in a nearby lake. Fortunately, Elder White's indisposition was only temporary and the following day they journeyed to Vergennes. A brother A. A. Dodge was to drive the wagon.

It was a very uncomfortable ride. Like many roads at that time, the one they were traveling on was built of logs laid closely together, well named a "corduroy road." The passengers received many a painful jolt as the springless wagon bumped over the poles.

Driving past a log house in the forest, James suggested that they stop and ask for something to drink. In response to their knock, a woman opened the door and invited them in. She gave them refreshments and asked where they were going. When James said they were on their way to meet preaching appointments, she begged them to stop and hold meetings in her area. She was hungry for spiritual food. She said that she had attended some spiritist meetings but couldn't accept the teachings because they didn't seem to square with the Bible.

Regretfully, James told her they had appointments to meet and people would be expecting them. Since it was Friday afternoon and they still had some distance to go, they had to leave. Placing some literature in her hands, they drove on.

For some distance, the driver and his passengers were deep in thought. James wrote in the *Review* that their feelings were indescribable, as they realized that all over that vast area there were thousands of souls hungering for the bread of life. They prayed that more workers might be sent into the harvest field.

Another incident took place while they were returning from Vergennes to Jackson. Because of excessive heat and a desire to spare the horse, they drove much of the night and rested during the daytime. Seeking a place where they might sleep, they stopped at another frontier home. They found a woman alone with her children. In response to their request for a short rest, she gladly made them welcome.

While James and Ellen were sleeping, Brother Dodge talked with the lady. Her husband, who was not at home, was a Christian but belonged to no particular church. Then she asked Brother Dodge a startling question, "What authority do you find in Scripture for resting on the first day of the week?"

"I will tell you before we leave," replied Dodge.

When James awoke, Dodge repeated the question. The surprised minister gladly outlined for the woman the Bible teachings on this important point of the third angel's message. She was deeply touched when Elder White suggested that they pray together. The mother and her children knelt while they prayed. The visitors then left Adventist publications with her, along with the address of the Rochester office so she might contact them if she wanted more literature.[8]

Two months later Elder White received a letter from the husband of the woman visited last. He had read the papers, had fully accepted their contents, and wished to be baptized as soon as possible. Is it any wonder that James White enjoyed traveling, preaching the gospel to the poor?

On this tour, James and Ellen White for the first time met with a company of Sabbathkeepers in Battle Creek. The Adventists in the vicinity met and half filled the living room of one of the believers' homes. Before parting from them, James remarked that if the brethren and sisters remained faithful, there might yet be a church raised up in Battle Creek. Prophetic words indeed!

In the fall of 1853 James and Ellen went on what was becoming their customary autumn "eastern tour." It lasted two months. Companies of believers were revisited, old friends were greeted and new friends were made.

Of all the visits made on this tour, none brought greater joy than the one they made at the home of Stockbridge Howland in Topsham, Maine. Joyfully they had anticipated a reunion with their first-born son, Henry. It had been so long since he had seen them that possibly at first he felt rather strange in their presence. Perhaps, when they told him he was going home with them to Rochester, he was not too sure that he wanted to leave his dear foster parents with whom he had lived for nearly five years. But, of course, during the days they stayed at Topsham, he became acquainted with his father and mother and, no doubt, looked forward to seeing his 4-year-old brother.

Before leaving the Howland home the Whites expressed their deep appreciation to them, particularly to the daughter, Frances, for having given their child such loving care and training. Now he was returning to his parents, a "well-disciplined, praying boy." [9]

A few weeks later, Henry and his parents arrived in Rochester. James and Ellen were happy to have their family together again, and James resolved to spend more time with his children in the future than he had in the past.

---

[1] *Review and Herald,* May 26, 1853.
[2] *Ibid.,* Aug. 19, 1852.
[3] *SDA Encyclopedia,* article "Smith, Annie Rebekah," p. 1200.
[4] *Review and Herald,* March 17-May 12, 1853.
[5] *Life Sketches* (1888), p. 301.
[6] *Ibid.,* pp. 302, 303.
[7] *Ibid.,* p. 303.
[8] *Review and Herald,* July 7, 1853.
[9] *Ibid.,* Nov. 1, 1853, p. 133.

Chapter Fourteen

TRAVELS AND TOILS

URING their three years in Rochester, James and Ellen White developed a yearly routine. The spring usually found them setting out on a "western tour," which would keep James from the office for several weeks. They usually reserved the autumn for their "eastern tour," when they could return to New England and revisit the field of their earliest labors.

During the winter, James followed a program that was different, but no less strenuous. Nearby churches often requested his services on the Sabbath. This meant closing his work early on Friday and driving perhaps thirty to fifty miles to spend the Sabbath with a group of believers. Sometimes Ellen went with him. At other times she remained with the children.

James usually conducted more than one service at these weekend meetings. On many Sabbaths he preached two or three times. In a descriptive letter to Brother Lyon, written in 1855, he wrote: "I am in hopes that I am improving [in health], but my lungs are not free from disease and pain. I preach loud and long, and am satisfied that it hurts me. I mean to be more temperate." [1]

He made similar resolutions many times throughout his life.

In his travels James labored early and late, robbing himself of suitable rest and sleep by riding the trains at night, and by attending long evening meetings. Most of his *Review* editorials were written during the hours between 9:00 and 12:00 P.M.

When he returned home from those trips, his desk was piled high with business matters demanding attention, and he spent days in the office handling a multitude of details. He also read proof sheets and examined materials submitted for the paper. It was frequently midnight before he could leave his desk.

During James's travels the editorial duties of the *Review* were placed in the hands of Annie Smith. But eventually she became too ill to do the work, for she developed tuberculosis and was forced to leave Rochester. She returned to her home in West Wilton, New Hampshire, where she spent her last days, being tenderly cared for by her mother. After her sad departure her brother, Uriah, took her place. Without the help of these two, James would have been confined to his desk.

The back page of the *Review* carried an ever-lengthening list of available Adventist publications. Some were written specifically for church members; others were prepared for missionary work among non-Sabbathkeepers. The hymnbook was 30 cents a copy. Twenty-five cents paid for a yearly subscription to the *Youth's Instructor*. Other tracts cost two, three, or four cents each. Thousands of copies of the little pamphlet *Elihu on the Sabbath* were sent out. After reading this well-nigh unanswerable tract a young man, S. N. Haskell, who later became a powerful preacher, joined the ranks of Sabbathkeepers.[2] Another pioneer, D. A. Robinson, became a Sabbathkeeper after reading the same tract.

By 1853 readers of the *Review* were requesting that it be published weekly. R. F. Cottrell, a leading Adventist minister, wrote a letter to James in which he stated he would prefer receiving the paper once in two weeks containing worthwhile material rather than weekly with inferior articles.

This was a point well taken, James admitted. He expressed the desire that Adventists who could write would use their talents more frequently for the *Review*.[3]

In the spring of 1854, James and Ellen returned to Michigan. During this visit they ministered to the church at Jackson, as well as other churches. While at Jackson they were both impressed that it was God's will for them to carry their testimony to the believers in Wisconsin. They decided to travel there by train. Inquiry revealed that one would leave Jackson at ten o'clock in the evening.

Before James and Ellen left for the train they had a season of prayer, asking for God's protection, which they somehow felt they especially needed. At the station James saw the trunk containing his precious store of Bibles, books, and papers placed in the baggage car. Then he and Ellen boarded the train. They walked through the forward car, hoping to find a place to rest, but that coach was full. They moved back through the train until they found two empty seats. Soon afterward the whistle blew, the bell rang, and the train moved out of the station. For some unexplained reason, Ellen did not remove her bonnet or put down her carpetbag, but sat holding it, as if expecting something to happen.

They had gone only three or four miles when the car in which the Whites were riding began to jerk back and forth. Then it stopped. They opened a window and in the darkness saw one of the cars ahead of them standing almost on end. Agonizing cries were coming from the forward section of the train. Later they were to learn that an ox had chosen to lie down on the track. The engine struck the animal and was derailed. Several of the cars were shattered.

Since the train would go no farther that night, James was anxious to return to Jackson. In the darkness, he and Ellen started for a road which they knew ran near the tracks. When they came to a swamp, James picked up his wife and carried her until he was able to set her down on the road. Along this road they walked toward Jackson until they came to a farmhouse.

"Our train has met with an accident," James explained to the man who answered their knock, "and there are many people injured."

They were invited in. Just then a man came along on his way to Jackson to find doctors to help the injured. James went along with him. At Jackson, James found an Adventist brother who, having heard his story, hastily found a team of horses, and he and James drove to the farmhouse where Ellen was staying. With Ellen with them they arrived back at Jackson at two o'clock in the morning.

After breakfast the next morning James borrowed a wagon and, with Ellen, drove out to the site of the wreck. They were very solemn as they looked at the last two cars, in one of which they had been riding, standing on the tracks more than 100 feet from the coach ahead of them. The coupling pin was not even broken but was lying on the platform of the intact car. Ellen was later shown that an angel removed the pin, thus saving the last cars from being wrecked.

Four persons died in the accident that night and many more were seriously injured. James retrieved his undamaged trunk full of books, and the next day they left by another train.[4]

After a fruitful visit to Wisconsin where they met many of the believers for the first time, the Whites returned to Rochester weary in body but rejoicing because of the rapid progress of the message in the West.

For Ellen White the trip had been a venture of faith. Her third child was due to arrive in August. He was born on August 29.[5] He was named William Clarence. But to the thousands of Adventists whom he met and to whom he ministered during his long life of 83 years, he was affectionately known as Willie White.

No sooner was James back in Rochester than he plunged into a conference. The meetings lasted from morning till night. If it was a strenuous time for James, it was more so for Ellen. Wives and children of workers came with the men to Rochester and to the house on Mount Hope Road. There seemed to be no end to the meals prepared and served to the guests.

"Oh, Ellen! If only we could have some quiet Sabbaths!" James lamented. She agreed, but could see no tactful way to bring their endless entertaining to a more normal level.

It was not only during general meetings that the Whites were overwhelmed with guests. Whenever workers became ill, they too fled to the White home in Rochester to recuperate.[6] One of these, Elder J. N. Andrews, arrived during the summer of 1854, completely worn out by his incessant labors. Long weeks passed before he was well enough to enter the field again.

After the death of her brother, Nathaniel, Anna White pondered her future. She did not wish to return to Maine. It might be difficult for her to return to Palmyra and be among Sundaykeepers. Both she and Nathaniel had accepted the Sabbath after joining the group in the big home. She had learned to love the girls working there, and wanted to stay with them. Although helping with the housework, she asked whether there was anything more she could do.

One day James asked his sister if she thought she could edit the *Youth's Instructor*. For Anna this seemed a most happy solution to her problem, and she gladly accepted. For the next year she cared for the little monthly paper.[7]

As winter drew on, it became apparent to Ellen and James that Anna was losing strength. Sadly they realized that she would probably follow her brother to Mount Hope Cemetery.

Realizing that his sister was failing rapidly, James invited his parents to come to Rochester to see her. They accepted his invita-

tion and spent some weeks at the home in the spring of 1854. Anna
repeatedly urged them to accept and keep God's true Sabbath.
After they returned to Palmyra, Anna remarked that she would
die happy if only she could know her parents were keeping the
Sabbath.[8]

In the November, 1854, issue of the *Youth's Instructor* Anna
wrote to her readers telling them that she was very sick, and admonishing them, "Try, dear young friends, to meet me in the
eternal home of the redeemed. Keep the commandments of God,
and seek to be washed from sin by the blood of Jesus."[9] A few
weeks later she was laid to rest beside Nathaniel.

Some time before Anna's death James's big family on Mount
Hope Road had lost another valuable member to tuberculosis.
Luman Masten, the foreman who had been healed of cholera, con-
tracted the dread killer and died after a lingering illness.[10]

---

[1] James White letter to Brother Lyon, July 18, 1855.
[2] *Footprints of the Pioneers*, p. 12.
[3] *Review and Herald*, July 7, 1853.
[4] *Ibid.*, July 18, 1935.
[5] *Life Sketches* (1888), p. 310.
[6] *Ibid.*, p. 309.
[7] *Review and Herald*, July 11, 1935.
[8] *Life Sketches* (1888), pp. 310, 311.
[9] *The Youth's Instructor*, November, 1854.
[10] *Review and Herald*, July 11, 1935.

Chapter Fifteen

CLOUDS AND SUNSHINE

JAMES WHITE was troubled as he walked slowly up the path, climbed the stairs and entered his Rochester home. He found Ellen busily sewing in the bedroom. Wearily he sank onto a chair. Ellen could see that something was troubling him. "What is it, James? What is wrong?"

"It's time to bring out another issue of the *Review,* but we have hardly any paper and no money with which to pay for the shipment that has come."

"How much money do you need?" she asked.

"Sixty-four dollars," he replied, "but it might as well be $10,000."

Ellen rose and walked to the closet. She opened the door, reached far in, grasped a black stocking hanging from a nail, brought it out and placed it in her husband's hands.

"What is this?" he asked, although he could feel coins inside the stocking. He tipped it up and a cascade of half dollars, quarters, dimes, and nickels poured out.

"Wherever did you get all this?" he asked in amazement.

"I've always believed a person should save something for a rainy day," Ellen answered. "For months I have been saving as much as I could. I hope it's enough." [1]

James counted the coins. It was enough! Through his wife's foresight a crisis was averted, and he was able to take delivery of the necessary paper.

Not all of their problems were resolved so quickly. Some hung on for weeks and months. For example, the Messenger Party was circulating its paper, *Messenger of Truth,* carrying falsehoods against Elder and Mrs. White. [2]

The pressure of work plus continual anxiety concerning finances and sickness in the home, all contributed to undermine the health of the leader. In *Messenger of Truth,* some writers taunted Elder White over his weakened condition; they expressed the opinion that God would remove him out of the way so that truth might triumph.

Roused by the taunt, James replied in words Wycliffe had used to address the friars who crowded about his sickbed urging him to recant because he was about to die: "I shall not die, but live, and declare the works of the Lord," and James added, "may yet preach at their funeral!" [3] Shortly after this, the leaders of the Messenger Party fell to quarreling among themselves, and the movement fell apart.

The circulation of the *Review* continued to grow, but the income did not keep up with it. The publishing committee appealed for help through the columns of the *Review:*

"On account of severe illness in the family of Brother White there will be no paper next week. . . . The health of Brother White is also much impaired by labor and care. We would at this time especially request the prayers of the people of God in his behalf.

"Brother W. is in want of pecuniary aid at this time. The publication of new and important works, together with the expenses of protracted sickness in his family make it necessary that the readers of the *Review* should comply with its terms, and that the friends of the cause should render immediate aid in this time of distress, by purchasing Tracts, et cetera.

Publishing Committee." [4]

Ellen wrote to friends: "James, poor James. I think he must leave the work sometimes and have quiet rest. I fear at times his life will fall a sacrifice to his incessant labors." [5]

Meanwhile, the number of publications available continued to increase. If each church member had purchased one copy of each of the more than two dozen publications listed on the back of the *Review,* including the *Review* and *Youth's Instructor,* the total cost would not have been much more than $2.00. [6]

By 1855, 2,300 copies of the *Review* were going out to members and friends. Of these recipients, fewer than two thirds were paying for their subscription. [7] Only a few months before, James had noted in the *Review* that the office was $1,000 in debt.

During trips into the field, James came to the conclusion that the *Review* was being sent free to many who would not pay for it, and who were not interested in its message.

"We have deprived ourselves of proper rest, and of many of the common comforts of life," he wrote, "till we are broken down as to health, that we might send out the *Review* richly laden with spiritual food for the flock of God. And now we meet those who say they are too poor and cannot pay for the *Review*. . . . Yes, too poor to help a brother send out the bread of heaven to the scattered flock, but have means enough to obtain tobacco, snuff and tea!" [8]

He resolved that this order of things should stop.

He did not want to deprive readers of the paper, for he felt it was a unifying force that all in the church needed. But if the paper was to make its way, something had to be done. So he gave notice that those not paying would be given a period of grace. When that was ended, as a final warning, their name would be written in red ink on the last copy of the *Review* they were to receive. [9]

Soon after he began publishing the *Review* James tried to alter the arrangements by which it was written, published, and circulated. He was aware of the hazards involved in his being essentially the only one responsible from the business viewpoint.

Actually, until the move to Rochester, there had been no assets to worry about. But at Rochester a hand press, a limited amount of type, and other printing materials were acquired. To buy these necessities, James had to use money lent by Hiram Edson and amounts subsequently sent in by dedicated believers. Since the equipment had to have an official owner, that owner became James White.

In time James's fears were realized. He was accused of putting into his own pocket money intended for the paper. But the publishing committee, composed of J. N. Andrews, R. F. Cottrell, and Uriah Smith, completely repudiated the charges. [10] James had urged the committee to assume responsibility for the business, but it did not do so.

While James and Ellen were traveling in Michigan in 1854, they visited a town named Locke, where evangelistic meetings were being held in a schoolhouse. However, the building was too small to accommodate those wishing to attend. As the group of leaders discussed the situation, it was suggested that a large tent would solve their problem.

"Perhaps next year we can make a special appeal and raise

A tent of the type used for evangelistic and camp meetings in the early days of Adventism.

enough money to buy one," James remarked.

As they continued the discussion someone remembered that two First-day Adventist ministers had used a tent the previous year, but were no longer working together, so the tent, now in Rochester, was not being used. Perhaps it could be purchased cheaply.

A number of the brethren in the Locke and Jackson areas donated various sums to buy the tent, so M. E. Cornell took the money, caught the first train to Rochester, bought the tent, and returned to Michigan.

Eighteen days after Cornell started for Rochester he and Loughborough pitched the tent in Battle Creek, Michigan, and began an evangelistic campaign.[11] The use of tents by our evangelists was a great step forward. Often people would attend meetings in a tent when they would not enter a church building.

Early in 1855 J. N. Andrews arrived at the Rochester house. He was completely broken in health, scarcely able to speak above a whisper, and with seriously damaged eyesight. He suffered from insomnia, depression, and stomach trouble. Five years of intensive activity in the field, frequently exposed to inclement weather, often

108

unable to find nourishing food, spending half the night writing articles for the papers—all these factors combined had left him prostrated. He was only 26.

Elder White described in the *Review* the condition in which this warrior found himself. At the same time he appealed for financial help to get him on the long road back to health. James made it plain that Elder Andrews was not making an appeal; he would never speak on his own behalf.[12]

Andrews went to his father's farm in Paris, Maine, hoping there to rebuild his strength, working in the open air. He found his family very poor, barely able to support themselves. But they were happy to have John with them again.

In the September 4, 1855, issue of the *Review* James referred to the trend of many Americans in the East to move West. "Many of our Eastern brethren think of moving West," he wrote.

"The advancement of the cause of truth should be the great object of all believers," he continued. Then he referred to a letter from a brother in Vermont who urged that those going West should settle at least forty miles from any other Adventist. In this way they could raise up the standard of truth and provide temporary homes for "the traveling servants of God."

James concluded, "With such views and feelings, we would say to those dear brethren in the East who think of going West, Go in the name of the Lord, and may your endeavors to raise the standard of truth in the great West be blest of the Lord."

Before the year closed, several families from Paris, Maine, left for Iowa. Among them was the Edward Andrews family and, of course, their son, John Nevins.

In the spring of 1855, James had put Uriah Smith in charge of the *Review,* and left the Rochester office. First he traveled to Michigan where he attended meetings in a number of places. The lightening of his burden, as a result of being away from the office, did him a great deal of good. "My health gradually improves," he wrote from Michigan, "and my spirit is getting perfectly free while freed from the care of the office, and mingling with the Lord's faithful, scattered ones."[13]

June found James in New York State, where he attended meetings at Mill Grove, Oswego, and other places. During the weeks following, he went into Vermont, crossed New Hampshire, and moved down the valley into Connecticut and Massachusetts. As always his heart was cheered as he met staunch and faithful families such as that of Otis Nichols, Stockbridge Howland, and the Chamberlains. Ellen was with him, and usually shared the preaching services.

From Topsham, they pushed on to Palmyra. Once again James visited the scenes of his boyhood. In a touching article he described his visit with his parents.[14]

"Come and join us in New York, or Michigan, or wherever we settle this fall," James urged the old farmer. But Deacon John said it was too late in life for him to think of moving.

In the same room where James and his brothers and sisters had first heard the voice of supplication, they bowed in prayer for the family they were soon to leave behind. James did not realize that his mother didn't share her husband's feelings of opposition to the Sabbath. She would keep it, but only if he did, for she believed the Adventist teachings with all her heart.

Ellen White reported their last prayer together:

"That night we talked the truth out as it is, and then James prayed and prayed out all his feelings. There was a whole sermon in that prayer. . . . Father was deeply moved."

Before James and Ellen left the next day, Deacon John told them that he had decided to move westward as soon as he could sell his farm.[15] He also gave strong indications that he believed the Sabbath.

1 *Spirit of Prophecy Emphasis Week,* 1966, 1967.
2 *Life Sketches* (1915), p. 155.
3 *Ibid.* (1888), p. 312.
4 *Review and Herald,* Nov. 21, 1854.
5 Ellen G. White letter B-5, 1854.
6 *Review and Herald,* Oct. 24, 1854.
7 *Ibid.,* June 12, 1855.
8 *Ibid.,* July 24, 1855.
9 James White, in *Review and Herald,* June 12, 1855.
10 *Ibid.,* Nov. 7, 1854.
11 William C. White, "Sketches and Memories," *Review and Herald,* July 18, 1935.
12 James White, in *Review and Herald,* Feb. 20, 1855.
13 *Ibid.,* May 29, 1855.
14 *Ibid.,* Sept. 4, 1855.
15 Ellen G. White letter 2, to Harriet Stevens, August, 1855.

Chapter Sixteen

JAMES WHITE, PROPRIETOR

THE time came when James could no longer hold up under the load of responsibilities he bore. Working from fourteen to eighteen hours a day, carrying the principal burden of producing the *Review*, the *Instructor*, and other printed matter, constantly burdened with financial difficulties, having the care of the large group of people in his home, and saddened by sickness and death in his family, he was finally brought, as he wrote in the *Review*, "very near the grave."

"We cannot expect a tolerable state of health without a complete change in many respects," he stated. "We are resolved on this change, even if we leave the office entirely." [1]

At about the time he was forced to this decision, actions on the part of the brethren indicated that the pillar of cloud was lifting, and that the press should move to some other place. James began to consider which direction the move should take.

When word got around that Elder White was thinking of moving the publishing work to another location, invitations came from Vermont and Michigan for him to move to those States. As early as March, 1855, the brethren in Vermont sent him a check for $492 and expressed the hope that the press might be moved to that State. [2]

The Michigan believers were not slow in stepping forward and inviting Elder White to move there. Of this invitation, he wrote:

"The brethren in Battle Creek and vicinity are generally awake to the wants of the cause, and are anxious to establish the Review office in that place. They are able and willing to do so, and manifest much anxiety to relieve us of those cares and responsibilities which we have too long borne. The climate, water, prices of rent, fuel, provisions, etc., seem favorable to the location." [3]

But before making a final decision James decided to visit Vermont in order that the brethren there might give their reasons why their State would be the better place to locate the Review. So, during the summer of 1855 James and Ellen made a tour of the eastern churches. That Elder White continued to keep an open mind in regard to the decision he would be making is evident from the following statement he wrote to a friend:

" 'Providence' does not open the way for the press in Michigan. The way is abundantly opened in Vermont." [4]

And in the August 7, 1855, issue of the *Review* he wrote, "Unless the friends of the cause in some more central position shall take their responsibility, it will be proper that the friends and supporters of the cause in Vermont should take it."

Two weeks later he was still undecided. He wrote to a brother of his perplexity. He hesitated about moving back to New England. He recalled Ellen's vision, when she had been instructed that the press should move westward. But he also hesitated about moving to Battle Creek:

"We must start right. I think I shall not settle at Battle Creek. My mind is west, say Wis. Ill. or Iowa or Minnesota. But I mean to stand by the press till it is well established." [5]

In the August 7 *Review* James repeated his resolution of February, no longer to carry the intolerable burden he had been bearing, and also reminded his readers that the publishing work was actually the responsibility of the church.

"We shall no longer bear the burdens we have borne in Rochester; neither shall we move the Office, East or West. The Office is the property of the church. The church must wake up to this matter, and free us from the responsibilities that have been forced upon us, and which we have reluctantly taken. We must have freedom and repose, or go into the grave."

Still, he knew that the final decision would be his. There was no organization as yet. Neither State nor general conferences had come into being. But God had blessed his movements thus far, and he had faith to believe that divine guidance would continue to light the way into the future. Finally, from Paris, Maine, he wrote to Abram Dodge, his friend in Battle Creek, indicating that he had made up his mind, and that the press should go to Battle Creek. A major reason for the decision was that four trustworthy Adventist believers in Michigan, Henry Lyon, Dan Palmer, Cyrenius Smith, and J. P. Kellogg, had decided to grapple with the problem and fill the need. They made up a fund of $1,200 with which to purchase land and erect a modest press building. After writing and directing these men to erect a building 32′ by 25′ two "story and a half, on three-fourths," James White went on to outline the conditions under which he proposed to make the move and the changes he foresaw:

1. The office would remain the property of the church.

2. Three or more persons would build an office and own it themselves.

3. Uriah Smith would be resident editor, while James White, R. F. Cottrell, J. N. Andrews, and J. H. Waggoner would be corresponding editors, all five to have an equal voice in conducting the paper.

4. There would be a finance committee of three men, C. Smith, Henry Lyon, and one other, who would receive all funds for the *Review,* pay all bills, and establish the prices of the papers and books.

5. The present inventory of books should remain in the hands of James White until his debts were paid off.[6]

At a meeting held on September 23, in Battle Creek, Michigan, of believers interested in establishing the publishing work in that city, these suggestions were accepted.

In his letter, White pointed out to Dodge that it was obviously impossible for any resident editor really to know the field. It would be the duty of the corresponding editors to supply reports and articles to Elder Smith. He suggested in conclusion that it might be difficult to move the press before the following spring. In this respect, he apparently misjudged the strong determination of the Michigan brethren, who moved with dispatch. A general meeting was called for November and representatives from the whole field were invited to discuss the situation. The proposals previously adopted were accepted and broadened. Joseph Bates served as chairman of the conference. At this meeting James was relieved of financial responsibility for the *Review and Herald.* A committee consisting of Henry Lyon, David Hewitt, and William Smith was appointed to examine the financial status of the *Review.* The name of Stephen Pierce was added to the list of corresponding editors. A vote of thanks was tendered to Elder White for his sacrificial work of the past six years.[7]

The last issue of the *Review* to be printed in Rochester was dated October 30. During November, all hands were busy moving the press and various supplies to Battle Creek. The building in Battle Creek had been erected, a neat two-story building. The first issue of the paper to be printed in Michigan was dated December 4.

With the move to Battle Creek another of James's wishes was fulfilled: The weekly publication of the *Review* began.

When the press moved to Michigan the publishing work was in debt, but this was more than covered by books on hand ready for sale. The committee appointed to investigate the finances of the Review office reported that Elder White had invested $311.89 in the publishing plant and urged that this amount be repaid.[8]

Twenty-five years later, and only a short time before his death, Elder White commented as follows in regard to divine guidance in locating the press:

"The publishing work increased gradually and safely all the way from Paris, Me., Saratoga and Rochester, N.Y., to Battle Creek where the Publishing Association has grown to be a powerful institution. Had we commenced at Boston, New York, Philadelphia, Chicago, or any other large city where our expenses would have been greater, and where the cause would have been sustained

at great expense, our work would have been crippled in its infancy, and we would have lost very much which we have gained by establishing ourselves in the little city of Battle Creek." [9]

Ellen White's comment throws light on the position held by her husband in his relationship to the publishing work:

"I saw that God had qualified him who had to stand at the head of the publishing for his station, and if he did not fill his place, God would remove him from it. God had oversight of the work. I saw that this was an important place. I saw that it was God who had rebuked the disease that was on James when nature had resisted as long as it was possible and could do no more, and disease had fastened upon him, and when Satan was exulting that he had his prey and that he would lay him in the grave, then God's hand interposed and He put bands around James and strengthened him to fill the place He had put him in." [10]

Looking back, Willie White commented on the manner in which his father had been divinely guided in settling the publishing work in Battle Creek, and of how, in God's good time, the headquarters were once again moved, this time to Washington, D.C.:

"How much would it have counted for our work in the United States if Father had gone to Washington at the time he established the printing work in Battle Creek? Then a few men with limited means went to a place where it was inexpensive living and where their work would not be despised; later on when the work had grown and many men had been called into it who were prepared to exert a decided influence wherever they were, the work was called to Washington." [11]

---

[1] William C. White, "Sketches and Memories," *Review and Herald*, Feb. 20, 1855.
[2] James White letter to a "Brother," March 13, 1855.
[3] ———, in *Review and Herald*, May 15, 1855.
[4] ———, letter to a "Brother," Aug. 3, 1855.
[5] ———, letter, Aug. 24, 1855.
[6] ———, letter to Abram Dodge, Aug. 20, 1855.
[7] *Review and Herald*, Dec. 4, 1855.
[8] James White, in *Review and Herald*, Dec. 18, 1855.
[9] *Ibid.*, Feb. 5, 1880.
[10] Manuscript 1, 1855.
[11] W. C. White letter to D. Hartwell, Dec. 29, 1903.

The first Review and Herald office in Battle Creek
was built in 1855.

Chapter Seventeen

HUSBAND OF A PROPHETESS

IHAVE a message for you." Ellen White addressed these words to hundreds of individuals during her ministry of seventy years. A large percentage of the individuals thus addressed accepted the message.

From time to time these significant words were addressed to Ellen's husband, James. In response to one such message, received in Dorchester, Massachusetts, in December, 1848, James began to print a "little paper." The following years brought crushing discouragements, and more than once he resolved to give up the paper "forever." But these decisions were reversed in response to messages from God through his wife, bidding him go forward in faith.[1] In response, James picked up the burden and pressed forward.

There was no question in James's mind as to the divine origin of Ellen's visions, which were to sustain and support him all through his life. To see her in vision was a fascinating experience to him. He observed the physical phenomena mentioned by Bible prophets—no breath, eyes open, no strength at first, then a strengthening which enabled her to hold out at arm's length large Bibles on more than one occasion.

Before their marriage, it was a source of satisfaction to James when the Lord told Ellen that she could trust him as he escorted her from place to place. This no doubt had a part in persuading Ellen to accept James's proposal of marriage in 1846.

Naturally, no other individual saw Ellen in vision more times than did her husband. As he listened to her pointed testimonies to individuals after these visions, his faith in their divine origin grew steadily stronger.

James and Ellen were both strong-minded individuals. Both were called by God to fill a crucial place in the church. It is difficult to conceive what James might or might not have accomplished had it not been for his wife's sympathetic encouragement as he set various projects in motion. On the other hand, Ellen needed someone who could not merely offer physical protection as she traveled but who could also put into motion Heaven's plans for the growing church.

Ellen realized the difficult position in which her messages at times placed her husband. It was not easy being married to a prophetess, who in certain ways outranked him. Concerning their relationship, she wrote: "Sabbath, June 6, 1863, I was shown some things in regard to my husband and myself. . . . I saw that we neither understood the depth and keenness of the heart trials of the other. Each heart was peculiarly sensitive, therefore each should be especially careful not to cause the other one shade of sadness or trial. Trials will come, but strong in each other's love, each deeply sympathizing with the other, united in the work of God, can stand nobly, faithfully together, and every trial will only work for good if well borne." [2]

While the doctrines of the as yet unshaped church were being hammered out, Ellen's role was a unique one. As leaders, the primary aim of James White, Joseph Bates, "Father" Stephen Pierce, Hiram Edson, and others, was to discover what the Bible taught. One by one the great doctrines now held by the Seventh-day Adventist Church were reaffirmed or established.

Ellen sat through these meetings, which sometimes lasted far into the night or even all night. But she could not grasp the theological topics dealt with. It seems that God caused her to have a mental block so that no one would later be able to make the claim that she influenced the form the doctrines of the Seventh-day Adventist Church took. So God had His plan, and He carried it out.

In later years, Ellen wrote:

"During this whole time I could not understand the reasoning of the brethren. My mind was locked, as it were, and I could not comprehend the meaning of the scriptures we were studying. This was one of the greatest sorrows of my life." [3]

When those godly scholars came to a point on which they could not agree, or where no solution was forthcoming, Ellen was frequently shown in vision the correct solution. Her statements were then accepted as Heaven inspired, for the men knew that when not

in vision she could not understand the matters, and they accepted the revelations as light from Heaven. However, as James pointed out, the doctrines of the church did not come by direct revelation, but by a diligent study of the Scriptures. In this Ellen White concurred:

"I recommend to you, dear reader, the Word of God as the rule of your faith and practice. . . . God has, in that Word, promised to give visions in the 'last days'; not for a new rule of faith, but for the comfort of His people, and to correct those who err from Bible truth." [4]

The papers sent out in the summer of 1849 were intended for the "little flock" who were still searching for light, and who were dedicated to keeping God's commandments and the faith of Jesus, as well as for their Sundaykeeping brethren who had been with them in Advent experiences culminating in 1844. A total of eleven numbers of this paper, the *Present Truth*, were printed in 1849 and 1850. In approximately half of them an article or a letter from Ellen White appeared. An examination of these articles reveals that she frequently used the expressions, "I was shown," "I saw," or "It was revealed to me."

By the time the Whites settled in Paris, Maine, in the late fall of 1850, the religious atmosphere was changing. Memories of the Millerite movement were fading. Evangelists, or messengers as they were more often called, were pushing northward into Canada and westward into the States lying along the Great Lakes. Into the hands of interested persons, these men were placing copies of *Present Truth* and the *Advent Review* that James White was printing.

It was in Paris, Maine, that James had decided to start a paper which he proposed to name the *Second Advent Review and Sabbath Herald*. He intended this to be a missionary paper, furnished to interested persons free, as their names and addresses should be sent in by the traveling messengers.

At the beginning he had one important question to settle. How much should be printed concerning the special mission of his wife, and should her writings be published in the *Review?*

It is not surprising that he should hesitate, and in the end decide against bringing Ellen White or her work into the columns of the church paper.[5] There would be no problems as far as Adventists were concerned. Most of them had become acquainted with the

James and Ellen White participated in the studies that rediscovered and re-affirmed the Bible truths held today by the Seventh-day Adventist Church.

work and mission of Ellen White as she had toured the churches throughout New England. But what would be the effect on strangers who would not understand her work?

The religious ferment prevailing during the mid-nineteenth century spawned a variety of would-be prophets and spiritual leaders. The Fox sisters were about to introduce modern spiritualism. Joseph Smith had brought forth the Book of Mormon and organized the Church of Jesus Christ of Latter-day Saints. There were others claiming to receive divine revelations, and promising to bestow eternal bliss upon their followers. So would not a paper containing Ellen's visions be tossed aside with the words, "Another prophetess! More visions!"

These considerations were weighed and James decided to exclude accounts of Ellen's visions from the *Review and Herald*. This practice continued for some five years. However, in order that the messages God gave her for the believers might reach them, James brought out in July, 1851, what he called a *Review Extra*, [6] or a supplement. He planned to publish others, but none appeared. James perhaps felt that there would be time enough after interested persons accepted the main teachings of Sabbathkeeping Adventists to present to them the convincing evidences proving that she was a messenger of the Most High.

The decision not to publish Ellen's visions in the *Review* curtailed, but did not stop, her work. Plans were set in motion to publish the visions in a little book. Also, she continued to write letters containing testimonies to members of the church and sent them out to ministers and laity alike. That lively interest in Mrs. White's supernatural visions was kindled widely is evident from what she wrote to Brother and Sister Abram Dodge of Battle Creek:

"There is a stir all around here since the conference reports are being carried. . . . Some are anxious to hear for themselves and will come to the meetings. The visions trouble many. They [know] not what to make of them. We shall have the visions published in pamphlet form, and if all the particulars are not published in the pamphlet, that I saw at Brother Cushman's, and if you desire it I can write it off for you." [7]

In July, 1851, the 64-page booklet, *A Sketch of the Christian Experience and Views of Ellen G. White*, appeared for circulation among the believers. This was followed in 1854 by the 48-page

supplement with more of the visions. Both were advertised in the
Review.

Actually, the columns of the church paper were not closed to
Ellen's writings. During the years prior to the move to Battle
Creek, she wrote several communications to brothers and sisters, to
the church, and articles on general subjects such as hospitality,
covetousness, and the duties of parents to their children. But the
words "I was shown," or "I saw," did not appear, although in several editorials James defended the visions.

Thus the *Review and Herald* went forth bearing what James
White described as the great Protestant slogan, "The Bible, and
the Bible only." Among the companies of believers, faith in the
Spirit of Prophecy was not made a test of acceptance. And with the
visions excluded from the paper's pages, the majority of church
members doubtless began to regard them as of little significance.

As the years passed, the proportion of Adventist readers of the
Review and Herald to new or non-Adventist readers steadily increased, and there was an ever-increasing desire on the part of members to know more about Ellen's gift.

James's faith in the divine origin of the visions never wavered.
But sometimes he found it awkward to step forward as Mrs.
White's champion. How could a husband boldly promote his wife's
books and seek to exalt her work before the world. For years he had
stood in the forefront of the battle, and he had no desire to give his
enemies a point on which to attack him. Perhaps he felt the less
said about the subject, the better for the time being. When, in
1856, he received a letter from a man in Vermont chiding him for
not putting his wife's writings more forcefully before the people,
James replied in the *Review:*

"My position has been one of trial. The relations I have sustained to the work in the rise and progress of the cause of present
truth, have exposed me to a thousand thrusts from those who were
opposed to the work.

"I have ever been slow to speak of Mrs. White's visions in a
public manner; but in consequence of the almost utter silence of
those who should have spoken fit words in season, I have felt compelled to speak." [8]

Several months previously, shortly before the publishing work
was moved from Rochester to Battle Creek, Elder White wrote a

The columns of the *Review* carried many articles from the pen of Ellen White that helped to strengthen the members of the growing Adventist Church.

series of short articles for the *Review* on the general subject of the gifts of the Spirit. In them he makes the significant statements:

"Can we for a moment suppose that God's people will pass through the perils of the last days, and face the time of trouble such as never was, and He not manifest Himself to them through those gifts which He Himself has set in the Church? Nay, verily." "The counterfeit and no genuine would be the greatest possible absurdity." "Let the visions stand upon their own merits." [9]

At a very important conference in Battle Creek on November 16-18, 1855—the same one at which the main editorial and financial responsibilities for the *Review* were taken from James's shoulders—many attending felt that proper attention was not being given to the visions. A committee was appointed to prepare a conference address on the subject. The importance of the messages from the Lord through His servant was strongly presented by Elders Bates, M. E. Cornell, and J. H. Waggoner. They felt a great burden to exalt the spiritual gifts. In the conference address it was declared:

"Dear Brethren, while we hold these views [regarding the inspired nature of the gifts] as emanating from the divine Mind, we would confess the inconsistency (which we believe has been displeasing to God) of professedly regarding them as messages from God, and really putting them on a level with the inventions of men." [10]

About two months later Ellen reported in the *Review* that visions were being given her less and less frequently.[11] She stated that she saw that the Spirit of God had been dying away from the churches.

To reverse this trend it was decided to bring together and print the visions given for the church. James, happy that the urging came from others, gladly cooperated in endeavoring to make the testimonies better known to the church members. The columns of the church paper were opened to her messages. However, it seems that during the subsequent five years, most of her testimony continued to be sent to individuals or published in Testimony pamphlets, later to be incorporated into Volume 1 of the *Testimonies for the Church*. During those years only nine articles from her pen appeared in the *Review and Herald*. The time was still future when nearly every week the *Review and Herald* would carry an Ellen G. White article.

James White did more than accept and print his wife's contributions. He prepared two series of articles on the subject. The first, entitled *Unity and Gifts of the Church*, appeared in December, 1857, and January, 1858.

The work of the Spirit of Prophecy played a vital role in bringing unity into the ranks of believers. In an additional article in the December 31 *Review*, James published *A Sketch of the Rise and Progress of the Present Truth*. In it he recounted the experience that had taken place at Volney, New York, in 1848, during a time of great confusion when every one attending a conference offered his own interpretation of Scripture. Graphically he described the situation:

"The meeting would have proved a failure, and the good brethren would have separated in confusion and trial had not the Lord worked in a special manner. The Spirit of the Lord rested upon Mrs. W., and she was taken off in vision. The entire congregation believed that it was the work of God, and were deeply affected. She related to them what she had seen, which was given to correct some errors among them, and in melting strains exhorted them to leave their errors, and those points on which they had differed, and unite on the important truths of the third message. And on that blessed evening, the brethren sacrificed their babel of sentiments, and united on the truth. And what was the result?

"Harmony began to prevail, and many came flocking to the standard of truth." [12]

Five years later, Elder White published another series of articles entitled "Perpetuity of the Spiritual Gifts," in the *Reviews* of February 4, 11, 18 and 25, 1862. In concluding them, Jesus urged readers to apply to the visions the Biblical tests, to follow the instruction of Paul to the Thessalonians not to despise prophesyings but to prove all things, and to hold fast that which is good. Anyone willing to do this would discover that the fruit of the gifts is beautiful, both for the individual Christian and for the church as a whole. [13]

---

[1] *Life Sketches* (1888), p. 281.
[2] Manuscript 1, 1863.
[3] *Messenger to the Remnant*, p. 39.
[4] *Early Writings*, p. 78.
[5] *Messenger to the Remnant*, p. 51.
[6] *Ibid.*
[7] Ellen G. White letter to Bro. and Sr. Dodge, July 21, 1851.
[8] James White, in *Review and Herald*, Feb. 14, 1856.
[9] *Ibid.*, Oct. 16, 1855.
[10] *Review and Herald*, Dec. 4, 1855.
[11] *Ibid.*, Jan. 10, 1856.
[12] James White, in *Review and Herald*, Dec. 31, 1857.
[13] *Ibid.*, Feb. 18, 1862.

Chapter Eighteen

THE GOLDEN YEARS

THE last issue of the *Review* published in Rochester was dated October 30, 1855. After it came from the press the machinery was crated and sent by rail to Battle Creek. The workers in the big house at 124 Mount Hope Road packed their possessions and followed the printing equipment to its westward destination.

James White was now 34 years old, and Ellen approaching 28. The three boys, Henry, 8, Edson, 6, and Willie only 15 months, were excited as, with their parents, they boarded the train for Michigan. They peered out the window at the passing landscape and the colorful autumn foliage.

At Battle Creek James found a house to shelter his greatly diminished family. The rent was only $1.50 per week, but the place lacked many conveniences. We "have to go a great distance for water; have no good shed for our wood," Ellen wrote.[1]

At last James and Ellen White would have more privacy than at Rochester. Although the days when they would provide food for large numbers of persons were by no means past, it was a relief not to have fifteen or eighteen at every meal.

Besides their three boys, they still had as members of their family Clarissa Bonfoey, who had been substitute mother for Edson, and Jennie Frazier, who soon became famous as one of the best bakers and cooks in Battle Creek.

The Whites' first winter in Battle Creek was a busy one, and one of great importance to the church. The messages Ellen had written out and sent to churches and individuals were collected, published, and advertised as "Testimony for the Church." One hundred and fifty copies were sent to various brethren without charge. An announcement of the publication, with a statement that "those who would encourage the circulation of such matter, can do so by assisting in its publication," appeared on the back page of the *Review* over Ellen White's name.[2] James perhaps felt it would be just as well to let her handle the circulation of her own books and pamphlets.

James's health, so precarious in Rochester, improved with the move to Michigan, particularly after the arrival of spring and summer. It was evident that the move benefited the whole family.

They soon established a regular routine. Henry and Edson attended the nearby public school, while Willie remained with his mother at home. James carried on his editorial work at the Review and Herald, no longer burdened with the task of looking over names and checking addresses or buying ink and paper. This now fell more and more into the hands of Stephen Belden. The finance committee looked after the major lines of business.

James now felt much freer to accept invitations to speak in churches in surrounding towns and communities. Ellen could not always go with him. Clarissa Bonfoey had died suddenly, and Ellen had to stay with her boys. She and James began seeking a solution to this problem.

Remembering the loving care that the Howlands had bestowed

on Henry, James and Ellen wrote inviting them to move to Battle Creek and take over the home during their absences.[3] However, the Howlands did not accept the invitation. They probably felt deeply attached to their Maine home. Besides, the responsibility for three lively boys would not be easy.

The members of the Battle Creek church were happy to have the Whites living in their town. Sometimes some of them may have wondered how long they would stay. Had not the press been moved no less than five times during the past seven years? Was there not a danger that it might be moved again? But it soon became evident that James intended to stay in town for a while. He began to look around for a house to buy to save on rent.

When this became known, the men who made possible the move to Battle Creek decided to help the Whites get a home of their own. An acre and a half of land about a mile from the Review office was bought for $200. After the land was cleared, a neat two-story house was built.

Later, an addition was made on one side for the three boys, and another on the other side for the Harmons, Ellen's parents, who came from Maine to live with their children. After the Harmons moved into a cottage across the street, Deacon John and Betsy came to Battle Creek also and lived in what came to be known as the "Wood Street House."[4]

Shortly after the Whites moved into their new house, Jonah Lewis, who lived on an adjoining plot of land, dug a well close to the White property line. He shared the water with the Whites and other neighbors.[5] A windlass and bucket were fastened over the top of the well with an oaken bucket to draw the water.

As the ice and snow disappeared after the first winter in the new house, James purchased garden tools and prepared to plant a vegetable garden. At the same time he set out a variety of fruit trees. The whole family worked in the garden, finding great satisfaction in learning how to make things grow. One of White's neighbors wrote, "The land is very rich. Such corn as Brother White raised there I never saw before. He planted it late, too, as it had to be grubbed out and fenced before he could plant."[6]

James was happy to have his parents in Battle Creek, and he was overjoyed when Deacon John announced one day that from then on he would observe the seventh day of the week as his Sab-

The box in which the Review and Herald hand press was shipped from Rochester to Battle Creek.

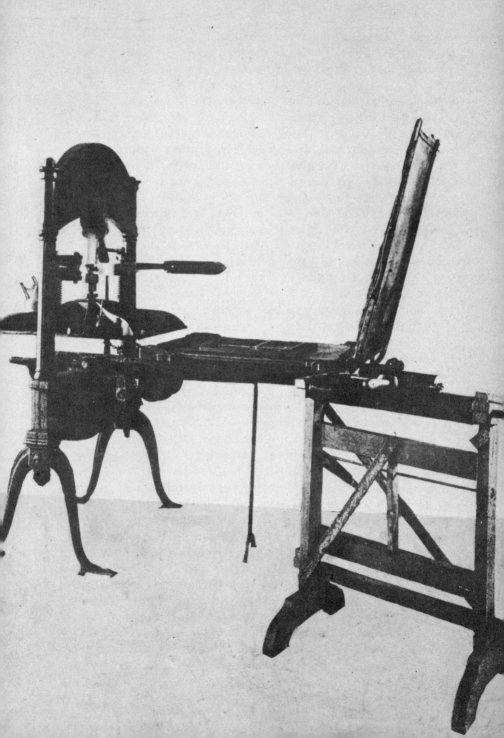

This house on Wood Street, Battle Creek, is the first one the Whites lived in in the town. Today it is Battle Creek's oldest Seventh-day Adventist landmark.

bath. Force of habit, however, was too strong to permit him to work on Sunday. The children noticed this, and wondered why Grandpa kept two Sabbaths.

Then came a Sunday morning when they saw Grandpa take out his shoe-making tools and go to work.

"Why, Grandpa," little Willie exclaimed, "don't you know this is Sunday?"

There was a twinkle in the old man's eye when he replied, "Yes, but I have decided one Sabbath a week is enough for me."[7] And he went on with his work.

Now that he had his own home, and the pressure of office work had eased, James had more time to spend with his family and to enjoy his surroundings. The land was fenced. In time his fruit

The Washington hand press used in Rochester and shipped to Battle Creek was soon replaced by a faster press.

9

Above: Deacon John White and his wife, Elizabeth, parents of James White.
Below: The home in which James's parents lived in Battle Creek.

trees began bearing. He grew strawberries, blackberries, raspberries, and grapes. It pleased the church members to see Elder White taking such an interest in the place they had provided for him and his family. The Sabbath-day preacher and editor and publisher was also a weekday gardener.

The time between the arrival of the Whites in Battle Creek in the fall of 1855 and the paralysis that prostrated James White in the summer of 1865 may well be called the golden decade for the family. Battle Creek was home for the boys. Henry, Edson, and Willie found work in the Review plant, particularly during the summer months. Then there were picnics, hikes, and swimming parties at Gogoac Lake.

Ellen busied herself both inside and outside the home. She sewed for her family and also for poor church members. She loved to make rag carpets out of cloth remnants. James did not approve of this activity. He felt it was beneath his wife's dignity to engage in such a task. One day he brought home a visiting minister, and to his dismay he found Ellen down on her knees putting another rag carpet together. His protests apparently were of no avail. He had discovered long before that Ellen had strong opinions of her own.

One day he hit upon a plan that proved to be effective in stopping the manufacture of rag carpets. As he neared his home on Wood Street, he began to chant loudly so that the neighbors could hear and his wife get the message at the same time, words set to a popular tune:

"In heaven above where all is love,
There'll be no rag carpets there—
There'll be no rag carpets there."

Ellen immediately ceased making rag carpets and took up knitting, an activity she continued to pursue for the rest of her life.[8]

Meanwhile, the work at the Review office was increasing. A spiritual and missionary revival was taking place among believers, prompting them to buy and circulate the literature coming from the press.

No matter how many hours they ran the old Washington hand press they could not keep up with the need. It soon became evident that something must be done to speed up the printing process. Three days each week were needed just to print the *Review*, and it was Elder White's hope that the number of subscribers would double during the next decade.[9]

Returning from a trip to Waukon, Iowa, early in 1857, James visited the stock room at the publishing house to find almost empty shelves. He discussed the shortage with Stephen Belden. The long hours demanded of the workers to print the literature was undermining their health, and there just wasn't money to buy all the supplies needed. James realized that a bigger press would have to be bought.

A conference was called in April to deal with the problem. The members willingly agreed that a power press was the answer to their need. With money raised, Elder White went to New York, purchased the press, and had it shipped to Battle Creek. He always had the ability to find money when it was desperately needed.

This press was operated by a large flywheel, turned by two men. It produced six times more printed sheets in an hour than did the hand lever press. Still that was not enough. So another appeal went out, money came in, and a steam engine was bought to turn the press.[10] Once this was in operation, the press workers felt they were in a position to keep up with the demands.

James and Ellen continued their ministry among the churches. Sometimes long tours to companies in the West and in the East caused them to be away from six to eight weeks. To help the churches nearer to Battle Creek, they would make weekend trips, using their own horse and carriage.

How the people loved to listen to those servants of God! It was their usual custom for James to present a doctrinal subject. Then Ellen would follow with words of exhortation and sometimes of reproof that the Lord had revealed to her for that particular congregation.

In a letter to W. C. White, Dr. A. D. Olsen described the speakers at those meetings:

"It is a very pleasant memory for me to recall my first meeting with you and your brother Edson, as well as your majestic father and your godly mother, at a Wisconsin camp meeting, years and years ago. . . . I can remember so well, way back in those anxious days, listening to the very earnest and powerful sermons of your beloved father and the beautiful discourses of your mother. You will not be surprised when I tell you that I preferred to hear her, because she talked so much about Christ and salvation and getting

ready for heaven. Very properly, Elder James White had a great deal
to say about our sins and about the heat of the 'hot place' to which
sinners would be finally condemned. That did not sound so good to
a little boy whose feet hung from the crude benches without reaching the floor." [11]

These trips were not without hardships and even dangers. The
following report printed in the *Review* indicates the nature of travel
conditions in the 1860's:

"We left Battle Creek at 3:00 P.M., changed cars at midnight
at Chicago; reaching the Mississippi River at 7:00 A.M.; crossed
the ice on foot, walking behind the baggage drawn on a sleigh by
four men, the ice being too weak to bear up horses; and felt relief
when we stepped upon Iowa soil. The late rain weakened the ice
very much, and even injured the railroad on the Iowa side, so that
the cars were detained the day before we crossed the river, detaining
our letters and the *Review*, so that our appointments were in the
mailbag on the same train with us. At Lisbon station we left the
train, and looked in vain for some brother to take us to a pilgrim's
home, so we returned to the train and passed on to Mount
Vernon." [12]

Meetings usually closed on Sunday evening. The members
might then escort their visitors to the train, to start on their return
trip to Battle Creek. One writer described the hour of parting:

"May God bless Brother and Sister White, and all the rest of the
dear brethren and sisters. It was hard to part with them; and as we
stood, with sad hearts, watching the train that was bearing them
from us, a brother remarked, 'Well, when we start for the kingdom
we shall all take the same train—all go together.' " [13]

There were delays caused by railroad accidents. One train was
derailed only nine miles from Battle Creek, and they had to wait by
the wreck for five hours for rescue. All the passengers were extremely hungry until James remembered that he had three pounds
of crackers with him. He divided them among the travelers, and
no one starved!

The White family lived in their pleasant Wood Street home
for six years. Then, in 1863, James sold the house and moved to
another, on the corner of Champion and North Washington streets,
nearer to the publishing house. The happy Wood Street years had
ended. There would be grief and trouble in the future, but that,

mercifully, was hidden from their eyes.

The Wood Street home still stands, the oldest Seventh-day Adventist landmark in Battle Creek, and now the property of the Battle Creek Tabernacle church. It is open to visitors.

1 *Lake Union Herald*, March 22, 1966.
2 *Review and Herald*, Dec. 18, 1855.
3 Ellen G. White letter to Bro. and Sr. Howland, July 15, 1856.
4 William C. White, "Sketches and Memories," *Review and Herald*, Feb. 13, 1936.
5 *Ibid.*
6 James White letter, Nov., 1856.
7 William C. White, "Sketches and Memories," *Review and Herald*, Feb. 13, 1936.
8 A. L. White letter to H. J. Thomson, May 25, 1944.
9 William C. White, "Sketches and Memories," *Review and Herald*, Jan. 30, 1936.
10 *Ibid.*
11 Dr. A. D. Olsen letter to W. C. White, Aug. 23, 1937.
12 James White, in *Review and Herald*, March 8, 1860.
13 Mary F. Maxson, "The Conference at Adam's Center, N.Y.," in *Review and Herald*, Dec. 8, 1863.

Chapter Nineteen

FATHER WHITE AND HIS FAMILY

J AMES and Ellen had four children, all boys. The first, Henry, was born in Gorham, Maine, in 1847. His brother, James Edson, arrived while the family was living in Rocky Hill, Connecticut. That was in July of 1849. A third son, William Clarence, was born in Rochester, New york, on August 29, 1854, and the fourth child was born in Battle Creek on September 20, 1860.

Shortly after the last child was born James went on a speaking itinerary to Wisconsin and Illinois. He and Ellen hadn't settled on a name for the boy before the father went away. While James was in Wisconsin he had a premonition that the baby's life was in danger. Shortly afterward he received a telegram urging him to come home; the baby was sick. James cut short his ministry and hastened to Battle Creek. He found the little one critically ill. In a few days the child died. Little John Herbert, the name they finally settled upon, was buried at Oak Hill in a plot of ground purchased by the grieving father.[1]

During the same trip, while in Wisconsin James had a dream concerning a certain company in Battle Creek in which he had deposited $1,500 of Review and Herald funds. He forgot this dream until just after the funeral of the baby. When he revealed his dream to his associates it was agreed that the money should be withdrawn from the company.

Two days after this transaction was completed the firm was declared bankrupt, and depositors in Battle Creek and vicinity lost $50,000. When James was asked how much money the Review had lost, he could answer, "Not a dollar." He knew that God had guided in that situation.[2]

The White home in Battle Creek became a Mecca to Adventists passing through the city. If they had kept a guest book, it would

have been quickly filled. Friends came to visit, and workers came to counsel with Elder and Mrs. White. During the year 1859, Ellen White kept a diary that makes interesting reading today. Under date of April 19 she wrote: "In the evening, Bro. Hilliard comes with his wife and seven children. We are glad to see them, and we keep them overnight, and . . ."

The record stopped there. Probably some interruption occurred.

At the time of the June 6 conference in Battle Creek, the diary reported briefly that "at dinner we had thirty-five." Is it any wonder that the following day the entry was extremely brief: "We were all very much worn out!" [3]

The nature of Ellen White's work during the pre-Battle Creek days necessitated her being away from her children much of the time, and this during their most formative years. Little Henry had spent five years with the Howland family in Topsham, while James Edson (called by his middle name so as not to confuse him with his father) was cared for by Clarissa Bonfoey. As has been noted, it was in the fall of 1853 that James and Ellen brought Henry home with them as they returned from an Eastern tour. Clarissa and Edson were already in Rochester.

The next year Willie was born and joined the family in the big house. So, during the last sixteen months that the Whites lived on Mount Hope Road, James and Ellen had their three children with them.

The situation in Rochester was not an ideal one in which to bring up children. With so much consumption among the office workers, it is not surprising that the Whites were concerned for their children's health. But there was a large yard in which the boys could play, and they were encouraged to spend much time outdoors.

Then came the move to Battle Creek. From the first home they could really call their own, Mrs. White wrote to her friends, the Lovelands:

"My husband enjoys good health, and my children are rugged. They never enjoyed so good health before. . . . I never took so much comfort with my family as now. Our family has always been so large. But now we only number eight and I can enjoy the company of my children, they can be more under my own watchcare." [4]

An 1864 photo of the White family. Willie, between Ellen and James, was 10 years old at the time. Edson was 15.

Miss Bonfoey's death brought perplexity to the Whites, and posed a threat to their mobility in ministering to the scattered churches. With three children in the house, ages approximately 9, 7, and 2, how could they answer the calls? Yet they dared not make their children an excuse for not responding. James decided to appeal to the church. He placed the following notice in the *Review:*

"We would say to those Eastern brethren who have been expecting a visit from us soon, that we can cheerfully leave our children in good hands and go abroad to labor. Is there not some brother and sister who have no small children who can come into our family, or settle near by, with whom we can leave our children safely?"[5]

There were no responses to this appeal, so the children were left with capable, loyal Jennie Frazier.

The traveling parents did not forget their children, but frequently wrote tender letters, describing their experiences and containing some serious admonitions to the boys.

Shortly after the birth of John Herbert, while in Wisconsin, Elder White wrote a letter to Ellen, expressing his deep concern for the boys:

"I hope our dear boys will seek to be good and right. Language cannot describe my anxiety for their welfare and future salvation. Hope they will seek to love one another, and to love and serve God."[6]

James and Ellen learned early that their children differed widely in disposition. Ellen wrote, "You have seen Henry, well, Edson [age 5] has more life and roughery than Henry so you must know my hands are full."[7]

There is no way of knowing how Henry White might have developed had he lived out his life. He was talented, a good scholar, extremely musical, and had a fine singing voice. In his youth he learned to play several instruments, which greatly pleased his equally musical father. But Henry died in 1863 at the Howland home in Topsham. Edson was 14 and Willie 8 when they sadly said farewell to their older brother. James and Ellen deeply mourned the loss of their firstborn. They referred to him as their "sweet singer."

Being human, the Whites made mistakes in rearing their children. Because, from boyhood, Willie was the model child, and by the most part his only lapses came when he was misled by his older

Henry, James and Ellen's first child, died in 1863, when he was 16.

brothers, there may have been a tendency on the parents' part to point out to Edson what a perfect little brother he had in contrast to his own sometimes sorry record. This must have discouraged Edson and done Willie no particular good, although his sweet disposition remained unimpaired. An example is found in a letter from James written to Edson, who was 11 at the time:

"I hope you are well and happy. You will not forget to mind and greatly respect Jane [Jennie] who does so much for you. . . . And my dear Edson, love to indulge Willie. Never plague him. Should he die, O how your heart would ache. He is the best boy you ever saw, and I hope you will always think a good deal of him, and of Henry " [8]

Ellen was deeply concerned for her second son. She wrote, reproving him for disobedience:

"Yielding to temptation to prevaricate—to speak plainly, to

deceive us. . . . When we went to Monterey last summer, for instance, you went into the river four times and not only disobeyed us yourself but led Willie to disobedience. . . . I became convinced that you could not be trusted." [9]

Willie was not always a model of perfection. One evening shortly before his third birthday, he was told it was time for bed. It happened that James had invited a number of friends from the *Review* office to his home that afternoon, and at sundown they began singing. Willie had changed since those days at Rochester when Ellen had described him as having "but one fault, that is, he is afraid of singing." [10]

Wanting to know what was happening, Willie crept down and sat on the steps, listening. His father saw him there, and commanded him to go to bed. Willie did so, but the pleasant sounds that continued to drift up interested him so much that he crept downstairs again. A second time he was told by his father to go to bed and stay there. He went, but before long slipped down the stairs once more, thinking to hide in a corner. His father's sharp eyes saw him. Willie described what happened next:

"Father took me out through the kitchen to the back steps, put his left foot on the railing, laid me across his knee and gave me such a spanking as I shall never forget." [11]

James and Ellen, being earnest, conscientious parents, ever sought to train their children for God.

"We prayed and labored for our children, and restrained them. We did not neglect the rod, but before using it we first labored to have them see their faults, and then prayed with them," wrote their mother. [12]

Naturally, the larger share of home training of the White boys fell on Ellen, and James knew that they were in good hands. On one of his trips to the West, he wrote her:

"I am in the path of duty. I am not anxious about home. I am happy to have you [give] so good a report of home, of our dear boys. I love my family and nothing but a sense of duty can separate me from them." [13]

James knew that the most reliable method of keeping the boys out of mischief was to keep them busy, so he had them work right along with him in the garden. Besides growing vegetables for family use, they raised small plants and sold them. They collected and sold vegetable seeds. Then, as they grew older, they worked after school in the publishing house. With the first $100 they earned they purchased a melodean [organ]. Then there was music in the home, sometimes perhaps too much to suit the studious parents.

Once, when James was away, Ellen and the boys entertained different ideas of what he had instructed them to do during his absence. Ellen wrote, asking him for a clear statement:

"Please write if you intended that the boys should have steady employment in the office until your return. Henry says you told him he could do as he pleased, work in the office or about home, after the hurry was over in the office. I told Henry I did not so understand it. I thought one day each week could be spent about home, the rest of the time in the office. Please write your wishes and all will be well. We want to follow as you think best in these things. I do not see much to be done at home." [14]

James White did not despise education, although from personal experience he might have felt that long years in school were not necessary in order for a boy to make his mark in the world. As they came to school age, the White boys enrolled in the Battle Creek public school. When John Byington opened a church school, they attended. But after a year the school closed for lack of popular support.

James was eager to give his boys every opportunity to make good, and gave them work at the Review and Herald. The practical experience Edson and Willie gained there during their student years prepared them to take over the management of the Pacific Press after their father founded that institution. Willie, in particular, acquited himself wisely when this responsibility was placed upon him.

As a teen-ager, Edson was beset with problems. He was more adept at spending money than at earning it. James was disheartened when he saw Edson purchase a coat for $26 * [15] so he might walk to the office in style. Ellen pled with Edson not to move rashly.

"May God give you a soft and tender heart to your poor, overburdened, worn, harassed father," she begged. [16]

When Edson was 20, his mother wrote to him concerning his

---

* At the time a man's pay for a day's work was about $1.

relationship with his father. "Father is utterly discouraged in regard to your ever making a success in anything because you won't be advised." She went on to point out that he had made wrong use of his father's liberality. James pitied Edson and mourned over him. He had promised Edson $500 when he was 20 if he would save an equal amount himself by that time. If Edson could earn $1,000, his father was prepared to give him a thousand dollars' worth of land. "He never will earn it," remarked James White gloomily to Ellen. "He can't keep means." [17]

It was a painful thought to James that his son lacked financial acumen. He decided to make Edson another attractive proposition. At this time Edson was nearing his twenty-first birthday. If he would raise $600, his father would give him $300. The father outlined his plan for Edson:

"You must excuse us from helping you to clothing, or in any other way. If you get sick, come home or let us know. . . . I will help you, unless it be for common debts. *I will not pay common debts.*

"Now, my dear boy, if you want me to help you, help yourself. . . . Be a man, a good man and a Christian." [18]

It was a deplorable situation. Estrangement grew between father and son, and James felt that the fault lay with Edson rather than with himself. From Boston, he wrote to Edson and his wife, Emma, for they had married on Edson's twenty-first birthday: "Edson lost, worse than lost, about five years of his life from 16 to 21, in rebelling and wandering from a course of right. Then his parents needed his help, instead of the terrible burden he was to us. He now can redeem the time if he will. . . . But if Edson will pursue an independent course, we shall in the future let him do it, at his own expense, and risk. I feel that it would be a sin to help him while he pursues an independent course, and cherishes hard feelings against me." [19]

One further misfortune was to befall the luckless Edson. This time it was caused by factors beyond his control.

In June, 1874, James started to publish on the Pacific Coast a paper he named the *Signs of the Times.* That same year he was elected president of the General Conference. The following year the California constituency voted to incorporate the Pacific Press. Willie White took over the management of the new press and operated it very profitably. This was largely a result of his steady management in financial lines. At that time, gold commanded a premium in the East. Willie could send a thousand dollars in gold to his father, who would take the money and with it buy paper, getting $1,300 or $1,400 worth in exchange for gold dollars. Thus the press profited by these transactions, and James was highly pleased. Later, Edson became manager, but did not do so well.

In 1872, when Edson was 23 and Willie 17, James sent them both to a short-term medical school in New Jersey, operated by a Doctor Trall. Both emerged with the coveted M.D. diploma. That their father considered that the degrees did not necessarily qualify them to practice the profession is evident from a letter he wrote to his sons:

"Boys, study hard. Bring home your diplomas. But never attach M.D. to your names until you enter your professional duties." [20] The following year he broached the subject again.

"One thing I wish to guard you both against. And that is not to think of writing for the *Review*, or professing any knowledge of the true healing art until you are fully qualified to master the whole subject." [21]

A. W. Spalding has well analyzed the characteristics of Willie and Edson:

"Edson and William exhibited diverse traits of character plainly derived from father and mother. William, the younger, was like his mother, constant, enterprising but cautious, a solid and careful builder. Edson, the older, had much of his father's enterprise and drive, and an overamount of his eccentricity. James White was saved from serious ill consequences of his enthusiasms both by his own balance of qualities and by his wife's counsel, but his son had not the same good fortune. He was resourceful, energetic, inventive, and he had a good deal of executive ability; but he was sometimes flighty and erratic. He built considerable businesses at different times, chiefly publishing enterprises, but they were liable to explode." [22]

It should not be forgotten that both these sons ran the race, both finished his course, both kept the faith. Both became ordained Seventh-day Adventist ministers. Edson later did a tremendous amount of good as he traveled up and down the Mississippi River on his missionary steamer, the *Morning Star*. The influence and accomplishments of Willie White went even farther.

Could James White have returned to earth at the close of the nineteenth century, he would have been proud of the achievements of both his sons.

[1] William C. White, "Sketches and Memories," *Review and Herald*, March 5, 1936.
[2] *Ibid.*
[3] *Ibid.*, Feb. 27, 1936.
[4] Ellen G. White letter to Br. and Sr. Loveland, Jan. 24, 1856.
[5] James White, in *Review and Herald*, Jan. 22, 1857.
[6] James White letter to Ellen G. White, Oct. 29, 1860.
[7] Ellen G. White letter 5, Dec. 16, 1854.
[8] James White letter, March 20, 1860.
[9] Ellen G. White letter 4, 1865.
[10] Ellen G. White letter 5, Dec. 16, 1854.
[11] W. C. White memories of the Wood Street House, DF 968a.
[12] Ellen G. White, *Testimonies*, vol. 1, p. 102.
[13] James White letter, Nov. 1, 1860.
[14] James White letter 12a, October, 1860.
[15] Ellen G. White letter 15, to Edson, June 17, 1868.
[16] Ellen G. White letter 2, 1871.
[17] Ellen G. White letter 6, June 10, 1869.
[18] James White letter to Edson, May 12, 1870.
[19] James White letter to Edson and Emma, Dec. 11, 1871.
[20] James White letter to sons, Dec. 30, 1872.
[21] James White letter to sons, Jan. 2, 1873.
[22] *Origin and History*, vol. 2, p. 344.

Chapter Twenty

MUSIC IN HIS SOUL

A SMALL boy sat on the front bench in the "Dime" Tabernacle church in Battle Creek. It was Sabbath morning and the congregation was waiting for the preaching service to begin. The boy's back was toward the street door through which the minister would enter.

Suddenly the silence was broken by a sweetly musical but strong, sure voice singing a hymn. The boy turned and saw the minister marching down the aisle, tapping on his Bible as he walked along singing. It was the speaker of the day, James White, president of the General Conference. The little boy's heart thrilled as he listened to the words of that song:

"When I can read my title clear
To mansions in the skies,
I'll bid farewell to every fear,
And wipe my weeping eyes."

Elder White launched into the chorus as he stepped onto the platform. The congregation rose and sang the second verse with him.

"Let cares like a wild deluge come,
And storms of sorrow fall;
May I but safely reach my home,
My God, my heaven, my all." [1]

That small boy grew up to become Elder William A. Spicer and a president of the General Conference himself. He never forgot the strength and uniqueness of his predecessor.

This was not the first time that James White had walked into the pulpit singing. Nearly forty years before, as noted earlier, he had used a similar method for catching and holding the attention of a thousand persons in a meeting at Litchfield Plains, Maine. There he had sung all eight verses of a song dear to the hearts of the Second Advent believers, "You will see your Lord a coming—in a few more days." [2]

During the time of the 1844 movement there was a power in Advent songs that captured and thrilled the soul of James White. He was determined that the sound of singing should be often heard among the scattered companies of Sabbathkeeping Adventists. Although not a composer he knew a good song when he heard one.

When James had stepped out by faith in 1849 and published the little paper, *Present Truth,* money came from its readers, providing means for its continuance. From his scanty profit on the paper he set aside a little fund for printing a hymnbook, which he felt was as much needed as the paper.

Carefully he studied the hymnbooks current in the popular churches of his time. He likewise studied compilations made by the Millerites, and chose songs he felt would be suitable for the use of Sabbathkeepers. He excluded two categories—hymns that taught the doctrine of the immortality of the soul, and those that displayed pleasure at the thought of the wicked being thrust into a fiery hell.

The first little hymnbook brought out by James White in 1849 consisted of only fifty-three hymns. It was published in Oswego, New York. No music was provided, and few of the songs in that small book are sung today. There were a few about the Sabbath, written by composers who regarded Sunday as God's holy day. This small book bore a rather lengthy title, *Hymns for God's Peculiar People That Keep the Commandments of God and the Faith of Jesus.*

Between 1852 and 1861 James issued three other hymnals bearing titles similar to the first book. The second and third hymnals were published in Rochester, New York, and the fourth in Battle Creek, Michigan.

Elder White did not forget the children's needs. In 1854, only a short time before her death, his sister, Anna White, compiled the little book, *Hymns for Youth and Children,* which was printed on the Rochester press.

Each edition became larger than its predecessor. The 1861 hymnal had 512 hymns, with music for some of them.

James White was a thoroughgoing democrat in all things pertaining to the church. Time after time he appealed to the members

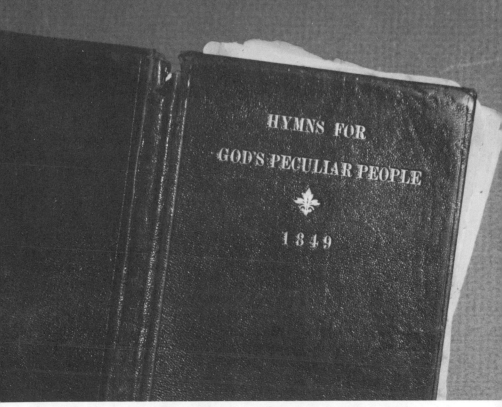

The 1849 edition of James White's compilation *Hymns for God's Peculiar People That Keep the Commandments of God and the Faith of Jesus.*

to send him their favorite hymns. He knew that songs that might please one brother would not satisfy his neighbor, so he compiled books containing a wide variety of hymns. Before issuing his 1861 edition, he wrote to the church members:

"Not a type is set on the new Hymn Book yet. Please send in good Hymns and Tunes, and point out defects in those in the old Book. We want the best Hymn Book in the world. We dare not take the whole responsibility of selecting. Neither have we the least idea of leaving this important work to any one or two men. Let us all take hold and have an admirable Book that will suit all so far as possible." [3]

An appeal of this kind was made prior to the publication of nearly every hymnbook James White published. He likewise invited those who had talent to write songs suitable for the remnant church. In all, some thirty songs about the Sabbath were produced and incorporated in Adventist hymnals.

The price of these hymnbooks was kept within the reach of all. The children's book sold for only ten cents a copy and the 1852 hymnbook could be had in cloth for thirty cents, or with paper covers at twenty cents. The 1851 edition sold for only twelve cents a copy, or twelve for a dollar.

Even with these low prices, James White came to depend on hymnbook sales to supply him with money for various projects he wished to undertake. Thus, prior to printing the 1861 hymnbook, he wrote to Ellen:

"The Hymn Book will be a good chance for me. I can get out 5,000 for $1,500 which will be worth to me at wholesale $2,000. But I will retail 1,000 in the east on which I will make $200 profit. I will have some advantages in that Office, so I can have something to do as I please, to help those I wish to help." [4]

From a study of the literature of the period it seems evident that people sang much more in those days than they do now. This was true not only during the regular church services but particularly in private homes. Many families had their old-fashioned pedal organs, around which they would gather to sing as they welcomed or bade farewell to the Sabbath day. Daily morning and evening worship usually began with a song. In the White home this came at seven o'clock each morning, and the hymn most frequently sung was Isaac Watts's familiar "Lord in the morning thou shalt hear . . ." [5] After the White boys bought their Melodean, two and even three songs were sung in the worship periods.

James frequently relied on music to lift the hearts of workers bowed beneath heavy burdens and perplexing problems. At such times, he would call to his wife, "Come Ellen, let's sing for them." Then standing side by side they would sing that most appropriate song:

> "When faint and weary toiling,
>   The sweat drops on my brow,
> I long to rest from labor,
>   To drop the burden now;
> There comes a gentle chiding,
>   That stills each mourning sigh:
> Work while the day is shining;
>   There's resting by and by."

Then everyone would join in the inspiring words of the chorus:

"Resting by and by,
There's resting by and by:
We shall not always labor,
We shall not always cry,
The end is drawing nearer,
The end for which we sigh;
We'll lay our heavy burdens down;
There's resting by and by." [6]

There were times when James and Ellen White needed encouragement themselves. Of such occasions, Mrs. White wrote:

"My husband used to say, 'What shall we do, Ellen? What shall we do? Now we have come to a strait place.' "

"Well," said I, "James, what shall we do?"

"Then he would laugh. Said he, 'Wife, we will pull together. And we will get out of this right side up with care, and we will have an influence here.' Well, so we have had." [7]

James White passed on his love for music to his children. Particularly was this true of the older sons. Henry both played and sang. Edson assisted his father in compiling at least one music book, and later published several attractive collections of his own.

Edson was also a composer, being the author of the music for Frances Havergal's beautiful poem, "I Gave My Life for Thee." [8] A nephew of James White, Franklin E. Belden, became the most prolific song writer produced by the Adventist Church. Belden compiled the very popular *Christ in Song*, a hymnal that served the church for more than thirty years.

James White felt that singing filled a very important place in the proclamation of the third angel's message. One day in June, 1870, Elder and Mrs. White, with a dozen Adventists from the Iowa Conference, were traveling by riverboat up the Mississippi River, all bound for the Minnesota camp meeting. Willie White, 16 years old at the time, thoroughly enjoyed watching the green countryside pass by as the boat chugged its way upstream.

In the late afternoon the band of Adventists gathered at the forepart of the ship and began singing hymns. Soon other passengers gathered, who encouraged them with applause and voices shouting, "Give us some more." Although the Adventist singers felt "sung out," from attending camp meetings, they sang another number, "Celestial Army."

This opened the way for Mrs. White to give a talk in the lounge, again at the request of the passengers.[9]

Thus James White passed through life, singing as he journeyed.

---

[1] William A. Spicer, *Pioneer Days* (Washington, D.C.: Review and Herald Pub. Assn.), pp. 145-147.

[2] *Life Incidents* (1868), p. 94.

[3] *Review and Herald*, Feb. 5, 1861.

[4] James White letter to Ellen G. White, Oct. 22, 1860.

[5] William C. White, "Sketches and Memories," *Review and Herald*, Feb. 13, 1936.

[6] *Origin and History*, vol. 1, p. 273.

[7] Document File, No. 2A, Board Meeting, Paradise Valley Sanitarium.

[8] *Church Hymnal*, p. 230.

[9] *Review and Herald*, July 5, 1870.

Chapter Twenty-one

IN SEARCH OF ORDER

TO EARLY Adventist believers, the idea of organization was anathema. It carried with it the idea of restraint, of heavy-handed authority and the rejection of Bible truth on the basis of church creeds. Organization would be too much like getting back into some of the problems in the churches from which many of them had suffered the ignominy of being expelled because they looked for Christ to come in 1844. Some of them had not waited to be disfellowshiped, but under the sounding of the second angel's message withdrew from what they chose to call "Babylon." George Storrs echoed the sentiments of most Adventists when he declared, "No church can be organized by man's invention but what it becomes Babylon *the moment it is organized.*"[1]

James White had not been treated by his church the way other Adventists had been by theirs. Ordained a minister by the Christian Church, he continued his labors without interruption until he accepted the seventh-day Sabbath. But he could not forget the manner in which the Adventists had splintered after the Disappointment.

During the decade 1844-1854 small companies of Sabbathkeeping Adventists sprang up in various localities, each inaugurating its own rules—or lack of rules—of conduct and practices. Whatever moves were made in Adventist ranks tending toward unity were reported in the columns of the *Review and Herald.* When the Fairhaven and Dartmouth companies decided to follow the New Testament practice and ordain deacons, this was reported by James White. Soon other companies followed their example and also began ordaining deacons.

Rapid expansion in the early 1850's convinced White of an additional reason for drawing the companies into some kind of unified

151

body. In three years, the membership in New York State grew
from apparently less than thirty to about a thousand.[2] A significant
growth also took place in Michigan and in other States farther
west.

More than once during the Rochester years James pointed out
to the believers that all the equipment for publishing the *Review*
was his personal property solely because there was no organization to
which he might give title. "The office is the property of the
church," he wrote. By this he meant that it should belong to the
church, but that legally it was impossible until some form of organization was set up.[3]

The move to Battle Creek necessitated the formation of a finance committee, whose responsibility it was to manage the business affairs of the Review office. But the property was still in the
name of James White. In response to his urging for the establishment of Christian order, many voices were heard protesting. He
laid it on the line in a hard-hitting editorial:

"We lack system. And we should not be afraid of that system
which is not opposed by the Bible, and is approved by sound sense.
The lack of system is felt everywhere. . . . [James then makes some
suggestions which would bring some organization out of disorder.]

"We are aware that these suggestions, will not meet the minds
of all. Bro. Overcautious will be frightened, and will be ready to
warn his brethren to be careful and not venture out too far; while
Bro. Confusion will cry out, 'O, this looks just like Babylon! Following the fallen church!' Bro. Do-little will say, 'The cause is the
Lord's, and we had better leave it in His hands, He will take care of
it.' 'Amen,' says Love-this-world, Slothful, Selfish, and Stingy, 'if
God calls men to preach, let them go out and preach, He will take
care of them, and those who believe their message'; while Korah,
Dathan and Abiram are ready to rebel against those who feel the
weight of the cause, and who watch for souls as those who must
give account, and raise the cry, 'Ye take too much upon yourselves.' "[4]

Until some form of organization was set up, there could be no
one authorized to deal with workers in the field who had to travel
from place to place. Some were very well treated, while others, laboring perhaps in isolated fields, often lacked the necessities of
life. James White wrote to his good friend, Abram Dodge:

"Brother Pearsall informed me that he helped Brethren Cornell and Loughborough $60.40 in cash. How could they receive it? Is this heeding the vision? . . . I hope dear Brother that you will be careful, as a church, how you use means. How you ruin these ministers." [5]

Many workers had the opposite experience. (Nor was Loughborough often treated so generously, as we shall soon see.) They did not receive sufficient to sustain themselves or their families. James pointed out the inequality in the payment of ministers, some getting much, others little. He knew of one minister who, after traveling 200 miles and preaching fourteen times in three weeks, was paid a total of $4. "Nobody is blamed in all this," Elder White remarked, "but is it not time that such evils were remedied among us? I think I hear the good brethren all say, YES." [6]

James wrote that he was tired of seeing statements concerning want among the preachers, coupled with appeals for funds in the *Review* columns. These general appeals, he pointed out, were actually aimed at everybody in general and nobody in particular, and so accomplished nothing effective. All they did was to fill up the paper and pain the reader. [7]

An experience of J. N. Loughborough offers a classic example of the results of fiscal policies of the time. Loughborough and two other workers had been preaching in New York and Pennsylvania during the summer of 1856. At the end of the summer Loughborough and another worker were given a sum which averaged $4 a week. The third man averaged $3. Discouraged, Loughborough gave up the ministry and went to Waukon, Iowa, to do carpentry. [8] James was concerned at losing him from God's cause, but it was not to be permanent. The Lord took a hand in the matter.

While attending a general meeting at Round Grove, Illinois, in 1856 Ellen White was shown that there was important work to be done at Waukon. The month was December, and 200 miles of ice and snow lay between Round Grove and Waukon. To make the long trip at that time of year in an open sleigh seemed to border on the impossible. But the Lord had spoken and they must obey. Just as they were ready to leave, it started to rain and it poured for an entire day.

"We must give up the journey," James declared.

"Sister White, what about Waukon?" asked Josiah Hart, the owner of the sleigh.

"We shall go," was her firm reply.

They left Round Grove, and so began what was to be called the "Dash to Waukon." The weather did not cooperate as they journeyed. It rained and it snowed. At one time they had to take refuge in an inn for seven days, until it cleared and they could travel again.

They came to the ice-covered Mississippi River. Crossing it would have been no problem, except that the ice was covered with a foot of water, rendering it extremely dangerous.

"Is it Iowa, or back to Illinois? We have come to the Red Sea," said Hart. "Shall we cross?"

"Go forward, trusting in Israel's God," declared Ellen White decisively.

"Go on," said James White.

They crossed the river, although they could at times hear the ice cracking beneath the sleigh. There was an outburst of "Praise the Lord" as the horses pulled the sleigh up the Iowa bank.

The weather turned bitterly cold as they pushed on. They had to keep rubbing their faces to keep them from freezing.

At last the travelers reached snowbound Waukon. They spent several days holding meetings and reviving the flagging zeal of the company there. Ellen White bore the message she had come to give to Loughborough, and J. N. Andrews, who had also settled at Waukon to regain his health. Before leaving, James White secured a promise from Loughborough that he would return to God's work no matter what personal sacrifice it might entail. Andrews likewise agreed to re-enter active service as soon as he was well.[9]

Pondering these experiences, White and other leaders became convinced it was time to find some equitable way to care for the needs of the workers. In 1858, with Loughborough and Andrews back in the work, a study group met in Battle Creek, led by Andrews, to discover what the Bible taught about the support of the ministry. The result was a method of giving that was called "Systematic Benevolence."[10] This plan called for each Adventist to lay aside a specific amount each week for the Lord's work. Those who owned property were also asked to give from one to five cents for each $100 value.

Systematic Benevolence was endorsed and soon established in all parts of the field. Churches had money with which to pay the expenses of visiting ministers. But James White urged them to exercise caution in regard to whom they supported. Only men willing to wear out, rather than rust out, should be financed. He wrote:

"We solemnly protest against supporting men on the old ground, doing little or nothing, and neglecting brethren, and letting them suffer, who are raising up churches, breaking into new fields, with poverty and destitution all around them, and sometimes thankful for 'Johnny-cake and string beans!' "[11]

Systematic Benevolence continued for approximately twenty years, until there was a change in the manner of reckoning the obligation. In 1878 the General Conference Committee recommended that, beginning with the first week of 1879, church members pay one tenth of their increase for the support of the ministry. This plan was accepted.

James continued to urge the church to take over legal ownership of the Review and Herald. Before this could occur, there would have to be a corporation formed to register with the State government. The *Review* became a sounding board for opinions of

James and Ellen's difficult trip to Waukon, Iowa, in
the winter of 1856 put new life into the church
there.

workers and laity alike. The greatest problem seemed to lie in the
necessity of choosing and adopting a name for the church body.
This was necessary before incorporation could take place.

R. F. Cottrell, one of the leading ministers, felt that a serious
mistake would be made if Elder White's plan was carried out. To
him, it called for involving the church in the questionable course
of making us a name, as the builders did at Babel.[12]

Uriah Smith, resident editor in Battle Creek, printed Elder
Cottrell's letter. James White was on a tour of Eastern churches
when it appeared, and he was greatly distressed by it. He telegraphed the office, "We are very sorry R. F. Cottrell's letter has
voiced his opposition before we had a chance to explain fully." [13]
At the same time he wrote to Uriah Smith requesting him to postpone publishing any further reference to the problem.[14]

Elder White showed his growing impatience in an article he
wrote for the *Review*. He expected an unsatisfactory situation to
continue for some time until "our brethren abroad become free from
their feelings of excited prejudice and become united upon a *plan
upon which we as a people can act,* then this church will move forward in harmony with the body." [15]

To settle the question, a general workers' meeting was called
in Battle Creek. Joseph Bates presided. A full report of everything
done and said there appeared in three succeeding issues of the
Review.[16] Speech after speech was made, both for and against
selecting a name and incorporating.

If a name was chosen, James White felt that the most appropriate one would be that title found in the Bible, The Church
of God.

There were strong objections. First, this title sounded exclusive,
and second, there were already several denominations calling
themselves the Church of God. In the end the name Seventh-day
Adventist was chosen, and it quickly gained well-nigh unanimous
support.[17]

Since the church now had a name—but, it must be remembered, was not yet an organization—it was possible to incorporate
the Review office. This was done and the Adventist Publishing
Association was incorporated. Elder White gladly turned over the
Review office and supplies to this Association on June 2, 1861.[18]

It took some time for the church members to come into full

harmony with the decisions taken at this Battle Creek meeting. But such was their confidence in the integrity of James White, that most believers rallied and accepted the plans as adopted by the leaders.

The cause of organization was carried one step further in October, 1861, when the Michigan workers met in Battle Creek to organize the first State conference. The first year Joseph Bates was chairman of the executive committee. He was followed in 1862 by William S. Higley. From then on the term president was used instead of chairman.[19]

As a result of organization, the work in Michigan moved forward rapidly. For a time, other States showed no indication of wishing to follow the example of the believers in Michigan. In 1863 James White pointed out the marked blessings that had come to Michigan as a result of the step taken by the brethren in that State.[20] While looking forward to a time when the States might all have conferences, he realized that until this took place, there could be no general over-all organization to care for the work as a whole. It was toward achieving this goal that he bent his efforts in 1862 and 1863.

---

[1] *Origin and History,* vol. 1, p. 291.
[2] *Review and Herald,* May 6, 1852.
[3] James White, in *Review and Herald,* Aug. 7, 1855.
[4] *Ibid.,* July 21, 1859.
[5] James White letter July 31, 1853.
[6] James White, in *Review and Herald,* Feb. 17, 1859.
[7] James White, in *Review and Herald,* May 26, 1859.
[8] *Origin and History,* vol. 1, pp. 281, 282.
[9] *Ibid.,* pp. 283-289.
[10] J. N. Loughborough, *Rise and Progress of Seventh-day Adventists,* p. 215.
[11] James White, in *Review and Herald,* Oct. 6, 1859.
[12] *Ibid.,* March 22, 1860.
[13] White's telegraphic message to Uriah Smith, April, 1860.
[14] *Ibid.*
[15] *Review and Herald,* June 19, 1860.
[16] *Ibid.,* Oct. 9, 16, 23, 1860.
[17] *Origin and History,* vol. 1, pp. 302, 303.
[18] *Ibid.,* vol. 1, pp. 303-305.
[19] *The SDA Encyclopedia,* Article, "Michigan," p. 779.
[20] *Review and Herald,* March 3, 1863.

Chapter Twenty-two

REACHING THE GOAL

WHEN James White turned over to the finance committee the handling of Publishing Association funds, aside from books, he did not thereby sever himself from all connection with the paper. His work as leading editor of the *Review* continued. With the exception of the period when he was suffering from the effects of a paralytic stroke, he continued to direct the editorial policies of the *Review* until his death in 1881.

The Adventist Church paper was a "sounding board" for James, a platform from which he addressed the remnant church. Through its columns he stimulated members to good works, warned them of dangers, and encouraged every move that might help to finish God's work and hasten the Advent of Christ.

In 1865 James expressed pity for Brother Uriah Smith who was substituting as editor while James enjoyed temporary freedom from office cares.

"It is all hurry, hurry, hurry with the Editor. He has no time to rest, or to be cheered and refreshed by visiting Christian friends. . . . He must be shut up to his task, and grow pale, and hurry on towards the grave. One who served you five years, but just escaped the grave, with his life, and now (having taken leave of his editorial post) is fast recovering his health and former freedom of spirits. He can feel for our present Editor, as he knows his cares, his confinement, his sacrifices, while shut up to his duties fifteen hours of the twenty-four." [1]

The formation of the Publishing Association, the selection of a church name, and the organization of the Michigan Conference had all been steps toward Elder White's goal—organization of the entire church body. James recognized them as such and looked forward ardently toward the formation of some type of organization that would bind every detail of the work together as a whole.

In a *Review* editorial, James attributed much of the growth taking place in Michigan to the fact that, like Israel of old, its members were united. Systematic Benevolence was operating beautifully, and for the first time workers were receiving a regular weekly wage, though it was small. With a gentle hint to other States, he concluded, "We would be highly gratified if preachers in other States would immediately give the subject a critical examination, and if they have suggestions to make, to freely make them without delay." [2]

As a result of this appeal, during the year 1862 State conferences were organized in Iowa, Vermont, Illinois-Wisconsin, Minnesota, New York, and Ohio. [3]

The stage was now set for the organization of the church as a whole. The officers in the Michigan Conference invited the other State conferences to send delegates to meet with them in Battle Creek, May 20-23, 1863, for the purpose of organizing a General Conference. The State conferences responded and appointed delegates. Of the 20 accredited representatives no fewer than half were from Michigan.

The appropriate committees were appointed. One, headed by J. N. Andrews, was entrusted with the responsibility of drafting a constitution for the new organization. Another committee was to bring in nominations for officers, and when they read their report, no one was surprised to hear that James White had been invited to serve as president.

But White politely, yet firmly, declined the position. For years he had been urging the formation of an organization. Now that it was coming into existence, enemies of the cause would say that his prime purpose in forming a General Conference was that he might seize the top position, and then he would be able to force his will and plans on the church body. He knew that some were already circulating such sentiments. Under these circumstances, he felt it would be better if some other individual were chosen for the position. [5]

Consequently, the delegates accepted his refusal and chose John Byington, a respected minister from New York. Uriah Smith was elected secretary, and E. S. Walker, treasurer. The General Conference Executive Committee would consist of three members—

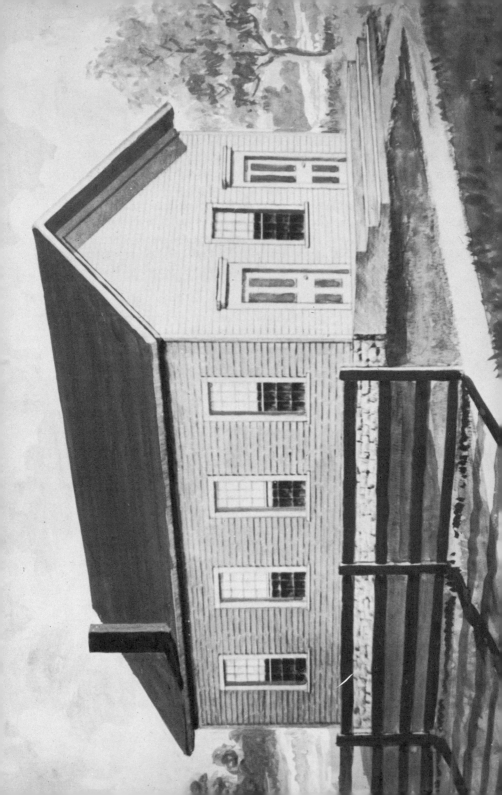

Byington, Loughborough, and White. Later, J. N. Andrews and G. W. Amadon were added to the committee.

The two-day conference drew to a close and the men returned to their respective States. Uriah Smith wrote, pointing out that "perhaps no previous meeting that we have ever enjoyed, was characterized by such unity of feeling and harmony of sentiment." [6]

It should be pointed out that a General Conference session in the 1860's and 1870's was vastly different from one held today, with its more than 1,000 delegates meeting, as it does, only once in four or five years. Between the first session in 1863 and the last one attended by James White in 1880, there were a total of twenty-four sessions in seventeen years. This means that in some years two were held. Two of these sessions convened in Lansing, Michigan, all the others in Battle Creek.

During those years the largest number of delegates, thirty-nine, attended the sessions held on October 4, 1878, and November 7, 1879. On December 29, 1871, there were only fourteen delegates. The General Conference president was elected (or re-elected) every year. During this period John Byington and J. N. Andrews served two years each, George I. Butler for three, and James White for ten years. Sessions usually lasted but one or two days and were almost entirely business meetings. A report of the proceedings of the General Conference session usually filled only one or two pages of the *Review and Herald.*

The battle was over, and James was cheered by the outcome. The church could now move forward as a united body. It was inevitable that changes would come in future years.

The General Conference treasury began with only $384.25 to work with. [7] To improve this situation, State conferences, as well as individuals, were invited to send funds to headquarters for use in supporting the work as a whole. But there was no compulsion. James White made this point very clear:

"No person is compelled to pay one cent into the benevolent treasury. Each person is left to assess his own property, and act freely in the fear of God. . . . Church treasurers in other States, send funds to their State treasurers wherever they may be located, to be used in their several States for the support of the cause. They are no more required to send their funds to Battle Creek than to Jerusalem or to Mecca." [8]

The General Conference was organized in Battle Creek in this meetinghouse in 1863. The denominational name, Seventh-day Adventists, was adopted at the time.

While concentrating their attention on the development of an organized church, Adventists were not unmindful of a political storm that was brewing in the nation. As the time for crucial elections drew near in the fall of 1860, Adventists, with their neighbors, found excitement growing. The fact that much of the discussion revolved about the slavery issue seemed to furnish Abraham Lincoln's party with a platform of moral issues. James White warned church members against allowing themselves to be carried away by political feelings. It was not wrong to vote, he pointed out, but he urged them not to enter into political strife.[9]

During the Civil War years, Adventist ministers were to find that interest in the great struggle tended to diminish interest in religious matters. Evangelistic tents pitched during that time did not attract as large attendances as in former years.

Also the war created many problems for Adventists. This was the first war in which they were confronted with the question of their duties and responsibilities toward the military establishment. A law permitted a noncombatant to pay $300 to the government, which then found a substitute to take his place. Many Adventists availed themselves of the arrangement. The church tried to help financially, but it could not cover all the demands.[10]

As casualty lists became longer, the calls for soldiers increased. Draft boards became increasingly reluctant to exempt Sabbath-keepers. Some Adventist leaders were advising those who were drafted to refuse to serve, regardless of consequences. But James White urged caution. It was a time for clear thinking, not rash action. He wrote:

"He who would resist until, in the administration of military law, he was shot down, goes too far, we think, in taking the responsibility for suicide. . . .

"But for us to attempt to resist the laws of the best government under heaven, which is now struggling to put down the . . . rebellion . . . we repeat, it would be madness."[11]

In time a solution to the problem of bearing arms was found, which has benefited Adventist servicemen ever since. At the direction of the General Conference Committee, Elder John Andrews went to Washington, D.C., in 1864, where he worked out an agreement with the officers of the Lincoln administration whereby Seventh-day Adventists would be exempt from bearing arms and would be recognized as noncombatants, a privilege that had already been extended to the Quakers.[12]

The long, terrible war drew to a close. The editor of the *Review* commented on the noble sentiments propounded by President Lincoln at the time of his second inaugural address on March 4, 1865. A few weeks later, after the end of the war, the nation was called upon to mourn the death of its great President. The General Conference Committee passed the following resolution:

"*Whereas,* Abraham Lincoln, the noble-minded and upright chief magistrate of this nation, has fallen by the hand of an assassin,

Resolved, That we hereby record our deep distress at the loss of this 'prince and great man,' . . . who was stricken down by his enemies at the very moment when he was studying how to forgive them all." [13]

---

[1] James White, in *Review and Herald*, Dec. 11, 1856.

[2] *Ibid.,* Oct. 15, 1861.

[3] *Origin and History*, vol. 1, p. 306.

[4] *Ibid.*, pp. 306, 307.

[5] Everett Dick, Ph.D., *Founders of the Message* (Washington, D.C., Review and Herald Publishing Assn., 1938), p. 186.

[6] *Origin and History*, vol. 1, p. 308.

[7] *Review and Herald*, May 31, 1864.

[8] James White, in *Review and Herald*, Dec. 6, 1864.

[9] *Ibid.*, Aug. 21, 1860.

[10] *Origin and History*, vol. 1, p. 324.

[11] James White, in *Review and Herald*, Aug. 12, 1862.

[12] *Origin and History*, vol. 1, pp. 323, 324.

[13] *Review and Herald*, May 23, 1865.

Chapter Twenty-three

CONTINUED LABORS AND REVELATIONS ON HEALTH

WITHOUT James White's dynamic leadership there would have been no organization of the Adventist Church in the 1860's. For week after week, month by month, year after year, through the columns of the *Review and Herald,* he presented the importance of gospel order and led the members forward step by step toward his goal. A problem that he had to face was that he could see farther ahead than most of his brethren. And, of course, he was married to Ellen White, through whom God spoke directly to him on many occasions, counseling, encouraging, and stimulating his thinking.

Ellen recognized the special talents God had given her husband. She wrote to him: "God has given you a good intellect—I might say a giant intellect. . . . The cause of God cannot spare you without experiencing a great loss." [1] On a later date she wrote to her son, "Your father does the work of three men at all these meetings. I never saw a man work so energetically, so constantly as your Father. God does give him more than mortal energy. If there is any place that is hard, your Father takes it." [2]

In the minds of some of the brethren, opposition lingered for some time after the General Conference was organized. There was, however, a general tendency, particularly on the part of the laymen, to trust Elder White's leadership. His manner inspired confidence. Elder W. A. Spicer beautifully described his gift in these words:

"James White had the gift of carrying the people along with him in joy and enthusiasm for the truth and work of God, and with a natural, unstudied grace and dignity that kept everything to the high, thoughtful, spiritual level. He had the qualities that were needed in a leader in those early days as the advent movement of the prophecy was taking form." [3]

The people indicated in a variety of ways their confidence in their leader. In response to a request for additional capital for the Review and Herald, one sister in Vermont sent $100. A receipt with the signature "Advent Review and Sabbath Herald Office" was refused by her. She indicated that she wanted a note signed by Elder White, not by the Publishing Association. James declined to accept the money on those terms, and it was returned to the sender.[4]

Although James was no longer in charge of the finances of the *Review* and *Instructor*, the responsibility for raising funds to ensure the publication of the papers rested, to a large degree, on him. It was over his initials that appeals appeared on the editorial page of the *Review*. He often found it necessary to reprove those who wanted the paper, but who declined to support it financially. Some of these persons were extremely unreasonable. James described one of them:

"A female subscriber in Wisconsin is a sample. Soon after we wrote with red ink the names of delinquents on the margin of their papers, and stated that the papers to all such would be discontinued unless they immediately renewed their subscription, this lady wrote to the Office in threatening style like the following: 'If you discontinue all the papers you write on with red ink, we shall withdraw our support.'

"Singular support that! We had sent them the *Review* one year *for nothing!*"[5]

The use of the steam press and engine made it possible to produce large quantities of books. The list of book titles available from the Publishing Association continued to lengthen. Most of them dealt with evangelical and doctrinal topics. James White spent many long hours preparing many of these publications for the press. Often his labors continued far into the night.

By the late 1850's nearly every conference owned its tent in which to hold meetings. Elder White urged the evangelists operating these tents to sell books and to aim at $200 worth for each place visited. This was so that the people might become established in the message after the evangelist left.[6] He himself always carried a trunkful of books whenever he left Battle Creek to hold meetings among the churches. The results were encouraging.

Ellen continued her trips to the churches with her husband, even venturing forth with him in the dead of winter. James describes one such journey made into central and northern Michigan in the winter of 1861:

When we gave our appointments for northern Michigan we expected to enjoy good sleighing. But the morning we were to leave for a trip of fifty-three miles that day by stage, the driver exchanged runners for wheels, and drove up to our door with an old mud wagon. The road was very rough, and we were seven hours getting twenty-seven miles. Here we met Brother Gerould with a wagon to take us twenty-six miles more that night. After resting fifteen minutes we got aboard; but we were so loaded down with our heavy trunks that Brother Gerould decided to go a-foot.

We had no time to stop and rest, or get meals, so drove on, refreshing as well as possible upon dried beef and bread. We were exceedingly tired as night set in; but how could we complain while Brother G. was walking or running by our side, or occasionally springing upon the trunks to ride down hill. In this way we pursued our journey till ten o'clock at night, when we reached the hospitable home of Brother and Sister G. We had been out fourteen hours without resting, and probably Brother G. had run eight or ten miles of the last twenty-six.

It was a question who was most to be pitied, we who had suffered the unaccustomed shaking in the old stage, and had finished out the fifty-three miles in the wagon, or Brother G. on foot, or the good horse who in tugging his weary load fell twice in ascending icy hills. The next morning, however, all could move about, and seemed quite comfortable, excepting Mrs. W.[7]

On many of these trips, it was long after dark before they reached their destination. Usually they carried a lunch with them, but were compelled to eat it cold. If they were meeting a distant appointment, they would travel by train. These often ran hours late, causing travelers to miss connections countless times. James and Ellen spent long hours waiting in lonely railway stations for trains that seemed never to run on time.

But calls for the help of the Whites seemed endless. Ministers and conference leaders, when announcing general meetings on the last page of the *Review*, often added the words, "We trust Elder and Mrs. White can be in attendance," knowing that such a notice would bring persons who otherwise would have remained at home. Then, rather than disappoint the people, Elder and Mrs. White would attend.

In Michigan they usually traveled by horse and carriage in summer or by sleigh in winter. To reach the New England States from Battle Creek they usually went by train. Many times journeys involved sitting up all night, since sleeping cars were just coming into use. Dining cars were unknown, and the contents of a lunch basket frequently had to last three or four days. It is no wonder that James's health suffered under the constant pressure.

James was not the only worker in those days who suffered from poor health. J. N. Andrews endured many afflictions. So did Loughborough, Smith, Edson, and others. There were times when so many of the Review staff were sick that it was impossible to print and distribute the paper on time.

Parents suffered, but their children frequently died. In those days one in four children died before reaching the age of 7, stricken with whooping cough, scarlet fever, measles, or often the deadliest of all, diphtheria. James and Ellen knew by personal experience the meaning of these statistics. Of their four children, only two reached maturity.

Early in 1863, James read in a newspaper an article written by Dr. J. C. Jackson, of Dansville, New York, describing how diphtheria might be cured by the use of water treatments.[8] When their two children manifested symptoms of the dread scourge, the Whites decided not to call in a doctor to prescribe the usual drugs, but to follow Dr. Jackson's directions. The children made a quick recovery. Impressed, James White reprinted Jackson's article in the *Review*.[9] Other Adventists tried it and often achieved successful results.

The time had now come for a great forward thrust along health lines. If the remnant people were to go into all the world and preach the gospel according to Christ's command, they would need healthy bodies and clear minds. God did not leave them to sift through the current medical journals for true health principles. Those journals contained much that was good, but they likewise promoted many nonsensical theories.

About two weeks after the Battle Creek meeting when the General Conference was organized, Elder and Mrs. White went with a group going to attend a series of tent meetings in Otsego, Michigan. One sunny Friday morning in early June, the group drove the thirty-five miles westward, reaching their destination well before sundown. The weary travelers were welcomed at the home of Aaron Hilliard. Besides being tired, Elder White had been suffering from poor health. His mind and spirits were depressed.

As the sun was setting, the family and the visitors joined in welcoming the holy Sabbath. An eyewitness described what followed:

> A chapter was read, and Sister White led in prayer, Brother White kneeling across the corner from her. Her burden in prayer was for him, and as she prayed, while still on her knees, she moved over to him, laid her hands on his shoulders, and prayed until she was taken in vision. This lasted for about three-quarters of an hour. At this time she was given the light on the health reform. Brother White also was greatly blessed and encouraged, and he was relieved of the burden he had been carrying.[10]

The light on health reform given Ellen that evening has proved a blessing to countless thousands around the world. The message was direct: "I saw that it was a sacred duty to attend to our health, and arouse others to their duty. . . . We have a duty to speak, to come out against intemperance of every kind—intemperance in working, in eating, in drinking, in drugging."[11]

It seems significant that intemperance in working was listed first. Certainly the workers, and perhaps James White most of all, needed to be admonished on this point. The eight-hour day was unknown for either workers or laity. On another occasion Ellen pointed out in a straightforward way the dangers of this course: "I was shown that Sabbathkeepers as a people labor too hard without allowing themselves change or periods of rest."[12]

The adoption of principles laid down in the health reform vision brought drastic modifications to the Adventist homes that accepted them. For example, dietary habits were changed. In regard to what took place in his own home, James White wrote:

> Returning to temperate habits restores the appetite, so that health reformers take their food with keen relish. We had a clear illustration of this matter in the case of our Willie. Before the reformation in our table, when it was set three times a day with flesh, the child's reply to his mother's interrogation at breakfast, "What will you have on your plate, Willie?" would frequently be, "I don't see anything on the table I want." But when the table was cleared of greasy, spiced, and saleratus cakes, flesh-meats, pepper, vinegar, pickles, mustard, et cetera, and the two meals a day were adopted, the boy's answer to the question, "What will you have on your plate?" was, "Victuals, mother, victuals." The simplest and most healthful food could then be received with a relish far exceeding that enjoyed in eating the greatest delicacy before his appetite was restored by proper habits.[13]

Ellen wrote out the instruction given in her Otsego vision,

which was later published in a thirty-page chapter in Volume IV of *Spiritual Gifts.* This book was in great demand. The Review office could scarcely keep up with orders. James White reported on one occasion, that, although there were two binders at work, not a single copy was on the shelf.[14] Ellen expanded the presentation in six articles, which appeared in six pamphlets entitled *Health, or How to Live.*

On August 24, 1864, Elder and Mrs. White left Battle Creek to spend three months, first in visiting Dr. Jackson's water-cure institution in Dansville, New York, and then touring the eastern States. Of their last meeting with the Battle Creek church, Uriah Smith wrote, "As they gave us their parting words of encouragement, exhortation and counsel, . . . the tears of the congregation showed to what an extent they are endeared to this people."[15]

On May 17, 1865, the third session of the General Conference met in Battle Creek. The nominating committee brought in the name of James White as president, and this time, although he protested, he accepted. However, he gave up his job as editor of the *Review.* Uriah Smith assumed the responsibility.[16]

Shortly after the conference adjourned the Whites received a request to visit Wisconsin, where they conducted important meetings. Their travels in that State involved many hardships. Meanwhile, two ministers in the Iowa Conference were encouraging disunion in the churches in that area. To meet this threat, the Whites traveled to Iowa and met with the disaffected members and their discontented leaders.

When they arrived back in Battle Creek, utterly weary from their strenuous labors, the Whites found an urgent message requesting their help at the Memphis, Michigan, church. They took the first train available and spent the weekend with the church. Sunday night's meeting was long. Since their train left early in the morning, they had very little sleep that night. They got up at three o'clock, took leave of their hosts, and walked a mile to the railway station carrying their luggage. Then their train missed connections in Detroit, and as a result, they arrived in Battle Creek at midnight. The next day James was at his desk early. He found a host of urgent matters calling for his attention, and was exhausted when he arrived home that evening.[17]

James seemed refreshed when he arose the next morning.

Deciding to take a walk, he and Ellen started out together. Along the way they stopped at a neighbor's home. Noting that the corn was ripening, James stepped into the field, broke off an ear, and began stripping it.

Suddenly Ellen heard him groan. Looking up, she saw him stagger as if to fall. Rushing to support him, she helped him as he staggered painfully into their neighbor's house. Inside, he could utter only one word, "Pray!" [18]

James's darkest hour had come.

[1] Ellen G. White letter 38, July 2, 1874.

[2] ———— letter 39, Aug. 17, 1876.

[3] W. A. Spicer, in *Review and Herald*, March 7, 1940.

[4] *Founders of the Message*, p. 184.

[5] James White, in *Review and Herald*, Feb. 5, 1857.

[6] *Ibid.*, July 2, 1857.

[7] *Ibid.*, Dec. 17, 1861.

[8] *The Story of Our Health Message*, pp. 63, 64.

[9] *Review and Herald*, Feb. 12, 1863.

[10] Martha Amadon, "Mrs. E. G. White in Vision," written Nov. 24, 1925, Document File 105.

[11] *Origin and History*, vol. 1, p. 346.

[12] *Testimonies*, vol. 1, p. 514.

[13] James White, in *The Health Reformer*, 1872. Quoted in *Pacific Health Journal*, Aug., 1888, p. 229.

[14] James White, in *Review and Herald*, Aug. 23, 1864.

[15] *Ibid.*, Aug. 30, 1864.

[16] *Founders of the Message*, p. 187.

[17] William C. White, "Sketches and Memories," *Review and Herald*, Jan. 7, 1937.

[18] *Ibid.*

Chapter Twenty-four

STRICKEN!

J AMES White lay on a couch in the Lunt home in Battle Creek, near which he had been stricken while he and Ellen were taking a walk. Ellen and Brother and Sister Lunt knelt by his side and pled with God on his behalf. In a short time the power of speech was restored and he could raise his arm.[1] A physician was sent for. Word spread rapidly through the Adventist community of Battle Creek that Elder White had suffered a paralytic stroke and that it might possibly be fatal.

Two days later he was taken to his own home. The doctors who examined him expressed fear for his recovery. They told Ellen that they had never known anyone suffering such a severe shock to recover.[2]

Eleven days after his stroke, on August 27, Elder White was dressed for the first time since his attack, and walked a few steps with assistance. Two weeks later he walked from his home to the office.

Dr. H. S. Lay, an Adventist physician on the staff at the Dansville water-cure institute, visited James in Battle Creek, and, since it was planned that James become a patient at "Our Home on the Hillside," accompanied James and Ellen there. The Whites had been at Dansville once before, as visitors.

James was not the only Adventist minister who journeyed to Dansville as an invalid in quest of health. With him, when he left Battle Creek on Thursday, September 14, in addition to Ellen, were Elder J. N. Loughborough and Elder Uriah Smith. Elder White stood the journey well, including a delay in Rochester because of bad weather.[3]

Dr. Jackson, chief physician at the institution, examined James and told him and Ellen that he would need to remain at Dans-

171

ville six to eight months. Because of overwork Elder White had suffered what could easily have been a fatal stroke. If restoration was to be achieved, complete rest, both mental and physical, would be necessary, the doctor emphasized.[4] The *Review* of October 3 carried a request from the General Conference Committee that Adventists set aside October 14 as a day of fasting and prayer for Elder White.[5]

There was much to commend in the health program carried out at Dansville. No meat was served to the patients, and there was an abundance of fruit, fresh vegetables, and nuts. Bread was made from whole-grain flour. Water treatments played an important part in hastening the curative process.

In Dr. Lay's report to the church through the *Review* he stated that the Whites and Elder Loughborough needed rest and time to recuperate. Elder White had suffered "a shock of paralysis, leaving his nervous system, as a matter of course, in a shattered condition, and his brain somewhat disturbed."[6]

Realizing that expenses at the institute were heavy, the Monterey, Michigan, church, led by Elder Joseph Bates, sent $60.00.[7] A Sister Gates sent $10.00 with the statement: "It is impossible for us to know that you are in affliction, and we not suffer with you."[8]

James's principal difficulty lay in his inability to rest, particularly at night. Sometimes his sleep would be limited to one or two hours. As healing began, it was evident that his mental powers were restored before the physical. There was never a moment's doubt in Ellen's mind but that God was guiding. But she no doubt knew that if her husband had been restored instantly, he would have very soon gone back to his program of crowding into one day the work of two.

The Whites found it difficult to harmonize some of the methods employed at Dansville with their religious belief. They agreed with Dr. Jackson's insistence that joy, happiness, peace of mind, and pleasure were conducive to health, while sadness and indulgence in feelings of discouragement tended to feebleness and poor health. What they objected to was the type of pleasures in which the Dansville patients were expected to indulge. These included card-playing, theatrical performances, and dancing. Naturally such activities conflicted with the religious principles of James and Ellen White.[9]

Following his serious stroke in 1865, James White spent some time recuperating at Dr. J. E. Jackson's "Our Home on the Hillside," Dansville, New York.

After James and Ellen had been at Dansville a while they decided that the children should be nearer to them. Consequently, they arranged for Edson and Willie to go to Rochester and stay at a home there. Ellen went to Rochester to spend a few days with them. During her stay at Rochester she expected James to write regularly. Apparently his affected hand, the right, had recovered enough for this.

Meanwhile, James's progress was not as fast as Ellen would have liked it to be. This, and her problem with the doctor's prescription of physical and mental inactivity for her husband caused her to decide to seek a different environment for him. This she proposed to find in the Lamson home in Rochester. [10]

Ellen returned to Dansville prepared for her next move. She told Dr. Lay of her decision to take her husband from the Home. He felt she was making a mistake, and stated that the patient was not strong enough to endure such a journey. Ellen stated that she would travel in several short stages, first stopping at Rochester, then Detroit, Jackson, and finally Battle Creek. To this plan the doctor reluctantly agreed, so on December 7 Ellen traveled with her husband from Dansville to the Lamson home in Rochester, where they remained for several weeks. [11]

James had great confidence in the prayers of J. N. Andrews, and requested that he come from Maine, where he was preaching. Elder Andrews came and led out in many earnest seasons of prayer around the bedside of the sufferer. A measure of relief was obtained. On Christmas Day three special seasons of prayer were held. During the evening season of prayer Ellen was taken off in vision. [12] She was impressed that she should take her husband and return to their home in Battle Creek.

On January 1, 1866, they left Rochester by train for Battle Creek. Back at home James began very cautiously to walk slowly around the town. Friends noted that he had lost fifty pounds. On pleasant days he and Ellen would drive out into the country.

On Sabbath, January 6, James and Ellen once again attended services in the Battle Creek church. Through the Lord's help James was able to speak for forty-five minutes, and tears were in many eyes as the congregation listened to him. That evening he conducted the Lord's Supper during another service. [13]

But to Ellen his total recovery seemed agonizingly slow. On

March 27 James White himself reported through the *Review*, "In some respects I consider my condition somewhat improved, yet I do not gain flesh. . . . I cannot read or write but very little, . . . I have no want of means, but at present must have rest from care and anxiety." [14]

On May 16 the fourth session of the General Conference was held in Battle Creek. The delegates indicated their faith that God would raise up Elder White by re-electing him to a second term as president of the General Conference.

But their leader was sadly changed. Gone was the buoyant optimism that had carried him through so many fierce struggles. One brother made the following observation: "Brother White is still about so. He seems better in many respects but does not think so himself. He looks upon the dark side a great deal. . . . He is very kind and takes no care whatever of anything or anybody but himself." [15]

James's illness had made it almost impossible for Ellen to continue her ministry to the church. She felt that her first responsibility was to bring her husband back to health. The same brother writing above noted her constant efforts to cheer her husband in his dark hours, wrote: "She is an exception to all women or mankind. I never saw a person brave through everything as she does." [16]

The next Sabbath, May 20, was appointed as another day of fasting and prayer on behalf of the stricken leader. Two days later, James wrote to the Review:

You will be able to form some idea of our sufferings, when we say that for the past nine months we have not been able to obtain sleep without artificial heat in some form, either a jug of hot water or a hot stone, or hot blankets applied to the feet; and that for the last five months we have not had more than one hour's sleep out of twenty-four, and that often disturbed by unhappy dreams. . . .

For two nights past since the season of fasting and prayer, Sabbath, May 20th, we have slept more than for the two weeks previous, and our feet were warm without the use of artificial heat. [17]

One friend, John Matteson, who visited Elder White at that time, has recorded his impressions.

When I saw him bowed down with disease and took his weak hand, I could not refrain from weeping. Like a mighty oak he had stood the storms of many winters, but a cruel tornado had broken the limbs, and even loosened the roots, so as to deprive the tree of its nourishment. He had stood foremost in the ranks, never fearing the bullets, nor terrified by the roar of the cannon, the bravest, and yet the humblest and most benevolent. He is now the most needed. Shall he sink down with the rest of our pioneers . . . ? He looks like a bruised reed. Yet God will not break the bruised reed. Brother White will recover.[18]

When a call came from the Monterey, Michigan, church for a visit by Elder White and wife, they decided to step out by faith and respond. Accompanied by Dr. Lay, they set out by carriage. The first day's travel of thirty-five miles brought them to the Hadden home. Traveling twenty miles farther the next day, they reached Monterey where they held weekend services. For two weeks they visited other churches in the vicinity, then returned to Battle Creek. Reported James White: "In point of health we sleep better, enjoy our food better, . . . and, we are gaining slowly in weight." [19]

But as the summer slowly passed, there seemed to be little improvement in his condition. Hearing that her own father in Maine was on his deathbed, Ellen decided to visit him. She would take James part of the way and leave him with friends in New York State. She felt that a change of atmosphere might help him. Ellen describes the hardships that her husband endured on that journey:

Either the operator at Battle Creek or at Detroit was negligent. We went on board the sleeping car by crowding and pushing and jamming our way through a crowd of people who could get no berths. We found two empty seats and occupied them, but they were taken and every berth was taken. I was sent to the forward car for a berth, but our names were not registered anywhere. I went back to the rear car and awaited the movement of events. It was all hustle and bustle.

James had endured the journey thus far well, but it was close and stifling in the sleeping car, and it was a long time past nine o'clock before things were in any degree settled. Your father seemed languid. I begged the man who had charge of the sleeping car to find us berths. He was kind. He did for us all he could. Said there were no berths. I told him one double berth I must have, for it was a case of absolute necessity. He finally prevailed upon a gentleman to give up his lower berth to your father.

After lying a short time in his berth and resting, he wished to go to the saloon [wash room]. I helped to steady him along. He seemed more languid, and while helping him back I saw his face grow very white and he was pitching forward to the floor. I raised and held him and called aloud for help. The manager in the sleeping car kindly, tenderly, and firmly supported your father to his berth. I succeeded in opening a window in his berth and a strong wind blew upon us all night. Willie and I could obtain no berths.[20]

At Brookfield, New York, Ellen left her husband and son with

the Abbeys and hastened on to the bedside of her dying father.
In the autumn of 1866, James was apparently losing ground in
his fight for life. Even Ellen's faith almost failed during that dark
time. She wrote to her son, Edson:

> Father grows feebler every day. He is very white and his face is
> pinched. I do not think he will live over a month. He is liable to die any
> day or any night. We have sent for your aunts Mary and Lizzie to come im-
> mediately if they would see father alive.[21]

But the crisis passed, and he retained his grip on life. Winter
arrived and still James lacked strength to return to his work at the
office. This did not prevent workers in the publishing house from
visiting him and referring many difficult problems to his attention.
Problems affecting the General Conference were likewise pressed
upon him. These cares resulted in his suffering many sleepless
nights.

By now Ellen had come to the place where she was prepared to
resort to heroic measures. She decided to get her husband completely away from Battle Creek for a time, settling where she could
put into practice those measures she felt sure would bring him back
to his former strength. What she did, and how friends and fellow
church members reacted to her plan, she described:

> I thought my husband should have some change, and we took our team,
> faithful Jack and Jim, and ventured a journey to Wright, Michigan.
> In this matter I was obliged to move contrary to the judgement of my
> brethren and sisters in Battle Creek. They all felt that I was sacrificing my
> life in shouldering this burden; that for the sake of my children, for the
> cause of God, I should do all in my power to preserve my life. His own
> father and mother remonstrated with me in tears. Physicians looked pity-
> ingly upon me and said, "You will not realize your expectations. There
> was never known a case where one afflicted with paralysis of the brain re-
> covered."
> I answered them:—"God will raise him up."[22]

As Ellen with her sick husband and 12-year-old Willie drove
out of Battle Creek that bitterly cold day, December 19, into the
teeth of a snowstorm, many friends and neighbors watching them
go felt that she was making a fatal mistake and would probably hasten her husband's death. Bitter feelings arose, which were to strain
the bonds of affection between the Whites and some members of
the Battle Creek church for some time to come.

But Ellen felt that no sacrifice would be too great if making it would result in the restoration of James White. Her faith was to be justified.

---

[1] William C. White, "Sketches and Memories," *Review and Herald,* Jan. 7, 1937.

[2] *Ibid.*

[3] Uriah Smith, in *Review and Herald,* Oct. 3, 1865.

[4] *Origin and History,* vol. 1, p. 355.

[5] *Review and Herald,* Oct. 3, 1865.

[6] *Ibid.,* Oct. 31, 1865.

[7] *Ibid.,* Nov. 21, 1865.

[8] *Ibid.,* Oct. 21, 1865.

[9] William C. White, "Sketches and Memories," *Review and Herald,* Jan. 7, 1937.

[10] Ellen G. White letter 8, to James White, Nov. 21, 1865.

[11] *Origin and History,* vol. 1, p. 357.

[12] William C. White, "Sketches and Memories," *Review and Herald,* Jan. 14, 1937.

[13] *Ibid.,* Jan. 9, 1866.

[14] James White, in *Review and Herald,* March 27, 1866.

[15] Letter to Lucinda Hall, Feb. 25, 1866.

[16] *Ibid.*

[17] James White, in *Review and Herald,* May 22, 1866.

[18] *Ibid.,* May 29, 1866.

[19] *Ibid.,* June 19, 1866.

[20] Ellen G. White letter 2, to Edson White, Sept. 12, 1866.

[21] Ellen G. White letter 16, to son Edson, Oct. 14, 1866.

[22] Manuscript 1, 1867.

Chapter Twenty-five

THE ROAD BACK

WITH a Brother Rogers at the reins, James, Ellen, and 12-year-old Willie rode northward hour after hour through falling snow. As daylight faded that brief December day, the weary travelers having driven 46 miles, began looking for a place to spend the night. The only accommodation they could find was a "rum tavern," as it was called, with provisions for guests. Next morning they drove fifteen miles to the home of a Brother Hardy, where they had breakfast. They had to cover another twenty-three miles in the afternoon before they would arrive at Wright, the home of Brother E. H. Root, where they were heartily welcomed as they thawed out their cold bodies before a cheerful fire.

On Sabbath, two days later, they attended the Adventist church, which was filled with attentive listeners. James was able to preach for 25 minutes from the text "Will a man rob God?" Ellen followed with an exhortation that lasted for an hour. They both spoke again in the afternoon and also the next morning.[1]

During the six weeks that the Whites made their home with the Root family James made steady improvement. He and Ellen traveled to various churches and held meetings on the Sabbath and "first day," as they called Sunday. As Ellen sat on the platform behind James and noted the return of his old-time power she, on one occasion, found tears trickling down her cheeks.

From Wright the Whites went to Greenville. To the editor of the *Review* James wrote:

We would express our gratitude to this dear people, who, among other smaller acts of liberal kindness, have given us a comfortable sleigh worth $75, and Brother Root has kept the three of us and team six weeks.[2]

The day they made the forty-mile trip to Greenville was bit-

The two-story section of this house was the Wright, Michigan, church when the Whites visited the area. The building has been moved from its original site.

terly cold and stormy. The travelers found shelter at the home of A. W. Maynard,[3] which they made their headquarters. Here they remained for another six weeks, visiting the churches in the area.

While at Greenville, James and Ellen decided that they would sell their Battle Creek property and move to Greenville. Brother Maynard was delighted at their decision and helped them find a small piece of farmland on which to build a house.

Although the Whites were now away from Battle Creek much of the time, they were still active in church work. In early March, James wrote to the *Review:*

Since we left home, eight weeks since, we have rode with our team one thousand miles, and have walked some each day, in all amounting to one hundred miles. This, with our preaching, writing, baths and rest hours, has filled our time.[4]

In March the decision was made to return to Battle Creek. In planning this, Ellen was happy that she would be able to bring her husband back in much better shape than he had been in when they had left some three months previously. She was aware of the attitudes of many in Battle Creek toward her actions in taking James away from there as she had. She was yet to learn how much the attitudes had developed in the intervening months.

Returning to Battle Creek, James and Ellen traveled by slow stages, visiting one church after another on the way. At a school-house on Sabbath, March 9, they found that three church groups had come together to listen to the preaching of the Word. The next morning they held another meeting. Attendance was smaller because of rain.

James described the last days of their trip, and summed up their accomplishments:

We reached home the 13th [March], over terrible roads by way of Marshall. We could have come through Monday, the distance of thirty-three miles, had we not been disappointed of our carriage from Battle Creek. But Monday night the roads broke up, and it took us most of three days to come this short distance in terrible storms, in which we nearly perished. . . .

We have been from home nearly a quarter of a year, during which time we have spoken about thirty-five times, and Mrs. W., at least, sixty.[5]

In a last-page note of the *Review* for March 19, the editor, Uriah Smith, called attention to a request he had received, signed by sixty-eight church members living in the counties of Montcalm and Ionia, that Brother and Sister White "locate in their midst." The editor continued, "Bro. White desires, as will be seen by his last two reports, to fix his residence near Greenville. . . . To this end he tenders his resignation of connection with the publishing department."[6]

At Battle Creek the Whites expected to be welcomed with open arms, as they had on previous occasions. Instead, they found alienation, criticism, and unfounded charges being made. It took a year before the situation was cleared up.

The three-month midwinter trip taken by James and Ellen and Willie marked the turning point in Elder White's recovery. The nagging question "Have the mental powers of James White been retained in spite of the stroke?" had been answered in the affirmative. There were still some hurdles to surmount, but never again did James White permit himself to sink into the degree of inactivity that marked practically all of 1866.

On March 16, James preached a kind of farewell sermon to the Battle Creek church. His subject was sanctification.[7]

While waiting to sell their Battle Creek home so that they might build at Greenville[8] the Whites did some more traveling. A note in the April 23 *Review* reported a visit to the Convis, Michi-

gan, church, where they spoke. Unfortunately the day was warm,
the ceiling of the room low, and there was a lack of air. James after
speaking "only about forty minutes," began to feel faint and sat
down. Ellen, ever ready to fill in for her husband, arose and spoke
with freedom for an hour and a half.

James wrote a protest to the *Review:*

> We plead for air in the house of God. Heaven has liberally given it
> without money and without price. We have not taken a cold for a year
> and a half, and the reason is simply this, we have a current of air through
> our bedroom and sitting room, and cannot speak in a close room. Again
> we say, we plead for good fresh air, such as fills all out doors.[9]

During that same month the Whites visited with some friends
at Allegan, Michigan, whose friendship they had made under interesting circumstances. Twelve years previously, in 1854, James
and Ellen were making a train trip from Rochester, New York, to
Jackson, Michigan. When they found seats on the train they noticed a couple sitting behind them. The woman was holding a baby
about the same age as Willie, whom Ellen was carrying. The babies
provided a subject of contact.

The name of the couple was Jones. It turned out that Mr.
Jones was a consumptive, in very precarious health. And, at the
time, James's friends had given him up to die. Elder White looked
at Jones, thinking he might live for a year. Mr. Jones decided
James had about six months.

The Joneses were on their way to Monterey, Michigan. As the
train traveled from Rochester to Buffalo, the two couples had an
interesting time together.

In those days train travelers going west from the Rochester area
changed trains at Buffalo and crossed over Suspension Bridge into
what was then called West Canada. In this way they took a short
cut across an area of Canada to Detroit, avoiding having to go
around the long south side of Lake Erie.

At the bridge the new friends said good-by, and each couple
set off to find seats on the next train. After James and Ellen had
found seats they looked around and, to their surprise, saw the
Joneses again seated behind them.

In this train they had several hours of visiting before reaching
Detroit, and their interest in one another deepened. James learned
later that the Joneses had had contact with a group called the

Age-to-come Adventists and had become disgusted with everything bearing the name Adventist. He had remarked to his wife, "That man is a Christian, [even] if he is an Adventist."

In Detroit the Whites once again said good-by to the Joneses, and went to a hotel. Then they learned that heavy rains had washed out the train tracks they had to travel on, and the train had not moved for forty-eight hours. More than 1,000 people were waiting to go west on the train. One would leave in the morning, and it would be a matter of first come, first served.

James and Ellen were early at the station, where a crowd of more than 500 persons were anxiously waiting beside a stationary train with locked coaches. The conductor came along and opened the doors, and the people surged into the carriages. The Whites managed to scramble aboard and find seats. Then to their utter astonishment, they found for the third time the Joneses sitting directly behind them. Another pleasant visit followed until the train reached Jackson, where the Whites got off and the Joneses continued their journey.

The next winter Elder M. E. Cornell conducted meetings in various towns in western Michigan. When he returned to his home in Battle Creek he told James about a man and his wife who attended his meetings in Monterey.

Elder White's eyes sparkled.

"Was the name Jones?" he asked eagerly.

"Right," replied Elder Cornell smiling. "When I posted announcements for my meeting the Joneses came to hear, hoping you might be the preacher. They came back every night, and at the close of the meetings were baptized."

Now, twelve years later, in 1867, the Whites and the Joneses met once more and spent a pleasant weekend together.[10]

1 James White, in *Review and Herald,* Jan. 15, 1867.
2 James White, in *Review and Herald,* Feb. 5, 1867.
3 *Life Sketches,* p. 174.
4 James White, in *Review and Herald,* March 12, 1867.
5 James White, in *Review and Herald,* March 19, 1867.
6 Uriah Smith, in *Review and Herald,* March 19, 1867.
7 James White, in *Review and Herald,* April 9, 1867.
8 *Ibid.,* April 16, 1867.
9 *Ibid.,* April 23, 1867.
10 *Ibid.,* April 30, 1867.

Chapter Twenty-six

IN JOURNEYINGS OFTEN

THE time came for the fifth session of the General Conference, which convened in Battle Creek on May 18. The estrangement that had arisen between at least some members of the Battle Creek church and James and Ellen White was still much in evidence. James's term as General Conference president expired, and J. N. Andrews was chosen to succeed him. James also withdrew from the Publishing Association. His place was taken by J. M. Aldrich. James's connection with the new Health Reform Institute that had begun operation only a few months before was also ended.

The care of the church and its institutions had rested heavily on James's shoulders. Now someone else could worry about the *Review* and the *Instructor* subscription lists. Midnight would no longer find him attending committee meetings. Now he could take time to write that book about his and Ellen's lives he had dreamed of writing. And he would be able to take time to care for his home, work in his garden, and enjoy his children more.

After the session the Whites set off by carriage for Greenville. At twilight they came to a dilapidated bridge that, to all appearances, was unsafe for use. However, heavy rains made fording the river impossible. After testing the bridge by walking across it, they decided to risk taking the team of horses and the carriage across. The horses were led slowly across without mishap.

It was now dark, and there were eighteen miles to go to reach their destination.

As they cautiously continued their journey in the dark they were abruptly halted on two occasions by running into tree stumps. Consequently, Edson went ahead of them, holding up a sheet of white paper to help them see where they were going. They finally arrived at their destination at midnight.[1]

Continuing their journey, they arrived at the Maynard home in Greenville just before sundown on Friday. Shortly after they arrived there James began to suffer from toothache, which persisted without letup. Finally, after putting up with the discomfort for three or four days, he went to a dentist and had five teeth extracted. A few days later he had his remaining six teeth removed. To help him pay for dentures J. N. Andrews and Uriah Smith sent him $10 each, and Mrs. M. J. Cornell sent $5.00.[2]

Some two weeks later we find the Whites visiting Brother and Sister Franklin L. Howe in Orange, thirty miles from Greenville. By this time James had become used to talking with dentures to family and friends. On this occasion he spoke for thirty minutes to the youth, greatly to his own satisfaction and relief that he could once again preach.[3]

On Sunday morning, after worship and breakfast, James requested that they fix a couch for him before the front door, where he could look at the outdoors. He hadn't been there long before Brother Howe heard his voice calling, "Ellen! Ellen!"

She came and stood, waiting for him to speak.

"Ellen, do you see Sister Howe out in the cornfield, hoeing?"

"Yes, I see her."

"Well, please get my trousers and boots."

"What are you going to do? Do you want to dress?"

"Yes. I'm ashamed of myself, a big strapping man like me lying here, and that woman with all her household duties out there in the garden hoeing corn. I'm going to help her."

The clothes were brought. James dressed and, with a hoe furnished by the owners of the farm, he took his place by Sister Howe's side and hoed a row of corn. Brother Howe always felt that the hoeing of that row of corn was the beginning of Elder White's return to physical activity.[4]

It was a beginning, but only a beginning. James could not rid his mind of the warning Dr. Jackson had given at the Dansville Sanitarium. Any return to physical activity, the doctor had assured him, would bring on another stroke, which would probably be fatal. As a result, he had carefully avoided physical work as much as possible. But according to the light given her, Ellen knew that physical exercise would play an important part in her husband's restoration. The question was how to persuade him to accept and practice this principle. Ellen did her best to help him see this point.

When the Whites' hay was ready to harvest James got someone to mow it for them, and planned to get the neighbors to help them get it in. But before he could arrange for this Ellen visited each one of them and, knowing they were very busy, asked them to tell him they were unable to help. They were reluctant to do this, but when she explained her purpose, they agreed. So when James sent to his neighbors for help with the hay he was disappointed to have every one of them say they were too busy to help.

Ellen then suggested to James that he, Willie, and she do the job. She and Willie would pitch the hay up to James. He could ride on the wagon and spread it as it was tossed up to him. When the wagon was full they would drive to the unloading area (they had no barn as yet) and build a haystack. Mother and son would do the stacking. And so it was done.

Townsfolk passing along the road in their carriages were surprised to see a woman they knew as a preacher busy pitching hay. But Ellen was not at all embarrassed. She would do anything to help her husband get well again.[5]

On Sunday, June 30, a group of Adventists from towns around the Greenville area assembled in a grove near the shore of a lake. For the first time in four years, James White entered the water and baptized four persons. One of them was his own son, Willie, who was nearly 13 years old.[6]

Now that it had been proved to him that exercise would not injure him, James became more active and as a result gained strength rapidly. One Friday, he drove to town to buy lumber and, with another man, handled nearly 3,000 feet of heavy lumber only recently unloaded from a river barge.[7]

One indication that James was steadily gaining ground physically was his increasing ability to sleep for longer periods of time. One day when he and Ellen returned from a weekend of meetings, they were presented with two gallons of fresh raspberries. Ellen thanked the friend who had been so kind and, as soon as she was home, set about to can them. James was tired and decided to go to bed around nine o'clock. An hour later he awoke and heard Ellen still busy in the kitchen. A fruity aroma was filling the house. Within five minutes he was sound asleep again.

At four A.M. he was awakened by the singing of robins. Refreshed, he got out of bed and dressed. That morning he viewed a gorgeous sunrise and murmured to himself, "Thank God for sweet sleep." [8]

James had no reason for feeling neglected in Greenville. He and Ellen found all their needs supplied by thoughtful neighbors. They were continuing their former practice of ministering in nearby churches. Friends, seeing them in their old, heavy, uncomfortable wagon, took James to Iona, where they purchased a light carriage so that they could travel to their appointments in comfort. Mrs. White, after taking a trip in the new carriage, reported that after riding fifty miles she was not in the least wearied. [9]

Then calls came, asking the Whites to attend conference meetings in distant States. For the first time since Elder White had been stricken, they agreed to take an eastern and a western tour among the churches.

Shortly after mid-September they left Battle Creek to attend camp meetings at Johnstown Center, Wisconsin, and Pilot Grove, Iowa. Not since their visit in July-August, 1865, had they been in Iowa. They were thrilled as they saw the large number of converts there. [10]

Returning to Battle Creek, they held revival meetings, and on October 22 Elder White presided over the communion service. This meeting closed with an earnest season of prayer, asking that God would richly bless Elder and Mrs. White as they set out for the East. As Uriah Smith wrote in the *Review*, the Whites,

> left for their eastern appointments, . . . bearing with them the prayers of this church for abundant help and spiritual prosperity among those for whom they go to labor. [11]

As usual, notices of the meetings were printed on the back page of the *Review*. Their first meetings were held at Roosevelt, New York, which they reached on Friday evening. Elder White described their labors in that place:

> On the Sabbath I preached twice and spent several hours in social meeting. First-day and evening we held three long meetings; preached in the forenoon one hour and a half, and appealed to the congregation many times during the afternoon and evening. Second-day we were in meeting nine hours, often exhorting the people. This morning [Tuesday] at six . . . , I spoke on baptism, took breakfast, packed up and rode twenty miles to Syracuse, and am now nearing Albany writing as the cars are moving at full speed. [12]

The Whites were on their way to New England, where they held meetings at a number of places during the following weeks. In these meetings James usually led out with a doctrinal discourse, and Ellen followed with what was called an "exhortation," or appeal for consecration. Sometimes she had personal testimonies for individuals present. These might be people she had never seen except in vision. There were times when she was obliged to give "straight testimony," which, according to a *Review* article by D. M. Canright, who was doing evangelistic work in Maine at the time, was accepted by each one to whom addressed.[13] Early on this tour Ellen and James had been joined by Elder J. N. Andrews, then president of the General Conference. It would be difficult to overestimate the good accomplished by this series of meetings.

Since Ellen had been given personal testimonies for some of the members of the Adventist group in Washington, New Hampshire, an appointment was made to hold meetings there. The announcement of this meeting in the *Review* carried some practical suggestions made by Elder Andrews:

> It will be necessary for those who attend to come prepared to take care of themselves as far as possible. . . . Brethren, come with your provisions, your blankets, quilts, comfortables, buffalo robes, and your straw ticks to be filled at the place of meeting. Barn room can be provided for lodgings for healthy men.[14]

Plenty of blankets would be needed—for these meetings were to be held at Christmas time! Meanwhile, Elder and Mrs. White held meetings in Portland, Maine, that city that had been home to Ellen many years before. From there the train took them to Manchester, where they were met by A. W. Smith and transported by carriage to his home. They were anticipating an early bedtime and a good night's rest, but at the Smith home they found eight young people who had come from Amherst, eight miles away. These were newly baptized converts who desired an interview with the Whites. Forgetting their weariness, Ellen and James spent some time talking with these young people.[15]

The next day James and Ellen went by train and carriage to Washington, New Hampshire. The Adventist church there, the oldest community of Sabbathkeepers in the United States, was practically in a dying condition. One of its members, Worcester Ball, openly opposed the Spirit of Prophecy. When the believers tried to hold a meeting Ball would interrupt, pouring out bitter complaints against Elder and Mrs. White. People had taken sides, and soon the membership was hopelessly divided. For months no Sabbath school services were held. William Farnsworth stopped attending church, and the young people, skeptical of such parental religion, stayed away from whatever services were announced.

It was to revive this church, to bring it to life again, that Elder and Mrs. White and Elder Andrews went there. Although it was Christmas time, and snow lay heavily on the ground, the members came to the meetings. Elder White in particular carried a heavy burden for the young people, but he realized that little could be accomplished for them until the older members repented of their sins and backslidings.[16]

Meetings continued morning, afternoon, and in the evening. Ellen White gave straight testimony to Brother Ball, and he began to see himself as God saw him. He repented and begged forgiveness of the church, and of the Whites, whom he had cruelly wronged. William Farnsworth, openly rebuked for his hypocrisy in using chewing tobacco secretly, promised that he would give up that health-destroying practice.[17]

Now that there was reform among the older members, Elder White could begin to work for the youth. One by one they took their stand for God. Eighteen said that they wanted to be baptized. Twelve of these, unwilling to wait for ice to melt on Millan Lake, cut a hole through thick ice, and one by one they were lowered into the frigid water and baptized. The church at Washington had indeed seen a revival in its midst.[18]

The importance of these meetings can be seen by a look at the record. Of the eighteen young people converted, no less than nine became church workers. Five became ordained ministers.[19]

The last stop on this tour was at Enosburgh, Vermont, where weekend meetings were held. At their meeting held on a Monday, forty-two persons, including a number of children, requested baptism. After questioning them carefully, James accepted eleven candidates.

Just as the wintry sun was setting, with the thermometer registering twenty degrees below zero, all the members and candidates walked to a stream about a mile from the meeting house. There Elder A. C. Bourdeau led the eleven into the icy water and baptized them. Among them was his aged father and mother.[20]

Exhausted by their labors on this eastern tour, but praising God for victories gained, James and his wife returned to Battle Creek, arriving there in early January. During their two month itinerary they had traveled 3,200 miles by train, 600 miles by private conveyance, and had held 140 meetings. James had preached at nearly all of them.[21]

For Elder White, a year that had begun in weakness closed in power. He summarized:

As we look back upon this battle-field of the past year, where so many have feared that many would be killed by the plain testimony, no one, no, not even one, has been driven from the church or from the Sabbath. Hence the plain testimony has united hundreds firmly, and we hope permanently, with the body, while no one has been driven from the body. . . .

Let God's servants raise one united voice in speaking the plain and pointed truth in love. And let all the people say, Amen.[22]

Later that month Ellen and James left Battle Creek for Greenville. It would be good to be home again.

[1] James White, in *Review and Herald,* June 11, 1867.

[2] *Ibid.*

[3] James White, in *Review and Herald,* June 25, 1867.

[4] F. L. Howe letter to W. C. White, July 11, 1934.

[5] Manuscript 1, 1867.

[6] James White, in *Review and Herald,* July 9, 1867.

[7] *Ibid.*

[8] ———, in *Review and Herald,* July 30, 1867.

[9] ———, in *Review and Herald,* Sept. 10, 1867.

[10] J. N. A., in *Review and Herald,* Oct. 8, 1867.

[11] Uriah Smith, in *Review and Herald,* Oct. 29, 1867.

[12] James White, in *Review and Herald,* Nov. 5, 1867.

[13] ———, in *Review and Herald,* Jan. 7, 1868.

[14] J. N. Andrews, in *Review and Herald,* Nov. 5, 1867.

[15] James White, in *Review and Herald,* Jan. 28, 1868.

[16] William C. White, "Sketches and Memories," *Review and Herald,* Feb. 11, 1937.

[17] *Ibid.*

[18] Mabel Robinson Miller, *William and His Twenty-Two* (Washington, D.C.: Review and Herald Publishing Assn., 1959), p. 101.

[19] *Review and Herald,* Feb. 11, 1937.

[20] A. C. Bourdeau, in *Review and Herald,* Jan. 21, 1868.

[21] James White, in *Review and Herald,* Jan. 14, 1868.

[22] ———, in *Review and Herald,* Dec. 31, 1867.

Chapter Twenty-seven

BETTER HEALTH

A VISION that outlined the principles of health reform had been given to Ellen White in Otsego, Michigan, on June 6, 1863. When the inspired information given in this vision was publicized, many Seventh-day Adventists made a radical change in their manner of living. Ellen had been shown that the great foe to good health is intemperance—in working, eating, drinking, and in drugging. Of these four forms of intemperance, many Adventists soon made drastic changes in the last three. Unfortunately, intemperance in working received scant attention, and the tragic results of this neglect were seen in the workers' ranks. Ellen White gave testimony after testimony to her husband and other leaders, urging greater moderation in their labors.

It was only natural that critics should ridicule an attempt to live without meat, tea, coffee, or drugs. When sickness struck they questioned the value of a way of living that had not been able to protect its leading adherents from its onslaught. If this system was so health-promoting, they argued, how did it happen that within two years after the vision was given, Elders White, Loughborough, Smith, Edson, and others were tottering on the brink of the grave?

James pointed out that it was his neglect to secure proper rest that had brought him to his weakened condition. His wife explained the situation:

The reform my husband had made in his diet, previous to his sickness, had a very beneficial influence upon his health. His head was generally free from pain and never felt clearer. By eating no meat, but grains, fruits and vegetables, simply cooked, his appetite was good, and he partook of his food with a keen relish. His brain felt so clear that he thought it safe for him to labor on, trusting much to the beneficial influence of his

191

simple diet; and in addition to the labors and burdens he had hitherto borne, he added the Health Reform—making extra efforts to teach Sabbathkeeping Adventists how to live to preserve health and enjoy the blessing of God.[1]

In 1865, while in Rochester with her husband, en route from Dansville to Battle Creek, Ellen White was given a vision that was to add another dimension to the Adventist message. She wrote:

I was shown that we should provide a home for the afflicted, and those who wished to learn how to take care of their bodies, that they may prevent sickness.[2]

At the General Conference session held in May, 1866, it was decided to open just such an institution. A committee was chosen to find a location for the project. Within a month after the conference closed, circulars were sent to all the churches, inviting members to purchase stock in what was to be called the Western Health Reform Institute. James did not take a leading part in promoting the new venture, but headed the list of stockholders by buying $500 worth of shares.[3] Simultaneously, with the opening of the institution a new journal was launched; dedicated to the promotion of health knowledge everywhere, it was titled the *Health Reformer*.[4]

A commodious house on five acres of land was purchased, with another plot of two acres being added later. Elder White was present on the September day the institution opened its doors. The staff consisted of two doctors, two bath attendants, one (untrained) nurse, plus three or four general helpers. There was one patient. The editor of the *Review* wrote:

In no enterprise ever undertaken by this people, has the hand of the Lord been more evidently manifested than in this thing.[5]

During the next two years, while recovering his own health, James White watched the development of the little sanitarium. For a time the patronage was excellent, and a building program was launched so that more patients could be housed.

But, unfortunately, when the institution was opened, there were no men available with the business experience necessary to operate it. Because of the institution's initial success, plans were made to erect a large addition. James protested this move, pointing out that without skillful, trained workers they were not ready for such enlargement. Yielding to his judgment, the managers not only

The Western Health Reform Institute, forerunner of Adventist hospitals around the world, was opened in 1866.

stopped work on the building but actually tore down the stone foundation that had already been laid.

By 1869 the sanitarium had only eight paying patients and was more than $13,000 in debt.[7]

James had pointed out that the most serious problem facing the enterprise was a shortage of trained personnel. He knew that the only way to make the Reform Institute what it should and must be, was to staff it with fully qualified nurses and doctors. He and Ellen began searching for someone with the intellect and natural ability who might be trained to operate the kind of institution they had in mind. They arranged for four young men to take a medical course, but eventually their choice fell on John Harvey Kellogg as the most promising.

In 1864 at the age of 12 young John had been invited by James to learn the printing trade in the Review and Herald shop. He set the type for the health tracts, *How to Live,* and for the first issues of the magazine *Health Reformer.* John lived in the White home for several months, and went on numerous trips with them, becoming almost like another son in the family. One day James confided to him that Mrs. White had been shown in vision that he was to fill an important niche in God's service. The boy was deeply impressed.

Years passed, and the day came when James White lent John Kellogg $1,000 and sent him to the best medical school in the United States—Bellevue Hospital in New York City—not for a

13

six-month course, but for a full three years of professional training.

As James White recovered his strength, various responsibilities were laid on him. One of these was to try to rescue the Health Reform Institute from bankruptcy. There was talk of closing the place, but James set his face against such a drastic move. He became editor of the *Health Reformer,* a position he held for some four years. Gradually circulation climbed until it reached ten thousand. Under White's judicious management the tide gradually turned. Debts were wiped out, and the institution began to prosper.

At the March, 1870, General Conference session a resolution was passed expressing gratitude for the flourishing state of the Health Institute:

> Resolved, that we deplore the errors and wrongs committed by those who had the management of the . . . Health Institute during the period of Brother White's prostration by sickness, and that we acknowledge the painful experience as teaching us the lesson that those who neglect the Testimonies of the Spirit of God, will be sure to commit serious errors in the work of the third angel's message.[9]

Two years later the secretary of the Health Reform Institute informed Elder White of an action taken by a recent meeting of the directors to the effect that "Brother and Sister White, be cordially invited to make it their home at the Institute, at their pleasure and also, to have a general oversight of it."[10] As patronage increased, more space was needed. James White urged church members to invest in the project of enlarging the building. Some years later he was able to point out that not a single dollar had been lost by any investor in the Publishing Association or in the Health Reform Institute.[11]

Reform in health aids prosperity, James declared. In a long article in the *Review* he emphasized the fact that 4,000 families of health reformers, by abstaining from tobacco, tea, coffee, and other harmful foods would save $300,000 a year![12]

Elder White did his best to practice what he preached, even while making long, tiresome train trips. In an article entitled "Reflections by the Way," he wrote,

> One hour since, we breakfasted luxuriously upon graham bread, pears, grapes, and nuts from our lunch basket. We slept well last night and are rested and refreshed. . . . Blessings on the health reform![13]

On another train trip, feeling the need of fresh air, James

stepped down onto a station platform at a railway stop and took a brisk walk in the warm sunshine. James wrote:

> God be thanked that there is a better way than to stuff one's self with chickens fried in swine's lard, greasy knicknacks, generally, and hot coffee, and get the headache and the blues.[14]

In the spring of 1875 John Harvey Kellogg completed his medical course and in a few weeks returned to Battle Creek. For a year he was one of the doctors at the Health Reform Institute. Then, at James White's urging, he accepted the position of medical superintendent. He soon changed the name of the Institute to that of the Battle Creek Sanitarium, by which title it became famous. Two years earlier Elder White had been happy to turn over to Dr. Kellogg the editorship of the *Health Reformer.*

With a skilled and competent man to lead out in the medical program at Battle Creek, James White declared, "We have our man. Let's build." And they did, soon greatly enlarging the sanitarium plant.

Shortly after Kellogg joined the Health Institute staff he paid tribute to the man who had built up the little sanitarium to its prosperous condition:

> Our readers will join with us in rejoicing at the prospect of so much able assistance. . . . Six years ago, the Elder [White] found the *Reformer* laboring under the greatest embarrassment, and with gloomy prospects. The change in its circumstances has been chiefly due to his able management. We are doing no one any injustice when we say that Elder and Mrs. White have done more to secure the practical adoption of consistent health principles than any other two persons in America. We shall be grateful for their assistance.[15]

The General Conference leaders were well aware of James White's organizational ability. Financial losses sustained by the publishing and health institutions during his illness and convalescence had been too recent and painful to forget. They were well aware also that he was again laboring under an extremely heavy load. This awareness and their desire to prevent a second collapse, led the session to pass the following resolution:

> Resolved, That in view of the long and untiring labor of Bro. White in the publishing department in connection with his other cares and responsibilities; and in view of our present facilities for publishing, we believe it to be just and right, and according to the mind of the Spirit of

God, that Brother White should no longer labor so hard and bear so many burdens of this work; that we consider it far more important that, as a counsellor and minister, his life and strength be preserved to the cause, than that the association should continue to increase its means to any great extent; and if the interests of our work demand a further extension of means and facilities for publishing the truth, it is better that the numerous friends of the cause supply the want from their abundance than that our most faithful and efficient laborer be utterly prostrated by overtaxing his mental and physical powers. [16]

As long as he lived, James received letters from numerous church members and friends in all parts of the United States. Occasionally he would receive one requesting information needed by the whole church. To that type of request he would reply through the *Review* columns.

In 1868 he received one such letter from a member in Monroe, Wisconsin, dealing with various aspects of health reform. From the answer that James published in the *Review,* it would seem that this conscientious brother was in danger of going to extremes. He had isolated the strongest statements available in the testimonies and was pushing them to the limit. In his reply, White pointed out that there have ever been two classes of believers—those whose fiery zeal carries them into extreme positions, and others whose sluggish natures make it almost impossible for them to move. He explained his wife's problem:

She [Ellen White] works to this disadvantage, namely: she makes strong appeals to the people, which a few feel deeply, and take strong positions, and go to extremes. Then to save the cause from ruin in consequence of these extremists, she is obliged to come out with reproofs for extremists in a public manner. This is better than to have things to go to pieces; but the influence of both the extremes and the reproofs are terrible on the cause, and brings upon Mrs. W. a three-fold burden.

But there was a way in which everyone could help God's messenger. James continued with emphasis:

We say to those who wish to help Mrs. W. in her work, you will not find her far ahead of the people, with a few extremists. No, she is back with the people, tugging away at the wheel of reform, and has to lift all the harder because of your extreme advance. Come back, good wholehearted souls, and stand by her side, and lift where she lifts.

Toward the end of the article he makes an appeal that is as

timely today as it was a century ago:

> Let the work go on, saith my soul, in all its branches. Not a piece at a time, lest it go all to pieces; but let it move on as a complete whole. Not fluttering and trembling in the wind, but like an old seventy-four-gun ship, let all the friends of truth and reform get on board and work together. Yet let all the friends of Jesus, His coming, and the future glory of the kingdom, patiently, cheerfully, joyfully unite and stand together in the work of preparation.[17]

He signed his letter: "A servant of the church, JAMES WHITE" —a very accurate designation.

The medical institution that Elder White had helped from its beginning, and which his hand had guided through troubled growing pains, grew strong and prospered. The message of health reform received increased attention as the years went by, and its truths have been affirmed by men of science and medicine in many parts of the world.

---

[1] *Review and Herald*, Feb. 27, 1866.
[2] William C. White, "Sketches and Memories," *Ibid.*, Jan. 14, 1937.
[3] *SDA Encyclopedia*, article "Battle Creek Sanitarium," p. 110.
[4] *Ibid.*, article "Health Journals," p. 511.
[5] *The Story of Our Health Message*, p. 132.
[6] *Ibid.*, pp. 154, 155.
[7] *Ibid.*, p. 159.
[8] Richard William Schwarz, *John H. Kellogg, M.D.* (© 1965), p. 25.
[9] *Review and Herald*, March 22, 1870.
[10] Salisbury letter of invitation, Document File 239 G.
[11] James White, in *Review and Herald*, June 13, 1878.
[12] ———, in *Review and Herald*, Aug. 20, 1872.
[13] ———, in *Review and Herald*, Oct. 7, 1875.
[14] ———, in *Review and Herald*, Nov. 1, 1870.
[15] *Health Reformer*, Nov., 1876.
[16] *Review and Herald*, Jan. 2, 1872.
[17] *Ibid.*, March 17, 1868.

Chapter Twenty-eight

CAMP MEETINGS

DURING most of the year 1867 the Whites lived in Greenville, where James worked in his garden and orchard, visited with friends, carried on wide correspondence, wrote *Review* articles, and responded to appeals for his ministry in surrounding churches. He also began work on an autobiography, which he was to name *Life Incidents*. It was published in 1868.

Although doing their best to answer all calls coming to them, the Whites found it necessary, in fairness to themselves, to try to conserve their strength. James, a man who had never shunned any hardship involving progress in God's work, was now constrained to plead for consideration from those asking his help. In August he put the situation plainly to the *Review* family:

> We are both worn, and must labor under the most favorable circumstances. We cannot ride in a springless open wagon. We cannot be up to late evening meetings. We cannot sleep on hard beds, or sit on hard seats. We cannot when weary from preaching, converse upon different subjects of little or no interest all the time we are out of meeting. Most of the brethren know how it is with me. Some do not know that I am but a shadow of what I once was. . . .
>
> I do not go to see the country or to please the people, but to declare the truth faithfully. Pray for us. If the Lord be with us, I can be a fraction of a laborer.[1]

J. N. Andrews, now General Conference president, had a great burden that James might be fully restored to his former condition of health. Ellen wrote concerning this longing of Elder Andrews: "At times he felt that he would give his life could my husband be in health of mind and body."[2]

Another burden that John Andrews bore was in regard to the spiritual condition of the believers. He feared that many were not making progress in the Christian way. During a visit he had with James in Greenville, Elder White, remembering the great Millerite camp meetings, suggested that Adventist churches have similar gatherings, where several companies could assemble and enjoy a blessed time together.

Knowing that camp meetings held by other churches had become disorderly and had fallen into disrepute, Elder Andrews had some doubts about the wisdom of holding them. But finally the General Conference Committee decided to hold one as a pilot program.

It was decided that the first camp meeting should be held in Michigan. A site was chosen at Wright, near the present town of Coopersville, a few miles west of Grand Rapids. The maple grove of Ephraim Root,[3] at whose home the Whites had spent two months in the winter of 1866-1867, was selected.

Fervent prayers were offered for the success of the gathering. The workers were asking for a revival. James knew that leaders of other conferences would be watching this first meeting, seeking to decide whether they should follow the example of Michigan.

James expressed the opinion that if this meeting proved a success there would be camp meetings all over the world until Christ should come.

When Tuesday, September 1, arrived, people began streaming into the grove. They came in carriages and in farm wagons, bringing tents and cooking supplies with them.

Ellen White opened the meeting with a solemn, soul-moving call for God's people to throw off the stupor enveloping the church, and with zeal prepare for Christ's return.[4]

James spoke six times and Ellen five. J. N. Andrews took four meetings, and another minister one, making sixteen in all. Having heard of Elder White's feebleness, the campers were pleasantly surprised by his vitality. One writer said:

> Brother White has regained his mental and physical powers, though he appears much older than before his sickness; and we were surprised at the amount of labor he performs; not with tottering steps, but with the firmness and elasticity of early life.[5]

Word of the success of the Michigan camp meeting spread rapidly. Within weeks similar encampments were held in Illinois and Iowa. The next summer the General Conference Committee suggested a series of dates over a period of ten weeks so that the camps would run consecutively without conflict. An August opening would allow for harvesting before the meetings began.

The Whites made the 1869 camp meeting circuit, sometimes suffering physical discomfort. The tents used were often homemade, constructed from cotton cloth. At the Wisconsin meeting held at Clinton Junction, there was heavy rain during the first day. Several tents were flattened by the wind and many more were flooded. Citizens of the town opened their homes to the drenched, shivering campers.[6] James and Ellen, in a canvas duck tent, managed to stay dry. They had to go to bed early, however, as there was not enough fuel to keep the fires going.

Every year camp meetings became more popular and more numerous. Before each season began, conference officials would write to the Whites urging them to attend their particular meetings. They knew that if they could publish the glad tidings that James and Ellen White would be present they would have a record attendance.

Year after year Ellen and James would decide that this season they would not—could not—face the weariness and toil involved in attending a string of camp meetings. But when the time came for the camp meetings, they would pack their trunk and would be on their way. From the first meeting to the very last one in late fall— they would be there, bearing their testimony. Elder White's pleadings for God's people to surrender their hearts and lives completely to Him were often touching.

On Sabbath afternoon a call was made by Brother White for those who felt that they had not a good hope in Christ, and who wished for a better, and sought the prayers of the people of God, to come forward. So general a move as then took place we have never witnessed in any assemblage of people. Nearly all in the tent, backsliders, as well as those who made no profession, came forward. Friend entreated friend, with weeping to come, and seek an interest in the Saviour. Fathers called for children, and wives for husbands; and they came pressing in with broken and penitent hearts. . . .

It was a scene long to be remembered.[7]

As he did so frequently, James White at that very first Michigan meeting gathered the children around him, told them stories, and presented a little book to each one.[8] When examining candidates for baptism he did his best to put the children at ease as they ascended the rostrum to be questioned. One little girl, Jessie, had asked for baptism the previous year when she was only 8, but the leader had suggested that she wait one more year. Now she was 9 and on the platform answering Elder White's questions. She knew her Bible and answered promptly. Suddenly he asked her another kind of question:

"Would you give up anything for Jesus?"

Jessie hesitated, then replied, "Oh, yes, I think so."

"How about those flowers on your hat?" asked Elder White. "Would you be willing to sacrifice them for Jesus?"

Jessie was dismayed. Her mother had dressed her in her nicest clothes for this occasion. Her little white hat was trimmed with ribbons and a small clump of artificial flowers. Although taken aback, Jessie hesitated only a moment. Resolved not to allow vanity to interfere with her baptism, she answered, "Yes." And her name was accepted for baptism.

As soon as the meeting was over, she rushed to her tent and cut off the flowers, never to wear them again. The next day she was one of a large group baptized in the Marion River.[9]

As James was preaching the evening sermon at one camp meeting a heavy rain began falling, making it almost impossible for the speaker to be heard.

"Let's sing while we wait for the storm to subside," James suggested. "It won't last long." So they all sang enthusiastically, "We Will Stand the Storm, It Will Not Be Long." He was right; the rain subsided as suddenly as it had begun, and the speaker went on with his sermon. So completely absorbed was he in what he was saying that he walked right off the platform. But this did not deter him. Picking himself up, he climbed back and built the incident right into his sermon so smoothly that many in the audience thought he had planned it that way.[10]

While preaching at another camp meeting in the West, word reached Elder White that a man had just been pulled out of the river, apparently drowned. Immediately the preacher left the desk, ran to the spot, and without a moment's hesitation, placed the victim in the proper position and administered artificial respiration as skillfully as though he were a member of a life-saving team. The man lived, and James went back to continue his sermon.[11]

Campers today would probably object to the strenuous pro-

gram observed at meetings of a century ago. For instance, at Marion, Iowa, the Sabbath morning bell awoke the campers at four-thirty. In this place there were 25 tents, and the first exercise of the day was family worship in each separate tent. This always began with a song, with the group in each tent choosing a different hymn.[12] The sound effects can be imagined. James must have smiled as he listened to the unharmonious bedlam, but he made no attempt to change the plan. Were they not all praising the Lord in their own way?

Gradually, over the years, the number of encampments increased until they totaled fifteen in the East and one in California. James continually endeavored to make these gatherings a time for concentrating on spiritual things. He pled with the women not to bring an oversupply of rich foods. To everyone he wrote, "Come to the camp meetings. Come with hands, hearts and purses open to help, to sympathize, and to push forward the great cause."[13]

It was not unusual for the preachers to hold protracted meetings. Elder White frequently suffered from hoarseness of the throat as a result. On one or two occasions, when he was unable to carry on, his wife stepped forward, took over and continued his sermon, which by repetition had become familiar to her.

During the years, while James and Ellen were traveling from one camp meeting to another and he was carrying heavy administrative burdens, he would vow that if others would carry more of the burden he would attend more camps. One way this could be done would be for the brethren in the field to write more frequently for the *Review*, thus easing his editorial load.[14] He admitted that there were times when the reading matter menu provided in the paper was not as might be hoped for. His own state of health prohibited much writing. He pointed out the need for a good reporter to attend camp meetings and write accounts of them for the *Review*.[15] Little seems to have come of the suggestion.

During the spring of 1873 Elder White suffered two minor paralytic strokes. Although they did no serious permanent damage he nevertheless regarded them as warnings that it was time to lighten his load. In 1874, when the time came for the South Lancaster camp meeting, he remained in Battle Creek, caring for the office work. Ellen went and spoke several times. She wrote to her husband:

A 1946 photograph of the site of the first Seventh-day Adventist camp meeting, held at Wright, Michigan, 1868.

"There was a great turnout, expecting Elder White and wife . . . there." [16]

Sometimes their travels took them through scenes of natural beauty and interest. Once, with Willie, they traveled up the Mississippi River from Iowa to the Minnesota camp meeting on a river steamer. Farms bordering the river were lush and green. Many lumber rafts on their way to St. Louis floating downriver passed their boat. As the first one went by, the men handling the raft shouted, "Papers!" Willing passengers gathered up old newspapers, tied them with string and tossed them into the water. Men from the rafts leaped overboard and rescued them.

A sudden thought struck Willie. He hurried off to return in a short time with some coal from the engine room, some string, and several pieces of gospel literature. Tying the literature to the lumps of coal, he threw them down to the raftsmen as they floated past. This was a unique type of missionary endeavor.[17]

In 1872, the Whites arrived in California just in time to attend a camp meeting held in Windsor. Before leaving the ground, the Whites were invited to visit and stay with no less than twenty hospitable California Adventist families.[18]

At the beginning of the 1876 season, James was carrying out his duties in Battle Creek, and Ellen was on the Pacific Coast. She wrote to her husband, telling him that unless the Lord indicated otherwise, she would not come East to attend meetings since she had a great deal of writing to do.

On May 23 of that year, James left Battle Creek, heading for the Kansas camp meeting. Two days later he received a telegram from Ellen stating that she would meet him there. And that was the beginning of the most arduous and difficult season in which the two had ever participated. For the most part, each camp continued for only five days; but there were fifteen of them across the nation, from New England to California. And James and Ellen did not miss one.[19] Perhaps only those who have had to travel and preach somewhat as the Whites had to can appreciate how exhausting it is.

For a layman attending only one camp meeting, the occasion was very pleasant. He carried no responsibility for the meetings. Between services he was free to walk about, purchase books, or chat with friends. How different it was for the speakers! James pictures their situation in an article he wrote for the *Review:*

Wet or dry, cold or hot, these very persons must do all, or nearly all, the preaching, and must be present at business sessions. And these are the very persons who feel the importance of the camp meetings, and take much of the care of them. And the time between the meetings is spent on the cars. We have gone from meeting to meeting for weeks at a time without stepping over a threshold, only that of the railroad depot. . . .

We live in our trunks nearly one-third of the year. We take our tent with us in a trunk. Could lumber be in reserve on the ground for us, some one be appointed to take us and our baggage directly to the ground, and persons ready to assist in putting up our tent, and we be visited by those only who should come to our tent to assist and cheer us, and none come in the confusion of breaking up, and packing for the cars, to bid us good-by, very much of the dreaded part of camp-meeting life would be removed. . . .

After a tedious journey shut up in the cars, or shut up in the woods speaking to the people, on committees, or attending business sessions, week after week, what an unspeakable relief to weary brain and trembling nerves would be the use of a horse and carriage for a few hours each day. But no one thinks of this, only the camp-meeting slave, who is shifted twice each week, first from the cars to the omnibus and to the ground; then away by the omnibus to the cars, to be dumped off in the ditch, perhaps, bag and baggage, beside the next camp-ground, after riding day and night for twenty-four, thirty-six, or forty-eight hours, in the dusty, smoky, stifled air of the cars.[20]

Is it any wonder that Elder White wrote, "Dear brethren, we cannot go the rounds of your camp-meetings any more, and we ask for one season's entire rest from camp-meetings."[21]

Yet so strong was his sense of duty and responsibility to feed the flock of God that the following summer found him attending no less than thirteen tent encampments!

---

[1] James White, in *Review and Herald,* Aug. 27, 1867.

[2] Ellen G. White letter S13, 1869.

[3] J. O. Corliss, in *Review and Herald,* Sept. 6, 1923.

[4] William C. White, "Sketches and Memories," *Review and Herald,* March 11, 1937.

[5] *Ibid.,* Sept. 22, 1868.

[6] *Ibid.,* Sept. 2, 1937.

[7] Uriah Smith, in *Review and Herald,* July 13, 1869.

[8] *Origin and History,* vol. 2, pp. 12, 13.

[9] Jessie F. Moser letter to W. C. White, Dec. 24, 1936.

[10] C. A. Parker letter to W. C. White, April 22, 1937.

[11] David Paulson, in *Review and Herald,* Nov. 12, 1901.

[12] James White, in *Review and Herald,* June 21, 1870.

[13] *Ibid.,* Aug. 10, 1876.

[14] *Ibid.*, July 18, 1871; April 4, 1871.

[15] *Ibid.*, Sept. 5, 1871.

[16] Ellen G. White letter 49 to James White, Aug. 28, 1874.

[17] *Review and Herald*, July 5, 1870.

[18] H. O. McCumber, *Pioneering the Message in the Golden West* (Mountain View, Calif.: Pacific Press Publishing Assn.), p. 109.

[19] James White, in *Review and Herald*, May 24, 1877.

[20] James White, in *Review and Herald*, March 29, 1877.

[21] *Ibid.*

Chapter Twenty-nine

A QUESTION OF INTEGRITY

O N THE evening of March 29, 1863, many members of the Battle Creek church met in their house of worship to consider a serious problem. The voice of slander was again being heard in certain quarters. The character and integrity of one of their most respected members was being maligned. Uriah Smith, one of the elders of the church, served as chairman of the meeting. In a pamphlet issued a few months later, the purpose of this meeting was described:

Whereas, There are certain reports prejudicial to the character of Elder White, as a man of upright and honest dealing, being extensively circulated through the country, and used to cut off his influence and that of his brethren, to shut the ears of the people against the truth, and steel their hearts against its reception; therefore,

Resolved, That we, the church of Seventh-day Adventists of Battle Creek, deem it our duty to take measures to ascertain the grounds of the charges, complaints, and murmurs that are in circulation.[1]

At this meeting it was voted to set up a committee of three members—U. Smith, G. W. Amadon, and E. S. Walker—to investigate the charges. They began their work by serving notice that they were prepared to receive reports of two kinds.

First, they would like to hear from those who knew of any charges against the financial integrity of James White. Any person who at any time might have felt himself defrauded or treated unjustly by Elder White was requested to present charges during the next six weeks.

At the same time persons who, having had business dealings with Elder White, were satisfied by his transactions and considered them honorable and above suspicion, were requested to submit their facts in testimonials to be considered by the committee.

Approximately seven weeks later, the General Conference was

organized in Battle Creek. By that time, the committee had received seventy-four testimonials to the honesty and fairness of Elder White, but not a single charge had been submitted. Thinking that perhaps those speaking against Elder White might require more time, the committee gave such persons until early August —two more months—to submit depositions. Not one negative word was ever received.

Elder Smith summed up the committee's findings: "And why have none come up with wrongs charged against Brother W[hite]? Simply because no such wrongs do in truth exist." [2]

Seven years later it was found necessary to meet similar charges, and again Uriah Smith was chairman of the investigating committee. The same procedure was adopted, but again none of those with accusations cared to submit them in writing. At the same time 54 individuals, many of them laymen with whom Elder White had had business dealings through the years, involving thousands of dollars, testified of their complete satisfaction with his financial record.

Why was James White singled out to become the recipient of a major share of whisperings and slanders circulated concerning the leaders of the Seventh-day Adventist Church? Smith provided an answer to this question.

The great enemy of all righteousness knows that one of the most effectual means by which he can hinder the progress of the work he hates, is to blast the reputation of those who are called to act a prominent part therein before the people. [3]

Ellen White, who leaned heavily on her husband for support, knew that if he were destroyed, her work would be permanently crippled. And this was Satan's objective. She wrote about the relationship between herself and James, "Without him I could accomplish but little, but with his help, in the strength of God, I could do the work assigned me." [4]

James White was a man in whose hands business enterprises prospered and grew. He might be compared with the man spoken of in the first psalm: "Whatsoever he doeth shall prosper." His prosperity, however, did not come easily. The cost was ceaseless vigilance and strictest economy, plus hard work fourteen to sixteen hours a day. His fertile mind grasped business opportunities when they came to him. Ellen freely acknowledged that this was not her gift. Three years after her husband's death she wrote, "It is a great loss to me, deprived of the wisdom and ability of my husband to help me plan, to bring in means, that mine is steadily decreasing." [5]

Most of the church members trusted James White. Prosperous believers were known to thrust large sums of money into his hands, requesting him to use it wherever it would do the most good.

Every worthy project needing support found James's name heading the list of contributors. His donation was often the largest. He led out in raising money to buy a home for Elder Andrews in Rochester, New York. When Elder John N. Loughborough, practically penniless, brought his family to Battle Creek after the experience in Waukon, Iowa, the Whites befriended them. James lent Elder Loughborough three hundred dollars with which to make a down payment on a home. At the time he did this, James had already borrowed five hundred dollars on which he was paying 10 per cent interest. But he refused to accept a penny of interest from Loughborough.

This was not all. When the time came for Elder Loughborough to repay the loan, James White told him that a purse had been made up that wiped out his loan completely. Such actions surely indicate that Elder White was not "insane on the subject of money" as had been charged. Loughborough was one of the many who wrote in testimonials to the kindness and generosity of James White.

When the time did come that Elder White needed financial help, he found it extremely difficult to accept the fact. Before being stricken with paralysis, he had asserted his independent feelings in the *Review:*

We have never been what might be termed a church pauper, and we expect, with the blessing of Heaven, never to be. By the grace of God we will eat no man's bread for naught. [6]

But the stroke he suffered in 1865 cost him dearly, especially during the weeks he spent at the Dansville Sanitarium. Even then he refused for some time to accept the donations raised for him by individuals and churches. Ellen wrote, "He had, during his sickness refused at different times to accept money from his brethren to the amount of nearly one thousand dollars, telling them that when he was in want he would let them know it." [7]

That time came. But before appealing for help, James and

Ellen sought to cut down their living expenses. First they sold $150 worth of furniture. Next, James offered to sell a sofa to the meetinghouse, but this was coolly refused. Just at that time, their only cow died. In that hour of dire need, Elder White wrote to a member who had previously offered to help, saying that if the church could make up the loss of the cow, it would be most gratefully accepted. The man approached did nothing except to accuse the stricken leader of being "insane on the subject of money." Of that sad hour, Ellen White wrote, "We were humbled into the very dust and distressed beyond expression." [8]

Since the very low wages received in Rochester were only slightly increased in Battle Creek, it was only natural that people should wonder where Elder White obtained the money he dispensed so generously in helping the poor, his fellow ministers, and in forwarding the work of the church. To his enemies it seemed logical to suppose that he obtained it from the publishing house and from cash sent in to the *Review* office. James wrote in reply that his financial transactions had been carried on in an open and aboveboard manner:

In justice, however, I would say that the *Review, Instructor,* and our publications, have not been a source of profit. Even now, with its numerous supporters and subscribers, the office is hardly self-sustaining.

What I this day possess I am indebted to a few personal friends, and rise of property on three places we have owned in this city, which is equal to what we possess. [9]

The property he referred to consisted of three houses. The first one cost $500 and he sold it for $1,500. The second cost $1,300 and was sold during the inflationary period of the Civil War for $4,500. The third cost $5,000 and Elder White sold it for $6,000. [10]

Mention might be made of yet another source of income. At the beginning of the Civil War, Elder White purchased $1,200 worth of stationery. He knew that the cost of this type of merchandise increases rapidly in time of war. Before the close of the war he disposed of these stocks for $2,400, thus doubling his investment. [11]

One question remained that critics could not answer. If the *Review and Herald* publishing work had been such a gold mine, would its owner have been so eager to turn it over to the control of the church, taking its profits out of his hands?

Other accusations made against James and Ellen White reveal

the nature of those who instituted charges. Naturally as stories went around, they grew and became more exaggerated.

One man, when asked point blank what he had to criticize, pointed to Elder White's fine pair of horses and comfortable carriage. Why did the Whites feel it necessary to own such equipment, he asked, when so many church members had to get along with farm wagons?

It was not for the sake of making a fine show that they had purchased a comfortable carriage, but rather to increase their own usefulness. The following incident, written by James White, illustrates this fact.

> Next sixth-day we drove our team to Monterey, fifty miles, over a dreadful rough frozen road. . . . Sabbath morning Mrs. W. was so lame from the violent shaking of the carriage, that she could hardly walk across the room.[12]

Another question involved the purchase of an easy chair, costing twenty dollars, during the time of Elder White's serious illness. Ellen did not deny the fact, but felt no necessity to defend her purchase. Anything that would soothe her husband's nerves and hasten his recovery was worth the price.

Still another charge, which would have been humorous if it hadn't been so petty, involved an incident that took place when the Whites were moving out of Battle Creek. In their cellar there was a large accumulation of glass bottles of assorted sizes. When Ellen asked James what she should do with them, he told her to throw them away.

Before she could do this, Willie asked whether he might have them. He proposed cleaning them up and selling them. Permission was given and he soon had a box of sparkling clean bottles. The next time James went to town, Willie went with him. On the way they picked up an employee of the Review office and gave him a ride.

Willie carried the box of bottles into a store, then came out to ask his father how much he thought they were worth. The Review worker was silent, but five months later the Whites met the report in Iowa that Elder White was "so crazy for money" that he was collecting and selling old bottles![13]

When Ellen took James away from Battle Creek in December, 1866, many bitter things were said about the move. Not only would such a midwinter journey result in his death, church members maintained, but she would kill herself caring for him, thus depriving the church of its two irreplaceable leaders.

When, after many months, they returned to what was rapidly becoming the hub of Adventism, some important meetings were held during which many heartfelt confessions were made by ringleaders of the unfounded gossip, which had done so much to injure Elder and Mrs. White. Even their own son, Edson, admitted having cherished hard feelings toward his father.

"I took part to a great extent in the prejudices that were then felt against him, and I fear, did more than any other one, to injure him," he said.[14]

The question may be asked: Did Elder White use the columns of the *Review* for conveying personal messages? He did.

When he wanted to dispose of his house, he offered it for sale in its columns. He intimated on more than one occasion that the White family would appreciate it if their friends in Michigan would can some fruit for them during the summer months. Was this not a reasonable request, however? He might well quote the words of Paul, "If we have sown unto you spiritual things, is it a great thing if we shall reap your carnal things?" (1 Cor. 9:11). These dedicated workers were busy from the beginning of the camp meeting season till its close, ministering to the spiritual needs of God's people. It was justifiable that they should cast themselves on the generosity of the saints.

At the 1872 General Conference session an effort was made to reimburse Elder White for his gifts to the Publishing Association. When relinquishing control of the papers, he had turned over the "good will" accumulated toward the Review office and its publications. This the brethren considered to be worth many thousands of dollars, and it was voted that a goodly payment be made to him in appreciation for his personal sacrifices. But James declined to accept a cent.

After his name had been cleared of the charges brought against him, Elder White was magnanimous enough to lay aside his personal feelings. He would press on with the work he had started in penury thirty years before. In 1873, while recuperating in the Rocky Mountains, he and Ellen covenanted to lay their all upon the altar. During the following five years "it has been their pleasure to put $15,000 into the several branches of the cause." [15]

When brought face to face with so many unproved and un-provable slanders, James White made one forthright statement and a confession, as was his right:

> As to my business career, it is a pleasure to me to state that I am not conscious of taking from the general treasury of our people, or from any church, or from any person, one dollar unjustly. If I have, I call upon my enemies, as well as my friends, to show *when, where,* and *how,* and I will restore four-fold.

> Our confession in this matter is simply this, that we have toiled on in the cause of God for more than twenty years unselfishly, and have carried out the most rigid industry and economy, have suffered excessive weariness, cold and hunger, to save means to the cause, and have given of our scanty purses, when we should have used the means for our own necessities. We now regret that we have robbed ourselves and family to help others, and have robbed the cause of God of more efficient service, by wearing out too soon, in the exercise of too rigid industry and economy. [16]

---

[1] *Vindication of the Business Career of Elder James White* (Battle Creek, Michigan, 1863), pp. 4, 5.

[2] *Ibid.,* p. 39.

[3] *Defence of Eld. James White and Wife* (Battle Creek, Michigan, 1870), p. 1.

[4] *Testimonies,* vol. 1, p. 575.

[5] Ellen G. White letter 61 to John White, Nov. 27, 1884.

[6] James White, in *Review and Herald,* Feb. 2, 1864.

[7] *Testimonies,* vol. 1, p. 582.

[8] *Ibid.,* p. 583.

[9] James White, in *Review and Herald,* March 26, 1867.

[10] *Defence,* pp. 10, 11.

[11] *Ibid.,* p. 11.

[12] James White, in *Review and Herald,* Jan. 27, 1863.

[13] *Testimonies,* vol. 1, pp. 605, 606.

[14] James White, in *Review and Herald,* Nov. 19, 1867.

[15] ———, in *Review and Herald,* Sept. 12, 1878.

[16] ———, in *Review and Herald,* Jan. 11, 1870.

Chapter Thirty

A GENEROUS SOUL

B E NOT forgetful to entertain strangers" (Heb. 13:2). All their lives, James and Ellen White would practice that injunction. No one was ever turned hungry from their door. Whatever they had they gladly shared. Both were generous-hearted, far beyond the average.

While Elder White was living in Greenville he heard that a woman named Hannah Moore had recently come to Battle Creek from New England in search of employment. Sister Moore had spent many years as a missionary in Central Africa working for another denomination. Someone had placed in her hands a copy of J. N. Andrews' book *The History of the Sabbath* while she was on furlough. She read it, and after her return to Central Africa began to observe the seventh day as the Sabbath. As a result she was dismissed by her mission society and returned to the United States.

She lived in South Lancaster, Massachusetts, for a time, then went to Battle Creek hoping to find employment there. She was not successful, and, finding no door open to receive her, accepted the invitation of a non-Adventist friend, a Mr. Thompson, who had also been a missionary, to go to his home in northern Michigan and teach his children.

When James heard of the cool, indifferent way the church members in Battle Creek had treated Miss Moore, he felt ashamed of them. He promptly wrote, inviting her to return and make her home with him and Ellen in Greenville. Miss Moore replied that she had spent all her money making the trip to her present residence. She would come when she had earned the fare, for she was eager to meet the Whites.

James replied that he and Ellen were leaving for New England to hold meetings, but when they returned in two months they would certainly send money so she could come and live with them.

214

Unfortunately, their trip lasted nearly four months, and by the time they returned to Michigan, winter had its grip on the land, and Miss Moore could not travel.

Before the next spring came, Hannah Moore died and was buried in northern Michigan. James and Ellen grieved deeply. They were convinced that her life might have been saved if some interest had been taken in her when she passed through Battle Creek.[1]

At the time of general meetings in Battle Creek, many old friends were entertained at the White home. On one occasion as many as thirty-five persons sat down to eat at their table, all at the expense of the generous host and hostess. There were no entertainment allowances in the 1860's.

One habit James White practiced was that of donating his own clothing to help others. The first time we read of this was in Vermont where the Whites had gone to attend a conference. James met a brother identified simply as N.A.H. James learned that this man was extremely poor, and from his own meager purse, he took twenty dollars, which he handed to this brother. But he went still further. He took off his own overcoat, the only one he had, and handed it to N.A.H. The act is even more impressive when we learn that this same brother had aroused an attitude of jealousy in others toward Elder White.[2]

J. O. Corliss was one of a number of young preachers whom James and Ellen took into their home to help train for work in the cause of God. This young man lived with them for two years. Concerning James White's generosity to the poor, Corliss reported:

> Elder White was very tender-hearted toward cases of need. I have seen him give no less than three overcoats in a single winter to poor preachers needing such garments. More than that, when he thought some hardworking messenger was being scantily dealt with by an auditing committee, he was not slow to appear before that board of award, to champion the misused one's cause, and always to good effect.[3]

It should be noted that James, who had scant sympathy for drones, did this on behalf of the "hard working messenger."

Young workers who received such generous treatment at the hands of Elder White, never forgot his kindness. Ten years after the death of his benefactor, L. R. Conradi wrote to Ellen White:

> It was my privilege to make you and your dear husband's acquaintance

shortly after embracing the truth [1878] and I shall never forget his kindness, as he bought me a coat in which I graduated and gave me the charts when I began to preach.[4]

That there might be money on hand when some worker faced an emergency or a church member needed immediate help, Elder White suggested the setting up of a fund for this purpose. Money was collected, and the first Benevolent Society was established, an organization that flourished for many years. Many worthy individuals had cause to bless Elder White for his part in the establishment of this society.

In those days there were many calls for the support of new enterprises. There was a book fund used for translating Adventist publications into foreign languages. The Health Reform Institute and the Review and Herald Publishing Association always needed more capital, and after 1874 there was the overseas European Mission needing help, as well as Battle Creek College.

The back of the *Review* carried many lists of persons who were contributing to these and other worthy causes. In those columns, Elder White called for "fifty dollar men" and "hundred dollar men," and, before he died, he was asking for a number of "thousand dollar men." The names of James and Ellen White headed nearly every list. This fact was acknowledged by the General Conference Committee:

Elder White . . . sold his property in Michigan and Iowa at a sacrifice in 1875, and is prepared to show that he has donated more than $5,000 to the cause during the past two years. . . .

These very grumblers do little or nothing for the cause themselves, while Elder White at the same time is giving a hundred here, and a thousand there. He pledges himself to give to the cause during the year 1876 more than all these murmurers put together from the Atlantic to the Pacific.[5]

James White, like Job of old, sought out the cases of the poor and the needy. In 1874 drought and grasshoppers devastated Kansas, reducing many farmers to penury. Wages of Adventist workers in that State were so reduced that they could not live on what they received. Hearing of this, Elder White protested that men could not feed their families on the low wages they were receiving. He promptly launched a fund for the relief of the Kansas workers. His and Ellen's generous donations of $100 headed the list. Workers in Kansas were deeply grateful.[6]

On several occasions James paid interest on money he borrowed from the bank to lend, interest free, to workers so they could purchase homes for their families. Among others helped in this way were Elders Loughborough, Mead, Waggoner, and Hull.[7]

When the cause of God prospered, James White rejoiced. When he saw excellent results obtained by Adventist preachers with gospel tents, James urged one conference after another to invest in them. For his own beloved Michigan, he purchased a tent costing more than five hundred dollars. This tent he was willing to lend to any minister who could use it for evangelistic meetings.[8]

In 1878 a heavy debt hung over the church in Oakland, California, and there was real danger that through bankruptcy it might be taken from the believers. Edson White, in California at the time, wrote to his parents, asking, Shall the church be sold to the "Campbellites" (who wanted to buy the building). Mrs. White said No, and James White said No. Sooner than allow that to happen, James indicated that he would sell his house in Oakland.[9]

Ellen's plan was somewhat different:

Let there be a Christmas tree in every church in California, to be covered all over with fruit in the form of cash, in sums all the way from a dime to one hundred dollars.[10]

At the same time she asked Edson to place $100 on the tree from James and the same amount from herself. She wrote to her other son, Willie, who was in Battle Creek, instructing him to place similar sums on a Christmas tree to be set up in the "Dime Tabernacle."

At the time of the death of White, in 1881, George I. Butler, General Conference president, referred to the generosity of the fallen leader:

There was a tender place in his heart toward the distressed and those whom he thought were wronged, which made him one of the most generous of men. How many there are among us who have been helped and encouraged by his means, his words, and his acts. How many times he has hurried away from busy cares to pray with the sick and sorrowing. Not every one who knew him was aware of the peculiar tenderness of heart which he really possessed, or gave him credit for this trait of character; but his most intimate friends know that I state the truth. I never knew a man who could more generously forgive a wrong when he thought it was truly repented of than he.[11]

During the years, James White enjoyed the blessings promised to the openhanded, proving the truthfulness of the statement, "The liberal soul shall be made fat: and he that watereth shall be watered also himself" (Prov. 11:25).

Uriah Smith, reporting in the *Review*, stated, on Elder White's funeral, "Memory brushes the dimness, accumulating through the lapse of time, from numberless deeds of kindness received at his hand." [12]

[1] *Testimonies*, vol. 1, pp. 666-680.

[2] *Life Sketches* (1888), p. 279.

[3] J. O. Corliss, in *Review and Herald*, Aug. 23, 1923.

[4] L. R. Conradi letter to Ellen G. White, Aug. 16, 1891.

[5] Administrative Pamphlets: *Dangers and Duties of Our Time*, General Conference Committee, pp. 42, 46, 47.

[6] *Review and Herald*, Nov. 4, 1875.

[7] *Defence*, pp. 19, 20.

[8] James White, in *Review and Herald*, June 8, 1869.

[9] *Ibid.*

[10] *Ibid.*

[11] George I. Butler, in *Review and Herald*, Aug. 16, 1881.

[12] Uriah Smith, in *Review and Herald*, Aug. 16, 1881.

Chapter Thirty-one

A WIDER VISION

A T A general meeting in Battle Creek in 1858 James White met a man who spoke English with a distinctively foreign accent. This man, Michael B. Czechowski, had only recently accepted the Sabbath while attending a series of meetings conducted by Elder G. W. Holt in Findlay, Ohio. He had been baptized by Elder Holt, and was now eager to begin preaching. Originally a priest in his home country, Poland, Czechowski came to the United States and had become a Protestant while in northern New York. He was very poor and found it difficult to find enough money to feed and clothe his family. Elder White raised enough cash to help him temporarily.[1]

Since D. T. Bourdeau was working among the French-speaking people in Eastern Canada, Czechowski, who was fluent in French, was invited to join him. He worked with Bourdeau for several years, but all the time he desired to go back to Europe to carry the message to Italy.

Czechowski next joined Elder J. N. Loughborough, conducting tent meetings in New York State. But, still thinking of his people overseas, he begged Loughborough to use his influence with the newly formed General Conference and try to persuade them to send him as their missionary to Europe.[2]

For a number of reasons the leading brethren hesitated to grant this request. Czechowski was a poor financier. His family was always on the brink of want. He was also inclined to be erratic. As a result, it was suggested that he be patient and wait a while.

Not willing to do this, Czechowski went to the leaders of the group of first-day Adventists and persuaded them to send him to Europe as their salaried representative. The fact that after reaching Europe he preached Seventh-day Adventist doctrines rather than those of the group who sponsored him was unknown in America for several years.[3]

Meanwhile, the Seventh-day Adventist Church in America continued to put down sturdy and growing roots. But while they recognized Christ's call to preach the gospel to all men, they were not at first able to envision Seventh-day Adventist missionaries fanning out around the globe. With their relatively small membership and an expectation of the near Advent, they thought this would be accomplished by preaching the gospel to representatives of all nations living in the United States. As early as 1859, Uriah Smith was declaring that "our own land is composed of people from almost every nation."[4]

That same year Merritt G. Kellogg, half-brother of the well-known Dr. John H. Kellogg, crossed the plains and mountains to California, where he made a home for his family. Probably the first Seventh-day Adventist in that State, Kellogg began spreading the truth while working as a carpenter. In the course of time a small group of Sabbathkeepers sprang up around him. As time passed, Kellogg continually urged the General Conference to send workers to California, assuring them that the golden West would prove a most fruitful field.

In reply to Kellogg's appeals, James White replied, "Do not be discouraged; we believe that in due time the Lord will provide men and means for the proclamation of His truth in California."[5]

In 1865, while James White was General Conference president, he received a letter from California. It contained a cash enclosure of $133.00. The letter specified that the money must be used to pay the expenses of an evangelist to California.[6]

But the General Conference Committee replied that there were fivefold more calls for help at their own doors than they could possibly fill.

In 1867 Kellogg traveled east to take a medical course in New Jersey. This gave him the opportunity to attend the General Conference session held in Battle Creek in May, 1868. Again he pressed his plea for workers to meet the needs of the far West.

What neither Kellogg nor Elder White knew was that two ministers attending that conference had been prepared by the Lord to go to California. These were John N. Loughborough and Daniel T. Bourdeau. Kellogg watched with mounting anxiety as workers suggested the various fields to which they felt God was calling them—to Ohio, Minnesota, Maine, Iowa, and other States. Finally, when only Loughborough and Bourdeau had not been placed, Elder White asked, "Has no one any impressions of duty relative to the California field?"

In response, John Loughborough arose and said he had come to the conference deeply impressed that his duty was in that direction. Elder White replied that when Jesus sent out His disciples, they went two by two. Was there another evangelist willing to accompany Loughborough to California? Bourdeau stood and offered his services. He and his wife had come to the session ready to go wherever he was asked to go. He was ready to go to California. Elder White asked the two men to pray over the matter. The next day when he put the question to them, "Brethren, what can you tell us?" They replied, "California or nothing!" [7]

James White published a notice in the *Review*, inviting church members to give $1,000 to equip the two missionaries with an evangelistic tent, and to pay other expenses.

Meanwhile the seed sown by Czechowski in Europe was beginning to bear fruit. After raising up a small company of Sabbathkeepers in Tramelan, Switzerland, Czechowski went on to Rumania without informing his Swiss converts that there was an organized Seventh-day Adventist Church in America. One day a member of this group in Tramelan looked over some papers left behind by Czechowski and discovered a copy of the *Review*. They were delighted to discover that there were many Sabbathkeepers in the United States. Albert Vuilleumier, one of the Swiss converts, wrote to the General Conference, where news of Sabbathkeepers in Europe came as a surprise. A letter was sent to Vuilleumier, suggesting that the European believers send a representative to meet with the General Conference session of 1869. A young German Swiss, James Erzberger (sometimes spelled Ertzenberger), was sent to make contact with the Adventist believers in America. [8]

Knowing no English, Erzberger bravely set out, carrying with him an envelope bearing the words, "James White, Seventh-day Adventist General Conference, Battle Creek, Michigan." In New York he was assisted by some kind-hearted person who helped him buy a railway ticket to Battle Creek.

Since Erzberger needed a working knowledge of English, the

James Erzberger, sent as a young man by Swiss Sabbathkeepers to contact Adventists in America, stayed in the White home for some nine months.

Whites took it upon themselves to teach him. Young Willie became one of his most faithful teachers. Willie would talk to Erzberger in English, then help him frame replies.

James Erzberger proved to be a very humble, teachable man. Elder White described his experience with this representative from Europe:

When they sent our much-beloved brother James Erzenberger to our country, we dare not risk him at Battle Creek. We took him to our then Greenville home, furnished an interpreter for a while, and a teacher, free of charge. He made our home his home at least nine months, for the blessed pay of having this godly youth in our family.

We can never forget his fervent French, then German, and finally English prayers, which he offered morning and evening.[9]

After studying English only nine weeks, Erzberger was sent to the Ohio camp meeting and invited to speak to the believers. James White also wrote of this experience:

222

One of the most interesting parts of our meeting was the good, humble, impressive, melting talks of our beloved Brother Ertzenberger, from Switzerland. Although he had been in America but nine weeks, and when he came he could not speak one sentence in English, he was able to speak to the people so as to be fully understood.[10]

After spending some fifteen months in America, Erzberger returned to Switzerland where he ministered to the believers in Tramelan. Later, the Swiss believers sent Ademar Vuilleumier, brother of Albert Vuilleumier, to Battle Creek to attend school and become thoroughly grounded in Adventist doctrine.

Then came a call for a man of stature to go to Europe, head up the work and superintend its development. James White placed the matter before the other two members of the General Conference Committee. As they narrowed their choices, the name of John Nevins Andrews began to emerge. Finally the leaders decided to request him to become the first American to cross the sea as a representative of the Seventh-day Adventist Church. This man, whom Ellen White later described as "the best man among us," [11] consented, and on September 15, 1874, John Andrews, with his two motherless children, set sail from Boston for Europe.

Three months later, on January 3, 1875, Ellen White was given a vision of tremendous significance. At first she saw only darkness everywhere. Then small lights began to twinkle. They brightened and expanded until the whole world was flooded with light.[12] When the vision was ended, her husband asked whether she could tell what she had seen. She was not ready at the time, but later she said that she had been shown printing presses operating in many lands. Eager to know just where the work was going to expand, James asked if she could name any specific countries.

At first she was unable to recall the exact location of the presses. Then her face brightened as she replied, "O, yes, I do remember, the angel said, 'Australia.'"

When he heard of it, J. O. Corliss, a worker in Michigan at the time, promptly wrote to Elder White offering his services for Australia. In describing the incident, Corliss stated that James's response was typical of the man. Under Corliss' signature he hastily wrote this brief message: "We are not ready to open work in Australia. When we are, we will let you know, James White." [13] Ten years later, Elder Corliss did become a worker in Australia.

This 1875 vision placed the church's world mission squarely

before all Seventh-day Adventists, but the burden came to rest most heavily on the heart of Elder White. The following year he wrote to his wife concerning his intense interest in the foreign mission program:

"O, my God, what a work is pressing upon our people! Three ministers in Denmark keeping and teaching the Sabbath. One reports six converts in one place. Brother Matteson must go to Denmark." [14]

James was aware of the fascinating sequence of events that led to the settlement of Pitcairn Island. He and Elder J. N. Loughborough decided to do something for Pitcairn. In 1876 a box of Adventist books and tracts was packed and shipped from San Francisco. The island had to wait another ten years before the arrival of a living preacher in the person of John I. Tay, who brought them the message of the Sabbath and other Bible truth. During his five-week stay on the island, he won the islanders to Adventism. [15]

James White did not live to see the tremendous expansion lying directly ahead for the church. It was not to be his privilege to see the lights go on in Africa, Asia, South America, and the islands of the sea. But he had the vision, and in the columns of the *Review* he frequently pointed the way to the future:

In the Progress Department of the present issue is a voice from old Denmark, by our beloved Brother Matteson. A great work is to be done in Europe. A man is wanted for England and Scotland. . . .

Calls come from all parts of the South. We think there is not a single State in the Union but has its little companies of Seventh-day Adventists. Five hundred men are wanted to enter all parts where calls are coming in for help. There are probably fifty Sabbath-keepers in the new State of Colorado, and not a man to respond to the many calls for help there. The same can be said of many good fields. [16]

He suggested that $100,000 be raised to establish the European mission. One can almost hear him appeal, in characteristic manner, "Come brethren, get out your pocket books and unroll the greenbacks." [17]

---

[1] James White, in *Review and Herald*, April 15, 1858.

[2] *Origin and History*, vol. 2, pp. 197, 198.

[3] *Ibid.*, p. 198.

[4] Uriah Smith, in *Review and Herald*, Feb. 3, 1859.

[5] J. N. Loughborough, in *Pacific Union Recorder*, Dec. 21, 1905.

[6] *Pioneering the Message*, p. 54.

[7] *Ibid.*, p. 59.

[8] *Origin and History*, vol. 2, p. 199.
[9] James White, in *Review and Herald*, Aug. 6, 1872.
[10] *Ibid.*, Aug. 24, 1869.
[11] *Origin and History*, vol. 2, pp. 203, 204.
[12] W. C. White description of Ellen G. White vision of Jan. 3, 1875, Document File, 105 B.
[13] John O. Corliss, in *Review and Herald*, Aug. 23, 1923.
[14] James White letter to Ellen G. White, April 21, 1876.
[15] *SDA Encyclopedia*, article "Pitcairn Island," p. 998.
[16] James White, in *Review and Herald*, Aug. 2, 1877.
[17] *Ibid.*, Jan. 25, 1877.

Chapter Thirty-two

BACK ON THE TRACK

WHEN James White was elected president of the General Conference in the spring of 1865, the publishing office, which had been situated in Battle Creek for nearly ten years, was growing and prospering. The post-Civil-War boom was still strong, and the printing office was busier than ever.

Three months after the General Conference session, James was stricken with paralysis. But for two years during his illness, his name remained as president of the Publishing Association. However, in 1867 he tendered his resignation. During the next two years the Association was under the management of J. M. Aldrich. Elder J. N. Andrews was elected president of the General Conference.

In the spring of 1869 James White, now recovered, was reelected General Conference president and also president of the Publishing Association. When he returned to the printing office he was dismayed at what he found. Not only had wages of workers in the press been increased far above ministers' salaries, but business had been conducted in such a manner that in two years the Association lost thousands of dollars. Prices for publications were kept down. The flow of cash into the Association was so low that the management had been obliged to borrow heavily in order to continue operating. On these loans they were paying 10 per cent interest.

Elder White immediately appealed to church members to lend money to the Association interest free so that all 10 per cent notes might be paid off.[1]

At the Health Reform Institute the situation was not much better. Ellen White's counsels had not been accepted. The management was attempting to operate the institution somewhat after the fashion of a popular water spa, copying the institution at Dansville, New York, in many respects.

As for the *Health Reformer*, its subscription list remained disappointingly low. Part of the reason for this was the radical health theories advocated in its columns. Among other items of diet condemned by the paper as injurious to the body was table salt. In November, 1870, the following statement appeared:

> In regard to salt, it must be said that in addition to its being absolutely indigestible, in even the least degree, it always is a great irritant, creating inflammatory action and consequent thirst in a high degree.[2]

Other items condemned by the editors of *Health Reformer* included sugar, milk, butter, eggs, cheese, spices, condiments, and many food combinations.[3] While we today might agree that for the most part they were correct, still their stand was premature, so it was not surprising that nearly every day the editor received requests from readers to cancel their subscriptions.[4]

Patronage at the Institute had dropped off sharply. By September, 1869, there were only eight paying patients and the institution was burdened with a $13,000 debt.[5]

Realizing that the Health Reform Institute was in a crisis situation, the leading men requested James to take charge of it. James knew that there was considerable sentiment in favor of closing the Institute, but he recalled the instruction given through his wife, calling for the establishment of just such a place as the one they had opened in 1866. We can almost hear James White speaking in typically emphatic fashion, "Come, brethren, we can't go on this way."

In an attempt to stabilize finances, James inserted a notice in the *Review* in regard to the policy of caring for the poor:

> We are . . . sorry to say that the Institute cannot treat the afflicted poor on as liberal terms as it has in the past. It will receive those destitute of means at half price, and thus give one half, if their friends will pay the other half. Payments must be made at the close of each week. The Institute has lost heavily by trusting patients.[6]

To implement these steps, John Preston Kellogg, father of John Harvey, was appointed treasurer of the Institute.

James made a number of other changes. The *Health Reformer* and the *Review* would no longer invite people to buy stock in the Institute, promising that it "will pay a large percent," or "it is a good investment," or "a paying thing." Instead, he invited those who could to buy shares, which would be sold at $25.00 apiece. He set the example by purchasing forty shares. Ellen bought twenty. This represented an investment of $1,500. James urged the *Review* readers to help get the Institute out of debt during 1871.[7]

Early in 1871, James took over the editorship of the *Health Reformer*. He relinquished the job to J. H. Kellogg in 1874. A more positive approach to health was emphasized, and contributed articles recommending radical diets and healing methods were confined to a less conspicuous portion of the paper. These improvements resulted in a quick reversal of the declining subscription trend. By July, 1874, 8,000 copies of the *Reformer* were being published monthly, and Elder White hoped that it would soon have 25,000 subscribers.[8]

The Battle Creek institutions soon began to prosper. Funds needed to build up working capital were forthcoming when Elder White appealed for them. He toiled early and late to continue the upward trend, and his efforts were successful.

For the remainder of his life, however, James regretted the losses that had been incurred by the publishing house and health institute during the years he was incapacitated. The financial loss was bad enough (though the situation was reversed when proper fiscal policies were adopted), but his deepest regret was over the loss of confidence brought about by the squandering of means at Battle Creek. Men who had stood nobly by the work withdrew their support as they saw money wasted. Elder White summed up what happened during the four-year period, 1865-1869:

> The paralytic stroke had so far touched the brain that for eighteen months we carried neither watch nor purse. And for the four years that immediately followed the war, we did not bear responsibilities at headquarters. During this time, sad changes took place at Battle Creek in the spiritual and financial condition of things. Although it was the best time to do business in the history of the cause, not less than $20,000 was lost during that four years at the Publishing House and Health Institute, when $30,000 should have been earned.

As the 1870 camp meeting season drew on, James and Ellen decided to attend as many as possible—first in the West, then nearer the Atlantic Coast. These early camp meetings all followed a more or less similar pattern. Conditions were primitive. The plan of locating in one place and returning to that spot year after year as facilities could be improved, had not occurred to the brethren.

They looked upon camp meetings as opportunities to evangelize previously unentered areas in their conferences, thus reaching larger numbers of non-Adventists. Ellen White supported this viewpoint.

James and Ellen thoroughly enjoyed camp meetings. Carrying a heavy burden for the spiritual condition of the church, their strong appeals for holy living were vibrant and effective.

Furthermore, the meetings gave Elder White a unique opportunity to promote the publishing work, a cause ever near his heart. In one notice in the *Review,* he promised to have "a good assortment of all our publications to sell, and to give, chargeable to the book fund. . . . We shall also expect to collect for the *Review and Herald, Health Reformer,* and *Youth's Instructor,* all dues from those on the ground who owe for these periodicals." It is difficult for us to conceive of a General Conference president handling such details today.[9]

If James had definite aims in mind when he visited a camp meeting, so did the laity who came. Many wanted to talk with Elder and Mrs. White, which imposed a tremendous demand on the two. For most members, camp meeting was a time for rest and relaxation, but not for them. On one occasion Elder White enlarged upon the problem:

Our good people mean to do their whole duty. But they are not able to see the difference between the fatigue of preaching and exhorting, business sessions, and morning and evening, and sometimes midnight, committees, during fifteen camp-meetings in succession, and the rest of the one only they attend each year, sitting and hearing, or strolling about the grounds with minds and hearts as free from anxiety and care as the gentle breezes that fan the groves. Many . . . come to camp meeting expecting to enjoy good long visits with Brother and Sister White.[10]

Repeatedly the Whites expressed the fear that they would be unable to attend so many yearly gatherings. Typical was an announcement in 1871—owing to a wornout condition they felt they would not be able to attend camp meetings.[11] But when camp meeting season rolled around that year, there were Elder and Mrs. White! Traveling from one meeting to another by train, river steamer, carriage or whatever means was available. Unfortunately, Adventists felt that a camp meeting was not really successful unless Elder and Mrs. White were present. "It takes the Lord to make a good camp meeting,"[12] James declared more than once. But many members refused to attend unless the Whites were present.

In the fall of 1870, after a long series of camp meetings, the Whites returned worn out to Battle Creek. But there was to be no rest for them there. For one thing, the editor of the *Review* was in another State suffering with fever. And other key personnel were away from the office sick. Thus, matters that demanded attention were left undone. [13]

Faced by this situation, James White was forced to plunge into work. For eight weeks he labored from five in the morning until nine each night, except on Fridays. Since he was expected often to preach on Sabbath in Battle Creek or in a nearby church, he had no rest day at all. In the *Review,* he pointed out that not only was he doing the work of "two businessmen, two editors, one minister," but that he and Ellen had been caring for a family of fourteen, which included his helpless mother, who was 82, and his father, aged 85. He had not even been able to take the time to winterize his house, as was needed. [14]

It is not surprising that James began to suffer the same symptoms he had noticed prior to his previous strokes. Feeling that it would be better to decrease his burdens before suffering another illness, he wrote begging for relief. He could do this now with a free mind, for the *Review,* the *Health Reformer,* the *Instructor,* and Health Reform Institute were all flourishing financially once again, thanks to his untiring efforts.

Therefore, at a meeting of the General Conference, held in February, 1871, he asked the officers to relieve him of some of his heavy work load. During the session he suffered another partial stroke, but performed his duties to the end. [15]

The General Conference passed a resolution expressing deep appreciation for the faithful and abundant labors of Elder James White. They went a step further. "We do, as an act of justice, request him to take a furlough that shall be sufficient to enable him fully to recover his wonted strength."

Having done this, they proceeded to re-elect James White president of the General Conference, and he was also re-elected or elected editor of the *Review* and the *Health Reformer,* president of the Publishing Association, president of the Seventh-day Adventist Benevolent Association, and president of the Missionary Society. [16]

As a gesture of appreciation for his labors and as a vote of confidence in his capabilities, this was magnificent. But as an exhibition of ecclesiastical statesmanship, it was extremely short-sighted. The leaders must have realized that no single individual could carry such a multitude of responsibilities without the danger of being crushed beneath the load.

But they did realize very clearly that James White commanded the respect and confidence of church members everywhere, and that as long as he stood at the head of these various enterprises the saints would continue to support them by their prayers and means.

---

[1] *Review and Herald*, March 29, 1870.
[2] J. W. C., in *Health Reformer*, November, 1870.
[3] *Ibid.*
[4] *Story of Our Health Message*, pp. 168, 169.
[5] *Ibid.*, p. 159.
[6] *Review and Herald*, Jan. 18, 1870.
[7] *Ibid.*, Aug. 22, 1871.
[8] James White, in *Review and Herald*, July 14, 1874.
[9] ———, in *Review and Herald*, May 17, 1870.
[10] *Ibid.*, Aug. 23, 1877.
[11] James White, in *Review and Herald*, March 21, 1871.
[12] ———, in *Review and Herald*, June 21, 1877.
[13] ———, in *Review and Herald*, Jan. 10, 1871.
[14] *Ibid.*
[15] ———, in *Review and Herald*, Aug. 29, 1871.
[16] ———, in *Review and Herald*, Feb. 14, 1871.

Chapter Thirty-three

BUSY HERE AND THERE

URING the years of their pilgrimage James and Ellen White lived in many different, and often widely separated, places. They owned homes in Battle Creek and Greenville, Michigan; Washington, Iowa; and in Oakland and Healdsburg, California. Sometimes they owned homes in two and even three places at the same time. The Washington, Iowa, home became theirs in early 1871. They called it their "Western home." Of course, for many years James's close connection with the publishing work made it impossible for him to stay away from Battle Creek for any extended period of time. But it was always a pleasure for him and Ellen, whenever it was possible, to go to a quiet place in peaceful country surroundings, where they could relax for a short time.

Rapid changes took place in the White home in 1870 and 1871. James Edson, second son of James and Ellen, married Emma Mac-Dearmon on his twenty-first birthday, in 1870. James was the officiating minister. This left only Willie in the parental nest, although that nest in Battle Creek was often bereft of the presence of his parents for weeks on end. Willie was now 16 and busy with his studies in Battle Creek.

Betsy White, James's saintly mother, passed to her rest on January 9, 1871, and was buried in the White family plot in Oak Hill Cemetery. Deacon John found life lonely indeed without his companion. Early in July, James, away from Battle Creek, received word that his father was sinking fast. He hurried back, arriving on July 6, only to learn that his father had died the previous day.[1] Following a poignant service in the Battle Creek meetinghouse, the body of Deacon John was borne to Oak Hill and laid to rest beside his Betsy.

In spite of the partial stroke James suffered in February, 1871, he recovered speedily so that he and Ellen were able to attend every Western camp meeting, with the exception of Illinois. By the time that one came around, both of them were temporarily ill, so they felt it expedient that they rest at their home in Washington, Iowa.[2] Then, with voices once again in working order, they proceeded to attend the Minnesota meeting.

The work continued to grow. Reports from California showed that Elder John Loughborough was attracting much attention to the truth in that faraway mission field.[3] One day James received a letter from California inviting him and Ellen to visit the golden West. James replied,

> It is in our hearts to accept the kind invitation of brethren in California to visit them this autumn, and spend the winter with them. This we can do after attending camp-meetings in New York, New Hampshire, Vermont, Maine, Michigan, Ohio, and Indiana, if the brethren will not load us down with cares and labors which do not belong to us. . . . Brethren, we are at your service.[4]

It is not always possible to know, when reading James White's reports to the church family, whether Ellen was in agreement with him. He was fond of using the "editorial *we.*" In many instances he was referring only to himself, although generally his wife was included in that expression.

Meanwhile, the summer of 1871 was passing and there was no diminishing of James's burdens, particularly in the Review office. His editorial stand-by, Uriah Smith, was in the East helping his brother-in-law, J. N. Andrews, complete work on his important *History of the Sabbath.* To help fill the gap created by Smith's absence, James invited J. H. Waggoner to join the *Review* staff as an editor. Elder Waggoner's first reaction was to decline, but he changed his mind when he met Elder White. He wrote:

> His careworn and emaciated countenance convinced me that he was near the point of entirely breaking down. . . . I felt willing to incur any personal risk if I could possibly relieve Bro. White of any of his burdens, so that he might secure rest, and so be spared to the cause which he has so long and faithfully served.[5]

James was able to visit the Michigan camp meeting, which opened on September 13. At this meeting he preached five times. For the next two months he remained in Battle Creek while Ellen and Willie traveled in the East.[6] Then he set out to join them at

South Lancaster, Massachusetts, planning to meet S. N. Haskell there.

The two long-time friends exchanged views on many subjects. Elder White knew of the New England Tract and Missionary Society, an organization for distributing Adventist literature, which Haskell had been promoting among the New England churches. James thought the plan an excellent one. Here was a solution to the problem of how to get books, tracts, and periodicals from the publishing house into the hands of the believers, and to all the world. White urged Haskell to journey to Battle Creek and explain his plan to the churches there and throughout Michigan.[7]

After James's visit to South Lancaster, he and Ellen attended meetings at Boston, at Washington, N. H., at Richmond, and Norridgewock in Maine, and also in Rhode Island. Then they turned homeward. No matter how far they might roam or how lengthy their absence, home for the Whites meant Battle Creek.

Once again James came to the decision that he must lay down some of his heaviest burdens. He felt sure that it was because he was so care-laden that he suffered depression, spoke discouraging words and murmured at times.[8] The time for another General Conference session was approaching. The opening date was set for December 29. During the session James hoped to try again to hand over to others some of his many official positions and duties.

During this session the delegates recognized the urgency and fairness of Elder White's request to be relieved of some of his burdens, and acted accordingly. However, their decisions may have gone differently than he had expected. Elder George I. Butler was elected General Conference president, and James was not even named as a member of the newly elected General Conference Executive Committee. His name, however, did remain as president of the Publishing Association. The brethren had learned the wisdom of leaving that position in his capable hands.[9] Four weeks after adjournment of the Conference, Elder White wrote in the *Review* that he would no longer accept correspondence regarding church business, for his health would not permit it. He added:

It is with feelings of grief that we feel compelled to lay the armor off for a while to rest. We have ever loved to labor in the cause of truth. . . . In God we trust, and hope for help and strength to work again in His vineyard.[10]

In spite of his appeals that his burdens be eased, was James taken by surprise when he was not re-elected General Conference president, or at least made a member of the Executive Committee? Certainly his plans underwent a drastic change that spring.

Between May 30 and June 4, Ellen and James attended the Illinois camp meeting, then one in Knoxville, Iowa, which lasted from June 6-11. The *Review and Herald* of May 28 carried notices giving dates for the Minnesota and Wisconsin meetings, with a brief statement that Elder and Mrs. White were expected to be in attendance. But this was not to be.

After attending two or three camp meetings the Whites went to their Washington, Iowa, home, planning to rest there until time for the Eastern camp meetings. "We hope to be able to be at these meetings, then attend the Seventh Day Baptist General Conference the second week in September, on our way to California," James wrote. He asked if some friend might lend them a carriage and team for a few weeks so they could visit the Iowa churches.[11] No doubt some kind friend felt honored to supply this need.

As usual, conference presidents had planned their camp meetings so that the dates did not conflict and that they might have the services of James and Ellen White. They were also writing letters to Elder Butler, asking him to synchronize schedules, thus guaranteeing the Whites' presence at all camps. Suddenly all was changed. Four weeks after James made his request for a carriage, the following notice appeared in the Review:

To the brethren, East, who are calling for Brother and Sister White to attend their several camp meetings, we would say that a letter just received from them reports them at Denver City, Colorado, on their way to California.[12]

What had happened?

---

[1] James White, in *Review and Herald*, July 18, 1871.

[2] ———, in *Review and Herald*, June 27, 1871.

[3] J. N. Loughborough, in *Review and Herald*, Nov. 22, 1870.

[4] James White, in *Review and Herald*, July 18, 1871.

[5] J. H. Waggoner, in *Review and Herald*, Aug. 8, 1871.

[6] James White, in *Review and Herald*, Aug. 29, 1871.

[7] Ella M. Robinson, *S. N. Haskell, Man of Action* (Washington, D.C.: Review and Herald Publishing Assn., 1967), pp. 30-32.

[8] James White, in *Review and Herald*, Nov. 14, 1871.

[9] *Review and Herald*, Jan. 2, 1872.

[10] *Ibid.*, Jan. 23, 1872.

[11] *Ibid.*, June 18, 1872.

[12] *Ibid.*, July 16, 1872.

Chapter Thirty-four

WESTWARD HO!

THAT June morning was warm and sunny as James White walked from his home to the Washington, Iowa, post office. Half an hour later he returned, carrying several letters. As he read them Ellen waited, knowing that he would soon share their contents with her.

"Here are no less than five invitations for us to attend camp meetings," he finally said, looking up. "Can we again go through what we endured last summer?"

"James, I don't think we should wear ourselves out," she replied. "Let me read you part of a letter I received only this week from Brother M. G. Kellogg, in California. He is deeply concerned about your health. Remember, he is a medical doctor and should know what he is talking about."

Taking a letter from a drawer, she read:

I am grieved to learn that Brother White is so poorly. He has worked himself down and must have rest. Do come immediately to California and rest. Brother W. MUST cease brain labor for a time. . . . I suppose he feels that he must WORK, WORK, WORK and that the cause will suffer if he does not work, but if he works into the grave, then we will have to get along some way without him.[1]

James looked surprised. "How long have you had that letter?" he asked.

"Only a few days."

"Why didn't you tell me about it before?"

"Because you were all wrapped up in plans to attend camp meetings, and I felt the right moment hadn't arrived."

"Well, I think the doctor is right," said James. "We must be sure we are doing God's will, but we were planning to visit California in the fall. Why not now?"

The prospect was exciting. Ellen and James had never been as

far west as the Rockies. And since there was no indication that they
should do otherwise, they decided to go.

The Michigan Adventists were sorry to learn that the Whites
were leaving their midst, where they had lived and worked so long.
To emphasize this fact the Michigan Conference passed a resolution
that must have assured the Whites that they would always have
many warm friends in the East—fellow believers who were eager to
see them again:

> This conference will esteem it a pleasure to defray all the expenses of
> himself [James White] and family in his efforts to regain health in the
> pure mountain air of the West.[2]

When they planned the trip James and Ellen had thought of
going almost directly to California. But as they thought about it
they received the distinct impression that there was work for them
to do along the way.

Their first stop was in Missouri, where they held some meetings. From there they went to Ottawa, Kansas, to visit Ellen's elder
sister, Mrs. Carolyn Clough, whom Ellen hadn't seen in twenty-
five years. They spent thirteen days with the Cloughs.[3] Then, at
the Cloughs' request, they agreed to visit their daughter, Mrs.
Walling, in Denver, Colorado.

James had a difficult time on the trip to Denver. We can imagine
that it was hot and stifling in "the cars" as the engine panted westward across the plains of Kansas and eastern Colorado that July.
When the train pulled into Denver, a town boasting at that time
about 12,000 inhabitants, James had to be helped from the train.
In the waiting room he stretched out on the floor, "our shawl for a
mattress, and traveling bag for a pillow," he wrote in the *Review*.[4]
Willie, who was with his parents, hurried out of the depot, found
Mr. Walling, and returned with him to the station. James was
helped into the carriage and driven to the Walling home, where
he and Ellen met two of Carolyn's children, Mrs. Lou Walling and
Miss Mary Clough. After a few days in Denver when James was
feeling stronger, Mr. Walling took the Whites to Walling's Mills,
about forty miles from Denver. There he had prepared a cottage
for them;[5] their nearest post office would be in a small settlement
called Black Hawk, and here they would receive their mail as long
as they stayed in the Colorado mountains.

James was thrilled by the grandeur of the mountains. Riding

through the pine woods he would exclaim, "Life! life! Breathe deep, Ellen; fill your lungs with the fragrant, life-giving atmosphere."[6]

Together husband and wife roamed the forests, followed sparkling brooks, and breathed deep of the pure, clear air. The natural wonders that God had created always appealed to James White more than any invention of man. His wife remembered that when he passed a colorful maple he "wanted to take off his hat in respect; but . . . when he saw a large house, he wanted to pass by as quickly as possible."[7]

When Mr. Walling suggested a pack trip over the snowy range and into the inner park, the group gladly accepted his invitation. With Ellen and James were Willie and Lucinda Hall, who for several years had been Ellen's assistant. On the trip the ladies rode on ponies, James and Willie on horses, and Mr. Walling followed, guiding a loaded wagon up the narrow mountain road. Ellen suffered what could have been a serious misfortune the first day, when her pony, frightened, bolted and threw her to the ground. She suffered considerable pain, but, fortunately, no bones were broken.[8]

Upward the party climbed until they reached timber line. On every side was a vast panorama of peaks. The travelers could not refrain from exclaiming in delight, "Magnificent! Sublime! Delightful! Glorious!"

At an elevation of 11,000 feet, the travelers were breathless in the thin mountain air. Suddenly they heard a shout from Walling:

"The storm is coming! Hasten on to the valley!"

Looking around, the climbers saw ominous black clouds massing in the sky. They urged their animals on as they descended a pass into a pleasant meadow. Fortunately, the clouds divided and the storm missed them completely.

While in Middle Park, the Whites received a letter from Elder Loughborough, uring them to come to California as soon as possible.[9] It was Loughborough's hope that James and Ellen might be present at a camp meeting planned to be held at Windsor, a small community about seventy-five miles north of San Francisco.

James was reluctant even to think of leaving Colorado. He had fallen in love with the mountains and could think of no place where he would rather spend his summers. During the following years he returned as often as possible to the health-restoring air and the grandeur of the Rockies. But now, when the call of duty came, he reacted in typical fashion. The party returned from the high country to Walling's Mills. The upward journey had taken four days, but only two were required for their return trip.

Walling returned with them to Denver, where they caught the California-bound train. On September 26 they reached their destination, where they were met and told that the camp meeting was soon to begin. Escorted to the site the next day, they arrived in time for James to preach the opening sermon. [10]

The newcomers were delighted by the reception afforded them and were greatly impressed by the intelligent attitude of the Californians. They had heard much about open-hearted Western hospitality. Now they experienced it.

And after the camp meeting, the California Adventists returned to their homes having feasted spiritually. They had heard James and Ellen White speak a total of thirteen times.

Between meetings the Whites, Loughborough, and Cornell discussed future plans for the work in the golden West. New believers in San Francisco were eager to have a series of tent meetings in their city. When Elder White was invited to lead out, he willingly agreed. A large tent was pitched on Market Street and the first meeting was held on November 8. James was astonished to find the tent so warm that it was necessary to roll up the canvas walls. He remarked on how much colder such an open-air meeting would be in Michigan at that time of year. The meetings continued until the last of November. One listener who came regularly was Mr. Holden, an ex-governor of California. The Whites had the privilege of dining with him in his San Francisco home. [11]

After James and Ellen had worked for the San Francisco church for several weeks Elder Loughborough wrote to the *Review*, "The labors of Brother and Sister White have been a source of great profit to the San Francisco church." [12] He described his feelings as he listened to Elder White on one occasion:

> While Brother White stood in the desk, worn in body, yet with the crowd before him, under the influence of the Spirit of God, powerfully impressing minds, I thought two things: first, Brother White is getting better fast tonight. Second, I thought, Oh! how needful that the minister of Christ have the Spirit of God, to go with the truth to hearts. [13]

James wrote glowing reports for the *Review* concerning the friendly Californians, their mild climate, fertile valleys, and the prospect of building up a mighty work in that State, so much so that friends in the East might have wondered whether they had lost their leaders for good. In one report he wrote:

> Our company . . . have been glad every moment since we met a cordial reception at the end of our long journey at San Francisco, that we were in California. The camp-meeting has not by any means changed our feelings upon the subject. And nothing but stern duty will ever call us from this country. [14]

On September 30 James wrote a letter to his son, Edson, which made it clear that he was not anxious to live in Battle Creek again:

> I am happily disappointed in California, both in the country, and in the condition of the cause. We may stay here till the spring of 1874, then sail to Europe and visit our people in Switzerland. I dread Battle Creek. [15]

The General Conference session at which G. I. Butler became president, had met in December, 1871. No session was held in 1872. When Elder Butler felt that it was time for another session, he placed an announcement in the *Review*, appointing January 8, 1873, as the opening date. He was most anxious for Elder and Mrs. White to attend this conference. But a few days after his notification appeared, he must have received some communication from Elder White, for the following issue of the *Review* carried the following item:

> Brother White has arranged to stay in California longer than was expected when the notice in regard to General Conference was given last week. It will not be held until his return, and the time is therefore postponed until further notice. [16]

As the days of the new year passed and there was still no word from the Whites indicating their plans, Elder Butler decided that the session must not be longer delayed. He therefore announced that it would begin on March 11, 1873, in Battle Creek. He included a further note in which he said, "We deem it of the utmost importance that Brother and Sister White attend this meeting." [17]

Such a plea could not be ignored. The Whites responded by leaving California on the last of February, arriving in Battle Creek on March 4 after a five-day train journey. [18] James came as the delegate representing the State of California.

Also, calls from Europe were increasing for someone to head up the work on the Continent. Adventist finances were in good shape.

Under Elder White's guidance, the *Health Reformer* had increased its influence and circulation. Now that these departments were thriving, Elder White was not so urgently needed to resume his former work, since others could care for the details. Elder Butler agreed. He wrote:

> We trust that Brother White will, under the sanction of the General Conference, be free to occupy that position in the future, so that as his strength will permit, that God has so evidently called him to occupy in the past, not to labor to the exhausting of his strength as heretofore, but to act as counselor, and to give to the cause the benefit of his mature judgment and experience.[19]

Elder and Mrs. White remained in Battle Creek for the remainder of the winter and spring. Two months after the close of the Conference, he relieved Uriah Smith of his editorial duties at the Review, due to "a disagreement . . . over administrative policies." Six months later the rift was healed, and Smith was once again secretary of the General Conference as well as resident *Review* editor.[20]

On April 27, 1873, James White suffered another minor paralytic stroke, and on May 13 yet another. He could but regard these as warnings that must be heeded. Once again he and Ellen, Willie, and Mrs. Hall hastened to the Colorado mountains where they visited their relatives the Wallings. The June 24 *Review* carried a brief note that the post office address of the Whites was Black Hawk, Colorado.

As premonitory winter chill began to descend, the Whites prepared to continue their journey to California. Taking the train northward from Denver they arrived at Cheyenne, a junction with the main overland line. On the train, on the way to Cheyenne, James received a distinct impression that he should attend the twelfth session of the General Conference, scheduled to convene in Battle Creek on November 14. Ellen agreed to go with him, and as a result the group split, James and Ellen going east, Lucinda Hall and other members of the party heading westward.[21]

In a *Review* article in which he discussed the General Conference session James wrote that Elder Andrews would go to Europe soon. "Brother Haskell," White reported, "by the grace of God, is making a great success of the tract and missionary work. This system puts a musket into the hands of every soldier."[22]

At the close of the convocation the Whites, eager to escape the

Michigan winter, prepared to return to warmer California. It was
with regret that the Battle Creek church said good-by to their beloved leaders. Elder Butler wrote, "We sorrow, many of us, at parting
with the servants of the Lord, as they go on their long journey westward." [23]

Just before the Whites' departure, the Battle Creek church
members took a unique step. Unanimously, they elected James
White as head minister of their church, in spite of the fact that it
might be many months before they would see him again. [24] Undoubtedly, James was deeply touched by this gesture.

About two weeks after the Whites left Battle Creek for California, 1874 was ushered in. This was to be a notable year for the
Seventh-day Adventist Church. Naturally, James White would be
involved in helping to make it that kind of year.

[1] M. G. Kellogg letter to Ellen G. White, June 6, 1872.
[2] *Review and Herald,* Sept. 16, 1872.
[3] James White, in *Review and Herald,* July 23, 1872.
[4] ———, in *Review and Herald,* Sept. 3, 1872.
[5] *Ibid.*
[6] Ellen G. White letter 293, 1904.
[7] Ellen G. White manuscript 50, 1902.
[8] *Health Reformer,* Jan., 1873; March, 1873.
[9] *Review and Herald,* Aug. 27, 1872.
[10] *Pioneering the Message,* p. 109.
[11] Ellen G. White letter 20a, to John Harmon, Jan. 21, 1873.
[12] J. N. Loughborough, in *Review and Herald,* Feb. 4, 1873.
[13] *Ibid.,* Dec. 3, 1872.
[14] *Ibid.,* Oct. 22, 1872.
[15] James White letter to Edson White, Sept. 30, 1872.
[16] *Review and Herald,* Dec. 10, 1872.
[17] *Ibid.,* Feb. 11, 1873.
[18] *Ibid.,* March 11, 1873.
[19] *Ibid.,* March 25, 1873.
[20] *SDA Encyclopedia,* article, "Smith, Uriah," p. 1200.
[21] James White, in *Review and Herald,* Dec. 30, 1873.
[22] *Ibid.*
[23] *Ibid.,* Dec. 23, 1873.
[24] *Ibid.,* Dec. 2, 1873.

Chapter Thirty-five

THE GREAT YEAR

I N THE history of the progress of the Seventh-day Adventist Church, few years stand above 1874 in importance. That year brought the founding of the Pacific Press, the sending of Elder J. N. Andrews to Europe as the first American Seventh-day Adventist minister to become an overseas worker, and the establishment of Battle Creek College in suitable quarters.

Although James was involved in all three of these events, he was most closely involved with the first. For some time he had pondered the feasibility of founding a press and printing a missionary paper on the Pacific Coast. He had broached the subject to D. M. Canright while vacationing with him in the Colorado mountains. At the time, Canright felt that the project was too huge for a small denomination to undertake.[1]

In 1868 J. N. Loughborough went to California and in four years built a flourishing work, raising up several churches. As he moved his tent from one location to another, he sold large quantities of Adventist publications. His orders for books from the Review office continually increased. James White was astonished.

"What are you doing with so many books?" he asked. "You are selling more books over there than all of the tent companies east of the Rocky Mountains." He began to consider whether it might be wise to set up a printing plant on the Pacific Coast, thus eliminating shipping charges.[2] Also he envisioned a religious news sheet, published by Adventists and circulated widely west of the Rockies.

During the eventful '70's, James White stood out in the church as a man of foresight and vision. Uriah Smith, who was present at the November, 1873, General Conference session, noticed the advance moves Elder White was recommending, and commented in the church paper, "Brother and Sister White were present with words of counsel and good cheer. The Lord is leading out the mind of Brother White in reference to the great work before us."[3]

Toward the end of December, 1873, James and Ellen arrived once more on the Pacific Coast. During the remainder of that winter they visited various churches. In April, while riding the ferry from Oakland to San Francisco, Ellen remarked to James, "Somewhere in Oakland is the place to locate the paper."[4]

At that time there were only a few Adventists living in Oakland. Certainly if the work was to be established there, a strong church must be raised up in that city. James was aware that Elders Canright and Cornell had decided to pitch their tent to hold meetings in the little town of Cloverdale, north of Healdsburg, but he and his wife both felt that the time was ripe to launch a strong campaign in Oakland. To do this it would be necessary to cancel or postpone the Cloverdale effort.

With a two-horse carriage, husband and wife set out from Petaluma to intercept the evangelists and persuade them to make Oakland their next field of endeavor. On reaching Healdsburg, they learned that the tent and supplies had been taken to a Mr. Seth Bond's place, en route to Cloverdale.[5] Night was approaching, but since the matter was urgent they continued their journey.

Arriving at the Russian River they found its banks overflowing. There was no bridge, only a drift where the water was usually shallow. The question was, "How deep is the water?" Not daring to drive through without knowing the answer, James unhitched one horse and rode him across. Finding the water not too deep or swift, he returned, hitched his horse to the carriage once again and they drove through the current.[6]

Farther on, they came to a wider and apparently deeper stretch of water. James again unhitched one horse and rode carefully through the drift. The water was deep, but he and Ellen decided to risk the crossing. They drove cautiously, the water reaching to the bottom of the carriage box. The Lord guided them that dark night and brought them safely to the Bond home, where they rested. The next morning they caught up with Canright and Cornell. As a result of their urging, the tent went south instead of north, and evangelistic meetings were held in Oakland.[7]

Meanwhile, Elder G. I. Butler, the president of the General Conference, was wondering whether the Whites would be available for the 1874 camp meetings. He knew that in 1872 they had attended only two—Illinois and Iowa. In 1873, James probably went to the Iowa encampment, but when two light strokes warned him of impending physical crisis that spring, he heeded the signals and hurried with his family to the healing of the Colorado mountains.

But the believers in the East felt that without the Whites something vital would be missing from their camp meetings. Elder Butler wrote, urging James and Ellen to attend at least some meetings.

Apparently his request bore fruit, for he was able to place in the *Review* the following notice: "We have received a dispatch from Brother White in California, dated April 10, saying, 'We leave for Michigan the first of next week.'"[8]

But after writing that letter James changed his mind. For in the May 26 *Review* he wrote: "Duties on the Pacific Coast compel us to decline the invitation of the General Conference Committee." We do not know whether the "we" referred to both James and Ellen. If it did, there were some changes made in their plans. For one day as the workers were gathered for a prayer season Ellen saw an angel pointing eastward. She regarded this as a divine indication that it was her duty to go, so on June 4 she started east, accompanied by Willie, leaving James in California.

Correspondence between James, Ellen, and Willie is revealing. For instance, from the deck of the steamer *Antelope*, bound for San Francisco, James wrote to Willie:

> The "HUB" is out here, much sooner than at Battle Creek. I think Brother Butler makes a mistake in making Battle Creek the hub, and making all the rest of the world whirl about it. . . . I am . . . gaining in strength. I milk, harness the horses, and go up and down hill as I have not been able for the past three years.[9]

James also emphasized the fact that once a press was established in California, there would be plenty of work for every member of the White family.

Through letters Ellen wrote to him during the ensuing weeks, James was able to keep in touch with her activities. Since she had so much writing to do, he felt it an imposition to ask for long letters, although he did appreciate frequent ones.

Since the penny-pinching days in Rochester, James had come to appreciate comforts unknown in his pioneering years. In this re-

spect he differed from his wife. Ellen never did reach the place where
strict economy lost its appeal to her thrifty soul. To her it was one of
life's crowning virtues. Knowing her convictions, James wrote to
Willie:

> Take the tenderest care of your dear mother. If she wishes to attend the
> eastern camp meetings, please go with her. Get a tent that will suit you,
> and get everything good in the shape of satchels, blankets, portable chair
> for mother, and do not consent to her economical ideas, leading you to pinch
> along. See that everything like her dresses, shawls, sacques, shoes, bonnet
> et cetera, are *good*. . . . Let your devotion to your mother exceed, if possi-
> ble, that which you manifested to me. She in every way deserves it.[10]

On June 4 the first copy of a new paper came from the Oakland,
California, press. James entitled it the *Signs of the Times.* Under the
masthead, beneath the printed promise that this would be a weekly
publication, a small pointing finger directed the reader to, "Terms:
Two dollars a year to those who choose to pay a subscription price,
and *free* to all others as far as the paper is sustained by the donations
of the liberal friends of the cause." In describing the objectives of
the new paper, White emphasized the fact that it was not intended
to supplant the *Review and Herald.* The *Signs,* he stated, should be
read both by Adventists and by those who knew nothing of their
beliefs. He appealed for help. "Let the true friends of the cause
everywhere" send in donations "from $2.00 to $100 each." He
likewise requested cooperation from the General Conference Committee and from State conference presidents.[11]

Elder White promptly sent copies of that first number of his
paper to Elder Butler, suggesting that he show them to believers
at the various camps. Butler cooperated and took 100 copies to
Iowa where they were bought up at once. Before that meeting ended,
$3,000 had been pledged to help establish a press on the West Coast,
where the paper would be printed.[12]

James revealed an even more ambitious plan for the *Signs* in a
back-page notice of the second number of the periodical:

> WANTED! Ten thousand subscribers wanted. For terms see first page.
> Money, or no money, let the names come in from the Pacific Coast, and
> everywhere else. This is missionary work. We offer no commission to
> agents. Go to work, friends, and get up lists of names. Look up your
> friends and acquaintances, far and near, those you know would read the
> *Signs* with interest and profit, and as you forward their names to this office,
> also notify them and get their consent to take the paper, money or no
> money. We would like to receive 1,000 names, more or less, from our Sev-

enth Day Baptist brethren. Wake up, friends. Let us unite our forces
and let our light shine. [13]

During a number of weeks in mid-1874 correspondence was
lively between Elder Butler and James. Elder Butler continued
urging James to return east to give assistance at camp meetings.
This experience would prove beneficial rather than otherwise to
Elder White's health, reasoned the General Conference president.

I have not yet given up Brother and Sister White's going to them. I
have held on in spite of all your discouraging letters that God would lead
your minds this way. I rejoiced at your telegram, and thought my prayer
was answered. But the letters are strongly setting the other way lately. My
mind has not changed that your only way back to returning health is cheerful, hopeful, *labor among God's people, in faith,* as the Lord has said. You
may rest among the mountains year after year and look down into the
grave, and in my soul I fear you will go there. [14]

James found it hard to resist such appeals, especially when they
started coming from his wife. She wrote:

"Dear Husband. . . . I have no special news to write you, except
I greatly desire to see your face and look forward to the time with
great pleasure." [15]

A week later she wrote again, "All will be rejoiced to see you
here and none more so than your Ellen." [16]

Finally the *Review* announced that Elder White would be leaving California on July 29, in time to attend the Michigan camp
meeting. [17]

While living alone in Oakland, James had ample time to ponder
his moves during the past years. In 1872 he had requested relief from
his heavy burdens. But he had been left with responsibilities—president of the Publishing Association, president of the Health Institute,
and head of many other committees. He had, however, lost the
presidency of the General Conference, and he had even been left off
the Executive Committee. Was this truly what he wanted? Would
it not have been better to wait for the Lord to provide the relief he
needed? In a letter to Elder Butler, James White expressed himself
freely:

O, that I had stood firm in the counsel of God, and had waited in faith
and hope for Him to open the way before me. I now heartily repent, and I
fully believe that God will forgive. But that He will restore me to the
position He designed that I should fill, remains a doubt in my mind. Sometimes faint hope comes up in my mind that God will restore me fully, and
let me finish my course with joy; then the feeling rushes over me, that it is

impossible. I am sorry, my dear brother, that you are compelled to fill the place God designed that I should occupy. I am the loser, you will be the gainer.[18]

By now James had reached the place where he was ready to say, "I will joyfully take any position where I can best serve the cause of God." It may well be that God permitted affliction to strike His servant to bring him to such an attitude. It must have come as a surprise to James White when, at the General Conference session held less than four weeks after he had penned the above words, he was re-elected president of the General Conference, a position he held until 1880.

Sermons he preached during this session made a vivid impression on his listeners. Uriah Smith reported in the *Review:*

The Word was spoken with great power and clearness. Especially was the speaking of Brother White thus characterized throughout. Never, we believe, did he make better points, or present the great truths of this message with more clearness and force.[19]

Another advance step taken at this conference was the final notification to J. N. Andrews that he was to go to Europe as the first regularly appointed Seventh-day Adventist missionary. Elder White commented on this significant event:

Elder J. N. Andrews, who has nobly defended the truth from his very youth, leaves for Europe, probably before these lines shall meet the eyes of the patrons of the *Review*. God bless him.[20]

On September 5, 1874, John Andrews and his two motherless children sailed out of Boston harbor, bound for Great Britain and Switzerland.

Meanwhile, James's plans for the advancement of the work in the West were being strongly encouraged. The generous support of the brethren in the East boosted the program, and it was hoped that $10,000 would be pledged by the California Adventists. Elder Butler, who had stepped down from the presidency, was invited to attend the California camp meeting and encourage the believers to get behind the program.

The camp meeting was held near the small country village of Yountville. Eighty-five tents were pitched. Between four and five hundred campers arrived. As Elder Butler inspected these men and women, many of them dressed in overalls or print dresses, he must have wondered how they could possibly give $10,000. Another

On January 4, 1875, James White gave the opening address marking the dedication of Battle Creek College.

visitor who felt that way remarked that such a motley group couldn't raise enough money to pay for the ink on the first edition of the paper. But pledging soon began, and within a few minutes nearly $20,000 had been given or promised.[21]

Reassuming his administrative responsibilities, James found an important item of unfinished business demanding his attention. The cause of Christian education had been under discussion for several years, and James was strongly convinced that the denomination needed a school in which ministers, printers, teachers, and, ultimately, missionaries, might be trained. That school should be established in the vicinity of Battle Creek.

As early as 1868 Prof. G. H. Bell had conducted a school in Battle Creek. Lacking adequate quarters, it met in the first Battle Creek print shop for a time. After that it moved into the Battle Creek Seventh-day Adventist church, and then into the new Review and Herald building. But if there was going to be a college worthy

of the name, better accommodations were imperative. To raise funds for a new building, Elder Butler and his associates toured the camp meetings, where they succeeded in raising more than $54,000.[22]

The big question was, Where shall the school be situated? Ellen White pled for a rural setting. But the Battle Creek leaders saw advantages in having a college near the *Review* and the sanitarium, as the Health Reform Institute was later called. Students could earn their way through school by working part time in these institutions. Ellen and James White were in California when the committee decided to purchase land in the city of Battle Creek on which to build the college. Ellen wept when she learned of this decision.[23]

Battle Creek College was erected during the last half of 1874. On a bitterly cold Monday morning, January 4, 1875, with the temperature hovering around ten degrees below zero, a large company of patrons and students crowded into the new building. In the chapel they heard James White give the opening address, launching Battle Creek College.[24]

Although Elder White had returned to the East during the summer of 1874, he found it impossible to attend the camp meetings, as Butler had hoped. He later wrote, "We have work for five winters that we would like to do in the very next. We are able to accomplish thrice the amount of labor at present that we have been able to do at any time during the past three years."[25]

As James began his third presidential term, it was with the hope that his days of physical weakness were past. Like any wife, Ellen was concerned about his lifelong habit of overwork, which he had found impossible to break. From the campground in Kirkville, New York, she wrote to him,

> Now dear Husband, do not, I entreat of you, do too much. . . . I think you might remain in Battle Creek if you would not do those things that God has not called you to do. God has not called you to lay sidewalks or move privies. . . . One touch, one word, one look from Him can remove disease, despondency and gloom. Look up, dear Husband. Look up, not down.[26]

Had James been able to accept and practice this advice, he might have enjoyed a longer life-span and been able to accomplish even more for God.

Adventists everywhere had confidence in the man chosen to direct church activities. Thirty years before this the angel of the Lord had

told Ellen, "You can trust James White." God's people knew this to
be true.

---

1 James White, in *Review and Herald*, Aug. 1, 1878.

2 *Pacific Union Recorder*, Feb. 1, 1906, p. 1.

3 Uriah Smith, in *Review and Herald*, Nov. 18, 1873.

4 *Pioneering the Message*, p. 119.

5 *Ibid.*

6 Ellen G. White letter 19e to W. C. White, cir. April 22, 1874.

7 *Pioneering the Message*, pp. 119, 121.

8 *Review and Herald*, April 14, 1874.

9 James White letter to W. C. White, July 5, 1874.

10 *Ibid.*

11 James White, in *Review and Herald*, April 21, 1874.

12 *Ibid.*, June 30, 1874.

13 James White, *Signs of the Times*, June 11, 1874, p. 16.

14 G. I. Butler letter to James White, May 3, 1874.

15 Ellen G. White letter 44 to James White, July 17, 1874.

16 Ellen G. White letter 47 to James White, July 23, 1874.

17 *Review and Herald*, July 28, 1874.

18 James White letter to George I. Butler, July 13, 1874.

19 Uriah Smith, in *Review and Herald*, Aug. 18, 1874.

20 James White, in *Review and Herald*, Sept. 15, 1874.

21 *Pioneering the Message*, pp. 129, 130.

22 *SDA Encyclopedia*, article, "Andrews University," p. 37.

23 Emmett K. Vande Vere, *The Wisdom Seekers* (Nashville, Tenn.: Southern Publishing
Assn., 1972), p. 22.

24 *Ibid.*, p. 25.

25 *Review and Herald*, Nov. 3, 1874.

26 Ellen G. White letter 51 to James White, Sept. 10, 1874.

Chapter Thirty-six

JOURNEYS EAST,
JOURNEYS WEST

FRIENDS and well-wishers thronged the Battle Creek station platform on January 27, 1875, as James and Ellen White, J. H. Waggoner, and young Miss Mary Kelsey boarded the train en route to California.[1]

The young woman in the group became a capable worker in the *Signs* office. Elder White had been aware of her abilities since, at the age of 12, she had entered the office as a folder. The next year she moved into the type-setting department, and ultimately into a responsible place as proofreader. Mary's mother was a widow. The Whites had helped and befriended the struggling Mrs. Kelsey and her children.

It was in the Review office that Willie White and his closest friend, John Harvey Kellogg, had become acquainted with the vivacious Mary. Both young men found her sparklingly attractive, and it was but natural that both should begin making long-range plans involving Mary's future. In 1873, however, John Kellogg went to New York City to attend medical school,[2] and the next year Willie moved to California to help with the new paper, *Signs of the Times.*

After Willie's departure, Ellen invited Mary to help take care of Addie and May Walling, two little nieces who were living in the White home. Each morning and evening Mary helped the children, getting them up and dressed, then getting them to bed at night.[3]

Mary was 17 when James White invited her to accompany him and his wife to California. At the same time he requested her help in the *Signs* building in Oakland. This must have been an exciting prospect for her. And who can say that the prospect was not brightened by the fact that Willie White would be working in the same office.

Little is known about the romance that developed between her and Willie in Oakland. But about twelve months after her arrival in California, the following news note, written by James White, appeared in the *Health Reformer:*

> Mary Kelsey. Marriage of, to W. C. White: On the evening of February 9, were married in Oakland, California, Willie C. White, youngest son of Elder James White, and Mary E. Kelsey, both of whom have resided until recently in this place. Both parties are persons of marked ability and numerous amiable qualities, which have won for them hosts of friends. The news of their marriage will not be received with any less pleasure on account of its having been long anticipated. We are happy to state that our friends are thorough hygienists. The *Reformer* extends to them its warmest congratulations and best wishes. We have unbounded faith in their future happiness and prosperity, and predict for them a career of wide usefulness.
>
> Mr. and Mrs. W. C. White are spending a short vacation in Petaluma, preparatory to another year's work in connection with the *Signs of the Times.*[4]

Before leaving Oakland in 1874, James and Ellen purchased a plot of land four miles out of the city. During their absence that summer and fall a modest home was built for them, and it was ready for occupancy when they returned. They remained in this home until 1878, when they bought land near Healdsburg.[5]

The first few issues of the *Signs* were printed on a commercial press in Oakland.[6] This was not a happy arrangement as far as James was concerned. He was reminded of the days back in 1851 and 1852 when he had to resort to such facilities when publishing the second volume of the *Review and Herald* in Saratoga Springs, New York. The same necessity that had led him to establish a denominational press then was now apparent for the *Signs*. The Adventist Church in California must have its own press, James declared.

Thanks to the generosity of the believers at the Yountville camp meeting, described in a previous chapter, and some assistance from members east of the Rockies, money was in hand for building a publishing office. A special session of the California constituency was called to decide on its location. Perhaps James made it known that Ellen had been shown that the office should be located in or near Oakland. At any rate, it was decided to build it there. An 80-by-100-foot lot was purchased on the corner of 12th and Castro streets. A Brother O. B. Jones, who had erected the new Review building, was invited to construct what came to be called the Pacific Press.[7]

James White led out in building the first Pacific Press plant, Oakland, California. It was patterned after the Review and Herald building, Battle Creek.

With camp meetings a vital part of Adventist life, James considered early in 1875 whether he should plunge into their demanding schedules that year. During the previous four years Ellen had attended some camp meetings, but he, scarcely any. The church's leaders remembered the exhausted protests made by him and Ellen after their last complete round of the camps, and were concerned at the prospect of losing James's services altogether. But James soon put their fears at rest for that year. In response to their question he inserted the following two notes in the *Review:*

"We hope to visit all our conferences and home missions during the present year in company with Mrs. W." [8]

"We hope to attend all the camp-meetings, closing up the season at the California encampment, and the North Pacific Mission." [9]

With this cheering information, conference presidents, confident that attendance at the 1875 gatherings would be the largest ever, proceeded to map out a schedule so that the camps would not overlap. *Review* readers rejoiced when they learned of the Whites' plans for the summer.

The Whites arrived in Battle Creek the first part of May, where they visited for a few days. By May 22 they were at Bowling Green, Ohio, starting their first camp meeting of the season. It would be tedious to describe every camp the Whites attended that summer. Ellen's description of one will suffice:

> Now you will wish to hear something about the meetings here. We have had excellent freedom. The people are hungry for the word of God. Some were one week coming in their large covered wagons. One man traveled in this way 300 miles; he spent ten days in making the journey, and did not reach the campground till the last day of the meeting. Delegates came from Missouri, begging for help in their State. Such entreaties I never heard before.[10]

Even while traveling, James carried on a voluminous correspondence with workers in all parts of the field—in California, Oregon, Europe, and elsewhere. Most of his writing was done on the train, while hurrying from one appointment to another. Written under such conditions his letters were not easy to read. Almost invariably he signed them, "In haste, James White." Regretfully he had to admit that he had not even found time to answer urgent letters from Elder Andrews in Europe. Because of such pressures he expressed the hope that he would be released at the next General Conference session from some of the offices he was holding.[11]

Between the eastern and western camp meetings, the Whites stayed with friends in Battle Creek. When word came that the new building in Oakland was nearing completion, James traveled to New York to purchase equipment for it. Since some of the pledges made at Yountville had not been redeemed, he found it necessary to sell both his properties in Battle Creek in order to raise funds to buy a press.[12] The equipment he purchased cost about $10,000.[13]

Sacrifices by the Whites such as they made on this occasion were not uncommon. Many times in the past they had felt compelled to act similarly. But there had been times when there was no lack of funds. James could recall meeting a man at a Vermont camp meeting who had $300 in his pocket to give to the cause. "What branch of the work most needs means?" he had asked.

James replied, "No branch of the work is in want of means." So his friend took his cash home with him.[14]

Now, in 1875, calls were coming from all sides. The Signs office in Oakland needed funds for additional equipment and to cancel a debt incurred in getting out the early editions of the paper. From

Switzerland Elder Andrews was appealing for money in order to establish a press in Europe. The sanitarium needed to be enlarged. The college, overcrowded and in need of additional equipment, could have absorbed thousands of dollars immediately. In addition, other fields were crying out for help.

Feeling almost a parental concern for the spiritual condition of workers, helpers, patients, and students at the three institutions in Battle Creek, James and Ellen were made especially happy to see John Harvey Kellogg, who had recently received his medical diploma, beginning practice as a staff physician at the Health Institute.[15] The young man was already working hard to raise the standards of the Health Reform Institute, which was later renamed the Battle Creek Sanitarium.

One Sabbath afternoon James and Ellen White with Uriah Smith from the Review office, Prof. Sidney Brownsberger from Battle Creek College, and Dr. Kellogg, went out of town to a grove not far from Goguac Lake. There they talked and planned and prayed. Each leader solemnly vowed that he would do everything in his power to "stand together for the right" against "disorganizing and distracting spirits." Unable to engrave their vows on nearby trees, they cut five notches with a jackknife in a trunk of a tree as a reminder of the promises they had made to God and to one another on that spot.[16]

One of James's peculiar strengths lay in his ability to choose workmen. He was a shrewd judge of character. The confidence he had in John Kellogg had led him to lend a thousand dollars to the young man to assist in his medical education.

James could forgive almost any failing except laziness. Had he been asked to read from his Bible a sentiment spelling out his philosophy of life in this respect he might very well have turned to 1 Corinthians 14:12 and quoted, "Seek that ye may excel to the edifying of the church."

An illustration of his methods in choosing and training men is seen in his experience with D. M. Canright. James told the story at a large gathering in Battle Creek:

When about 21 years of age, he [Canright] came from Coldwater to talk with me on the subject of his preaching. I spent about an hour with him. I said to him, Do not content yourself with being a small preacher, but be somebody, or die, trying. Do not go out to be a pet, but go out into the field, with the weight of the work upon you, with steady principles, and stand your ground. The last thing I did, was to present him with one of our English Bibles, and a pair of charts, saying as I did so, Here, Dudley, take these, and go out and try it. When you become satisfied that you have made a mistake, bring them back. The next May at the Conference, I met him, and asked him, What about those charts and Bible? He replied, "Brother White, you have lost them." Thank God! I would like to lose more in the same way. We raised means to purchase a library for Brother Canright and Brother Van Horn. And I said to them, When you study, study with all your might, and when you visit, visit with all your might, and exercise briskly. Whatever you do, do it with all your might.[17]

James was re-elected president of the General Conference at the annual session held at Battle Creek in mid-August.[18] Then he and Ellen were out in the field again, hurrying from meeting to meeting in Vermont, Maine, New York, and Michigan.

James and Ellen were saddened to note that the majority of those present at the New England and New York camp meetings were middle-aged or elderly people. The youth from Seventh-day Adventist families, having attended non-Adventist schools, had drifted from the church and could now hardly be reached by the message. James challenged the church to get behind the college at Battle Creek and make it possible for more Adventist youth to attend.[19]

The Whites were to attend camp meetings in Kansas and Missouri, which were scheduled to be held the end of July. But they were postponed because the grain harvest would come just at that time.[20] This meant the Whites would miss those meetings.

Having engagements in California to meet, they hurried to Battle Creek to prepare for their long journey to that State. There was, in James White's words:

Rush, packing trunks, valises, and baskets, for nearly a week's journey, giving ourselves but four and five hours' sleep each night. . . . But we are not weary of the work. We are filled with hope, courage, and faith, and design to extend our labors, and what influence the Lord gives us, as never before.[21]

They were returning to California to spend the winter. The train wound its way over the Sierra Nevada Mountains, then down onto the lowlands. As they were nearing Oakland, James opened the window and began tossing out scraps from their food basket. That was, of course, in a time when the population was sparse, before people realized the urgency of environmental protection. He picked up an empty bottle and prepared to hurl it out onto the right-of-way, when Ellen exclaimed, "Stop! Please, James, I can use that bottle."

James sighed. He looked at the bulging overhead racks, the floor, the aisle, all crowded with their luggage. Where could he put the bottle? With a hurried, "Oh, what's the use?" he tossed it quickly out the open window.

Understanding his mood and yet reproachful, Ellen remarked, "Well, James, you might at least have saved the cork."

On September 24 the couple arrived in Oakland. The next day was the first Sabbath of the California camp meeting. James preached during the eleven o'clock service.

James was pleased to find the presses running smoothly and the work in the Signs office progressing well. His two sons, Edson and Willie, with their wives were at the press. It had been a long time since the White families had lived and worked so closely together.

[1] Uriah Smith, in *Review and Herald*, Jan. 28, 1875.

[2] Richard William Schwarz, *John Harvey Kellogg, M.D.*, p. 149.

[3] Ellen G. White letter 78 to Lucinda Hall, Dec. 2, 1874.

[4] *Health Reformer*, March, 1876, p. 96.

[5] Ellen G. White letter 40 to Willie and Mary, Dec. 5, 1877.

[6] *Pioneering the Message*, p. 128.

[7] *Ibid.*, p. 131.

[8] James White, in *Review and Herald*, Jan. 8, 1875.

[9] *Ibid.*, April 1, 1875.

[10] Ellen G. White letter 16a to Edson and Emma, October 1870.

[11] James White, in *Review and Herald*, June 17, 1875.

[12] James White letter to W. C. White, June 2, 1875; *Review and Herald*, July 29, 1875; July 22, 1875.

[13] *Review and Herald*, July 29, 1875.

[14] James White, in *Review and Herald*, Nov. 4, 1875.

[15] *SDA Encyclopedia*, article, "Battle Creek Sanitarium."

[16] James White, in *Review and Herald*, June 1, 1876.

[17] *Ibid.*, May 20, 1873.

[18] *Review and Herald*, Aug. 26, 1875.

[19] James White, in *Review and Herald*, Sept. 30, 1875.

[20] *Ibid.*, July 8, 1875.

[21] *Ibid.*, Sept. 23, 1875.

Chapter Thirty-seven

FAMILY HEARTACHES

URING the year 1876, the General Conference met in session no less than three times—March 31, September 19, and November 12. So rapidly was the work expanding, so urgent were the appeals for help that Elder James White, General Conference president, felt it essential to summon the leaders frequently for planning sessions.

At this time James was at the height of his powers spiritually and mentally. He had progressed greatly during the past twenty-seven years, since that day when the paper *Present Truth* had been launched in Middletown, Connecticut. In every forward move of the church he had played a vital role—beginning with the publishing work, organization, choosing a name, development of the Health Reform Institute. Also, a college had been started. Missionaries had been sent to California, where a strong work was developing. A missionary paper had been born in the West and a publishing house had been built and was operating there. Elder Andrews was in Europe grappling with awesome problems, yet moving ahead in strong lines.

Behind all this stood Ellen White, counseling, warning, guiding, and inspiring her husband. Many times when he faltered, James would have given up the struggle had it not been for messages sent by God to him through her pen and voice.

Each owed a great deal to the other. Ellen's heroic move in the winter of 1866-1867, of taking her husband to workers' meetings and then on short preaching tours after his stroke, helped restore his mental powers and made him realize that God still had an important work for him to do. The following spring, by moving to a farm, she helped him rebuild the physical powers he would need for the struggle ahead. When well, James was a tower of strength to his wife. He provided well for his family. He assisted her in preparing her books and testimonies for publication and circulation.

Alike in their complete dedication to the cause of God and in many other ways also, their personalities were nevertheless very different. James recognized this when he first thought of marrying Ellen. He said that although he was her complete opposite in nearly every way, still he could see they would make an excellent working team.

James believed in and practiced the three rules for a happy life laid down by John Wesley: Earn all you can, save all you can, give all you can. Ellen had no difficulty with the second and third principles, but found the first one more involved. She admitted that she lacked the ability her husband possessed, that of bringing in means. Both were generous with whatever they had and shared it freely with others.[1]

All through their married life their home relationships were tender and close. When separated by the demands of the work they greatly missed each other's companionship. A few months before his death James could write:

> Marriage marks an important era in the lives of men. "Whoso findeth a wife findeth a good thing, and obtaineth favor of the Lord," is the language of wisdom. Proverbs 18:22. . . . We were married August 30, 1846, and from that hour unto the present she has been my crown of rejoicing.[2]

A few weeks after her husband's death, as Ellen sought a little rest and retirement in a cabin they used as a retreat in the Rocky Mountains, she commented in a letter to her son William:

> I miss Father more and more. Especially do I feel his loss while here in the mountains. I find it a very different thing being in the mountains with my husband and in the mountains without him. I am fully of the opinion that my life was so entwined or interwoven with my husband's that it is about impossible for me to be of any great account without him.[3]

One problem that James faced at times was how he should receive counsel and instruction from his wife, dealing as it did with a wide spectrum of subjects. There was no question in his mind when she said, "I have a message for you." He wrote that on hearing God's message as given to him through Ellen, he trembled and obeyed. When they did not perfectly agree in regard to matters of lesser importance, such as the purchase of land or furniture, she went along with his decisions, taking the position that ordinary opinions of hers might be wise but not necessarily inspired. In between, there were other areas where differences of opinion might prevail, just as in any other marriage. And, it will be remembered, they were both strong-minded individuals.

In 1878, when James was looking for a man to head up the work in England, Ellen wrote to him:

"Why are you thinking Elder Loughborough [is] the man for Old England? . . . I should select others before him. . . . Hurrying Loughborough to Old England is in my mind an oversight in judgment." [4]

In his later years, when well and with buoyant spirits, James could accomplish wonders. When ill, he quickly became discouraged and felt that he could accomplish little or nothing. His severe stroke had left its marks. There were times when he even seemed unreasonable.

One subject over which James and Ellen disagreed was the course pursued by their son Edson and how they should handle him. This young man, in spite of his parents' repeated warnings, spent money far too freely. In his youth and after his marriage he was always getting into debt. Time after time ambitious enterprises involved him in financial loss. His father repeatedly settled Edson's financial obligations. But to a man with the financial acumen James had, such irresponsibility was well-nigh unforgivable—particularly so when so frequently repeated. In the end, the father lost all patience with his elder son and tried to keep as far away from him and his problems as possible.

Ellen's mother heart went out to Edson. She wrote him almost nonstop, letters containing motherly counsels, caution, and advice. She did what she could to soften the attitude of James toward Edson when his son became involved in his oft-repeated shaky financial ventures. The fact that Willie was so different—steady, upright, cautious—made it all the more difficult for the older of the two boys.

It may seem strange, but both James and Ellen confided freely in Willie. One letter revealing this confidence, written from the East by the heartsore father to the 21-year-old Willie, helps throw light on a complex situation and the involved inter-family relationships.

I have read your mother's letter in another envelope. She can go to California. . . . But I shall wait for radical changes before I go. If mother would not always blame me when Edson abuses me, and would take a firm stand for the right with me, I think I would consent to live in the same State where Edson may reside. But until I see a radical change in both Edson and mother, I do not expect to go to California.[5]

In the spring of 1876, James traveled eastward alone. In a letter to him Ellen, deeply involved in her writing, explained her reasons for not accompanying him:

I would enjoy attending the camp meetings if God said Go. I have no light as yet to go. The pillar of fire is here yet, when it moves I would move also. I want to follow it. I have no will of my own, I want to do God's will. At present His will is to tarry in California and make the most of my time in writing.[6]

Accepting the situation, James replied,

I trust the Lord will lead you in duty. If you feel free to write, and are not urged by the Spirit to attend camp meetings, by all means stay. . . . Should you come, I shall join you.[7]

Although at this time they were separated by almost the width of a continent and their communications indicate divergent points of view, Ellen kept her sense of balance and her spirit, refusing to be upset. Always tender in their relationships and each deeply concerned for the other, they kept in touch by letters when separated. One day the mail brought a post card from James. In replying to it, Ellen first quoted what he had written, then commented on it: "Battle Creek, April 11. No letters from you for two days. James White."

Then, in humorous vein, she replied: "This lengthy letter was written by yourself. Thank you for we know you were living. No letter from James White previous to this since April 6. . . . I have been anxiously waiting for something to answer."[8]

In a letter to his wife written about this same time from Battle Creek, James indicated his feelings:

Dear Ellen. . . . As long as your strength holds out, and you are free, stick to your writing. But don't try to write when strength fails, and you do not feel called out to write. . . . I am very strong and active. [I] Walk much. I never felt so free. . . . I think I shall speak [Sabbath]. I am perfectly free here.[9]

Ellen replied,

I get no light in dreams or in any other way to attend camp meetings. I pray for light. . . . You are happy and cheerful. I am the same. The Lord has in His providence arranged matters that we both can work and not get in each other's way.[10]

This was neither the first nor the last time that the Whites felt it expedient to work apart. On several occasions in the last few years of his life, as James became more dominating, Ellen knew that the only course she could take to spare her writings from outside influences was to work alone. But the periods of separation were followed by close association at home and equally close teamwork in the field.

Of one such time, when she chose to work in California while her husband carried responsibilities at Battle Creek, she wrote to him:

Although I miss you very, very much, and love you, yet I feel at present I belong to God to wait for and do His will. I tell you freely it is a great sacrifice to my feelings to have you separated from me as you are, and yet it seems to be that it is as God would have it, and I must be reconciled. It has been hard, so hard.

I wept and prayed and pondered and wept again, and the steady conviction forces itself upon me that it is right as it is. God's work is great. It demands our first attention. Separated as we are, we shall not be influenced by each other but we shall look to God separately and do our work in His fear and to His glory.[11]

After writing that she would not attend camp meetings that year, 1876, Ellen later reversed her decision; her "pillar of cloud" must have moved eastward. A telegram was received in Battle Creek announcing that Mrs. White and her niece, Miss Mary Clough, would arrive at the Kansas camp meeting on May 26, and that she hoped to see her husband there. In concluding a report on this development, James wrote:

"We shall probably go the rounds of the camp meetings for 1876, and retire from the Northern climate in October, either to the South or to California." [12]

He then took the next train for Kansas, where he and Ellen joined forces. It was the beginning of the last continuous camp meeting tour for the Whites, going from one to another in rapid succession. Never again did James's health permit him to make such a circuit.

The couple soon adopted the by-now familiar pattern of camp life. Pack boxes, board the train, ride for hours to the next campground, be met at some out-of-the-way crossing, preach—three,

four, or even five times. Then camp would close, and they were
on the road again. It is surprising that they kept as well as they did.
On a train bound for Maine, James wrote in a letter to Willie some
of the problems travelers of that day had to face:

> I found time to take a bath the other day, the first in twenty-five days,
> and was surprised to find my skin as white and clear and fresh as a babe's.

> Your mother is splendid. The terrible hot weather, with the help of
> beet tops, string beans and the like, took her down "right smart," but she
> is coming up, and is cheerful, with us on the train.[13]

All that summer they continued their ceaseless pace, attending
fourteen out of fifteen camp meetings. One, held at Groveland,
near Boston, was the largest Seventh-day Adventist camp meeting
ever held up to that time.

It was estimated that 20,000 persons poured out of Boston and
surrounding cities for the Sunday meetings. Mrs. White spoke that
afternoon. Special trains brought throngs, and loaded river steamers pushed up the Merrimac to Groveland. Ellen was unusually
blessed with vocal ability. Her message was well received, and her
voice carried clearly to the far limits of the crowd.[14]

Camp meetings over, the Whites, exhausted, took the train for
Oakland, California. On the trip James had a premonition that this
was the last time he and Ellen would do the camp meeting circuit,
and he was correct. Deeply concerned, Ellen wrote to her son about
James:

> I am worn; your father is worn. We both work too hard. . . . I look
> all over the field and I see none who could fill your father's place. His head
> to plan and his life of experience to balance the inexperienced is very es-
> sential. God has a work for us to do, and we need the help, the encourage-
> ment and confidence of our people to do this work.[15]

The next spring the Whites returned to Battle Creek where
they spent much of that summer. James worked hard trying to fill
the various positions to which he had been assigned. He and Ellen
did attend some of the later camp meetings, though multiplying
symptoms indicated to James that he might soon be on the receiving
end of yet another stroke. But just doing the things that had to be
done kept him hard at work on his heavy program.

S. N. Haskell had been particularly eager to obtain the services
of James and Ellen at the New England camp meeting, which was
to be held again at Groveland in northeastern Massachusetts.
James almost decided not to go, because of worry about his health.

In preparation for the trip East he had labored early and late, then suffered what proved to be a light stroke, though at first not clearly perceived as such.[16] In their Battle Creek home, after praying earnestly for guidance, both James and Ellen were impressed to follow their practice of former years, stepping out by faith and trusting that God would sustain and strengthen them. So they went. James's health did not improve, but neither did it deteriorate.

After resting a few days at the Haskell home in South Lancaster, they were to go north to attend the Vermont camp meeting. At a small gathering held in the Haskell home on the evening of their arrival James reviewed his experience. He confessed that he had not always viewed matters in the right light[17] and, remembering his weakness and many mistakes, he felt deeply humbled. Ellen declared that "In much care and in the many burdens he has become unsympathizing and too severe."[18]

At the camp meeting in Vermont, James became ill. Lying on an invalid's bed he had time to think seriously. Reviewing the events of the previous years and the ten years since his crippling stroke in Battle Creek, he came to some important conclusions. He talked freely and frankly with Ellen, and she wrote to the boys, who had been well aware of the problem, particularly from events of the previous year. In her letter to Edson and Emma she wrote:

> Your father is painfully conscientious, which makes it hard for him to cling to faith for himself but he is steadily coming up and he views the case of your mother very differently than he has for the last ten years. He thinks he must have been blinded by the enemy. The scales have fallen from his eyes. We are in perfect harmony in views and feelings. I never enjoyed his company so much in years as I do now.[19]

She wrote to Willie and Mary in a similar vein:

> He does not suffer bodily pain but his great trouble is battling with depression of spirits. He seems to feel that he has wronged me very much. He goes back to the letters he wrote me when he was in California, and you and I attended the camp meetings. He feels that he has committed a great sin that the Lord can hardly forgive. My work is to comfort him . . . to speak cheerful, loving words to him and soothe him as a little child.[20]

She knew that her husband was in precarious health. But by the time the two were ready to turn their eyes westward, he was making a slow comeback.

It was in early October that the Whites, with Miss Clough, left Battle Creek for Oakland, where they planned to spend the winter.

A few days after they arrived in Oakland, James and Ellen, Miss Clough and Mrs. Lucinda Hall, set out on a tour of Adventist churches in the Sonoma and Russian River valleys. On the first Sabbath in December they met with the San Francisco church. James White preached, then Ellen "exhorted" for forty minutes. The next Sabbath they spent in Petaluma. There was scarcely a Sabbath during that winter when these workers did not have a church appointment.

Weekdays were spent in Oakland. As long as James White was nearby, the editors and manager of Pacific Press brought their problems to him. Ellen, sensing that her husband would be in danger healthwise if this situation continued, wondered whether there was any refuge where they might obtain rest and find time for recuperation of health.[21]

[1] Ellen G. White letter 61 to John White, Nov. 27, 1884.
[2] *Life Sketches* (1888), pp. 125, 126.
[3] Ellen G. White letter 17 to W. C. White, Sept. 12, 1881.
[4] Ellen G. White letter 39 to James White, July 8, 1878.
[5] James White letter to W. C. White, June 7, 1876.
[6] Ellen G. White letter 4 to James White, April 7, 1876.
[7] James White letter to Ellen G. White, April 18, 1876.
[8] Ellen G. White letter 5 to James White, April 11, 1876.
[9] James White letter to Ellen G. White, April 21, 1876.
[10] Ellen G. White letter 23 to James White, May 10, 1876.
[11] Ellen G. White letter 32 to James White, June 24, 1878.
[12] *Review and Herald,* May 25, 1876, p. 168.
[13] James White letter to W. C. White, July 19, 1876.
[14] *Origin and History,* vol. 2, p. 13.
[15] Ellen G. White letter 41 to Edson and Emma, Aug. 24, 1876.
[16] Ellen G. White letter 19 to Edson and Emma, Sept. 28, 1877.
[17] Ellen G. White letter 11 to Dear Children, Aug. 31, 1877.
[18] *Ibid.*
[19] Ellen G. White letter 16 to Edson and Emma, Sept. 7, 1877.
[20] Ellen G. White letter 13 to Willie and Mary, Sept. 3, 1877.
[21] Ellen G. White letter 40 to Willie and Mary, Dec. 5, 1877.

Chapter Thirty-eight

OUT OF WEAKNESS MADE STRONG

BY THE beginning of December, 1877, Ellen knew that her husband was a very sick man. The cause and nature of his illness was difficult to determine; probably James was in danger of nervous collapse. But one thing his wife did know—they must get away from Oakland, where Adventist leaders continually pressed their problems upon him. For the same reasons, they had fled Battle Creek ten years before. So Ellen persuaded her husband to take a trip with her into the beautiful Sonoma Valley, about forty miles from Oakland, where they might purchase a small acreage and build a quiet country home.

Two miles from Healdsburg they found what they were searching for. A fifteen-acre plot of land was offered to them. Much of it was in forest—manzanita, madrone, and evergreens. There was one tiny cottage, and into this they moved in December. There they would live until a more adequate home could be built.[1] Mrs. Lucinda Hall was with them, helping Ellen all she could to make the sick man comfortable.

Meanwhile, another interesting development was taking place in the Napa Valley, about thirty miles from Healdsburg. Six months previous to this, J. N. Loughborough and I. D. Van Horn had secured from a new convert, W. A. Pratt, ten and a half acres of land on the slopes of Howell Mountain on which to erect a health retreat similar to the one in Battle Creek.[2] These men invited Elder and Mrs. White to visit the site and give their advice. The Whites were happy to comply.

While in Napa Valley they were entertained in the William Pratt home, nestled just under the hill below the proposed Health Institute. Seven years later, on a nearby site, Robert Pratt, brother to William, built a house that would in later years be visited by thousands of Seventh-day Adventists from all over the world. This house was purchased in 1901 by Ellen White and it was her home until her death in 1915. She named it Elmshaven, and by that name it has become world famous. Certainly she and James could never have dreamed of such a possibility as they sat relaxed before the fire in the Pratt parlor that chill December day.[3] James and Ellen loved their Healdsburg cottage. They found the change from city bustle to country serenity very relaxing. James was not well, and his wife was distressed by some of his strange ideas. She wrote courageously to Willie and Mary, who were in Battle Creek:

> We are seeing already the beneficial effects of this move from Oakland. Father's mind is diverted. He eats more liberally and it does not injure him. . . . He is cheerful. He is so pleased with his home. He tries to do what he can and is busy from morning till night about something. . . . I am glad for every step he advances, climbing the hill of health.[4]

The road back to the summit of that hill was to prove long and wearisome. Accustomed to activity, James was both puzzled and dismayed by his frailties. When circulatory difficulties attacked his hands and feet, he tried every possible remedy. When one form of treatment failed to bring quick improvement, he tried something else. In her perplexity, Ellen again confided in Willie:

> I have felt greatly perplexed to know just what to do in the case of your father. He seems to have mind enough, but is forever studying his own feelings, which eclipses faith. He gets habits and notions, such as wetting his head and hands and feet. All these are innocent, but carried to excess are doing him great injury. . . . The restlessness, wanting to be riding continually, is very difficult to manage. . . . All these habits keep his mind centered upon himself.

She concluded her letter pathetically—"I feel so sorry for poor father."[5]

James was also suffering from the recurrence of a troublesome problem he had experienced when recovering from his stroke in Michigan—insomnia. Often he went two and three nights at a time with no sleep at all. On one such occasion he, Ellen, and Lucinda climbed a nearby hill where they had a season of prayer. When they returned to the house James lay down, but sleep still refused to come. Following Biblical instruction, they then anointed him and prayed again that he might find rest. But there was no change. A third time they prayed. After that, James lay down and almost immediately fell asleep.[6]

His hands and feet became swollen and sore. Seeking relief, he visited treatment rooms in Oakland operated by an Adventist, Andrew Brorsen, and found some help. He also went to the nearby well-known Litton Springs, where many sufferers found relief in the hot mineral baths. He wrote to Dr. Kellogg, describing his symptoms and asking advice. But for a while everything he tried brought only temporary relief.

Meanwhile the General Conference was virtually leaderless. Facing complicated problems, the leading men in Battle Creek met in a special General Conference session on March 1, 1878.[7] Unable to face the journey or the problems to be met at its end, James sent regrets. S. N. Haskell was appointed as president pro tem. James did prepare an address which he sent to be read. He stated that this was the first session since the organization of the General Conference that he had failed to attend. The address arrived too late and had to be printed in the *Review*.[8]

Gradually the rheumatic pains in James's hands and feet lessened, and he felt sufficiently improved to be able to attend an annual meeting of the Publishing Association in Oakland. Reporting to *Review* readers, he wrote that his hands and feet troubled him, but that he had gained eleven pounds and was feeling better. He hoped to spend some time in Colorado, and hoped to attend the General Conference session to convene in October.[9]

But even when suffering most severely, James had not been inactive during that winter he spent in Healdsburg. He and Ellen often visited among the churches, traveling as far as Oakland and San Francisco to meet with the believers. When James spoke, he could feel the healing, strengthening hand of God upon him. Ellen watched with intense eagerness the gradual disappearance of James's symptoms. It had been a nerve-racking time for her as well as for him. She wrote to Willie: "For eight months I have been on a constant strain of anxiety and now I feel the care lifted somewhat. I feel as though I was running down like an old clock but I shall rally again soon."[10]

Meanwhile, the work in Oregon and Washington territories to the north was just getting started. Eager to help, Ellen decided to respond to an invitation from believers there that she attend camp meeting, to be held near Salem. She was relieved that James's recovery was such that she might safely leave him for a time.

Shortly after Ellen left by ship for Oregon, James boarded a train for Battle Creek. When he arrived there on June 5, the brethren in the various institutions rejoiced to see their leader again. To promote the continuing return to health, Elder White went to the Sanitarium and took treatments regularly. The *Review* editor reported to his readers,

He spends much of his time in the open air, but gives considerable attention to works which he is preparing for the press; and we have been happy to have his counsel in some of the board meetings of the different institutions located here.[11]

During his stay at Battle Creek, James foresaw that the time would soon come when the local church building would be far too small to house the regular congregation, let alone the students that would attend Battle Creek College, and the large number of believers who might wish to attend general assemblies there. He suggested that a structure be built that would accommodate 3,000 people. To finance such an ambitious project, he suggested that each Seventh-day Adventist lay aside a dime a month for a year. If this were faithfully done, the building could be paid for in twelve months.[12] His plan was adopted and the church erected. As long as the large building stood it was known as the Dime Tabernacle.

James described the dimensions of the large, imposing building:

The main auditorium will seat 900 persons. This is surrounded by a north, an east, and a south vestry, seating respectively 250, 350, and 250 persons. These rooms are separated from the main auditorium by ground-glass sliding partitions, which can all be raised when necessary, throwing the entire lower floor into one room, capable of seating at least 1,750 persons. A gallery running around three sides, seats 800; wall-seats and chairs, 650 more; giving the entire building a seating capacity for 3,200 persons. The height of the central dome is 66 feet, clock tower, 108 feet. . . . The cost of the tabernacle was less than $27,000.

It was dedicated April 20, 1879, and by actual count, 3,649 persons were present. For our own use, the Battle Creek church does not need so large a place of worship, but on special occasions, which will become more frequent in the future, there is need of just such a house as the Battle Creek Tabernacle.[13]

James was not present at the dedication. About the time it was dedicated, he wrote to Willie from Denison, Texas, where he was preparing a caravan to travel to Colorado via Kansas. In his letter he barely mentioned Battle Creek doings: "Your report of Tabernacle

The idea for the Dime Tabernacle was conceived by James White. It was dedicated in 1879 and destroyed by fire in 1922.

and the various funds is rather encouraging." [14]

But his heart was at the center of Adventist work. Now, whenever he visited Battle Creek, he was impressed and pleased by the flourishing condition of its institutions. An addition was built on the Sanitarium, which could now treat three hundred patients. The Publishing Association likewise was prospering. [15]

Commenting on the stability of our institutions, James pointed out that no one who had taken stock in them had ever lost a dollar, while over a five-year period, Adventists had lost no less than $100,000 through poor investments. [16]

As the hot summer drew on, James found himself longing for the coolness of the Colorado mountains. He decided to go there, and he asked D. M. Canright and Mary, Willie's wife, to accompany him. On the evening of July 4 they boarded a train headed for Denver. Willie, working in Battle Creek, could not get away just then, but hoped to join the group later. [17] Mrs. Canright was suffering from tuberculosis. At first her husband hoped to take her to Colorado, but when the departure date arrived, she was too weak to travel.

Once more in his beloved mountains, James made excellent progress healthwise. Returning from Oregon, en route to the Eastern camp meetings, Ellen enjoyed a week of relaxation with her husband and daughter-in-law in Colorado. Then with Emma, her other daughter-in-law, as a traveling companion she went on to meet her appointments.

When Willie managed at last to get away from his responsibilities and join the party in the mountains, James felt that his cup of joy was full to overflowing. A letter from Ellen brought cheer also. She urged the vacationing group to enjoy themselves, so that they might be rested and refreshed when they took up their work again.

On August 12 Elder Canright left for Battle Creek, having received word from the sanitarium doctors that his wife, Lucretia, was fast losing strength. [18] But Edson's arrival brought joy to the father's heart. Differences reconciled, father and two sons enjoyed vacationing together. All too soon, however, crisp fall days began, and they had to travel to Battle Creek to attend the forthcoming General Conference sessions scheduled for early October.

Hundreds of visitors were flocking into town. Since the local

The Whites' cabin near Boulder, Colorado, where James and Ellen savored the mountain atmosphere.

church building was far too small and the Tabernacle would not be built until the following year, a large tent was pitched that would seat 1,000 persons.

Sabbath was a long-to-be-remembered day for everyone. In the morning, Elder White spoke with power to the large congregation for an hour and ten minutes.[19] His wife could scarcely believe that the speaker was the same man she had nursed through a torturing period of invalidism eight months before. She praised God for His mercy, and for His lovingkindness to the children of men.

Elder White also had much for which to be thankful. His fatherly heart was touched as he saw his son, Edson, leading the congregation in song, using the latest hymnbook compiled by himself—the *Song Anchor*. Emma was present also. James White often referred to this musical pair as his two canaries. That summer James was very hopeful for his two sons. From Colorado he had written to Willie, boasting a little: "You and Edson will come out all right. If you did not put your whole soul into what you are doing, you would not be like your father. Neither would you amount to much."[20]

For the time being, Edson, who had given his father so many heartaches, was a source of fatherly pride.

18   It must have seemed like old times to the delegates at the

General Conference session to have James presiding. It is not surprising that the Committee on Resolutions introduced one expressing gratitude to God for the recovery of James White and for
his return to active service.[21] Then they proceeded to re-elect him
as president of the General Conference, a move which surprised no
one. In addition, he was again appointed chairman of committees
or boards governing the three large Battle Creek institutions.

Besides his Sabbath sermon, James preached five other times.
On October 8, seventy-three persons were baptized; James baptized several of them.[22]

After the General Conference session James, Ellen, and Edson's
wife, Emma, and D. T. Bourdeau started west for Kansas. That
year four meetings were held in the State—one in May, the others
in October and November. The last two were held near Richmond,
in the vicinity of Topeka, and at Sherman. James attended the
latter, which began October 31. Ellen was at the Richmond meetings, which were conducted October 24 to 29. Then she joined
James at Sherman. James found the Kansans responsive and the
weather pleasant.[23] The latter would change.

---

[1] Ellen G. White letter 40 to Willie and Mary, Dec. 5, 1877.
[2] *SDA Encyclopedia*, article, "St. Helena Sanitarium and Hospital," p. 1132.
[3] Ellen G. White letter 40 to Willie and Mary, Dec. 5, 1877.
[4] Ellen G. White letter 43 to Willie and Mary, Dec. 25, 1877.
[5] Ellen G. White letter 18 to Willie, March 20, 1878.
[6] James White letter to Dear Daughter, Jan. 15, 1878.
[7] *Review and Herald*, March 7, 1878.
[8] *Ibid.*, March 14, 1878.
[9] *Ibid.*, May 9, 1878.
[10] Ellen G. White letter 65 to Willie, April 2, 1878.
[11] *Review and Herald*, June 27, 1878.
[12] James White, in *Review and Herald*, July 11, 1878.
[13] *Life Sketches of J. White*, 1888 ed. Quoted in *Appeal in Behalf of Dime Tabernacle at Battle Creek, Michigan.* Document File 453-A.
[14] James White letter, April 20, 1879.
[15] *Review and Herald*, July 4, 1878.
[16] James White, in *Review and Herald*, June 13, 1878.
[17] James White, in *Review and Herald*, July 11, 1878.
[18] James White, in *Review and Herald*, Aug. 22, 1878.
[19] *Ibid.*, Oct. 3, 1878.
[20] James White letter to W. C. White, July 15, 1878.
[21] *Review and Herald*, Oct. 17, 1878.
[22] James White, in *Review and Herald*, Oct. 17, 1878; Oct. 3, 1878.
[23] *Ibid.*, Nov. 21, 1878.

Chapter Thirty-nine

TEXAS ADVENTURE

ROM Kansas, the Whites and their daughter-in-law, accompanied by S. N. Haskell, took a train for Dallas, Texas. There was a brief interval before the Texas camp would open, so James and Ellen went with Emma to her home in Denison, some 100 miles north of Dallas. They found the situation in the McDearmon home desperate. Illness had prevented the family from working, and they were on the verge of starvation.

"They all looked like corpses," remarked Ellen. James thought it would take two of them to make a shadow. Naturally, Emma's parents were overjoyed to see the visitors, especially their daughter.[1]

Before Ellen and James left for the Texas camp meeting, they did what they could to relieve the McDearmon family. Ellen gave them forty dollars, and James bought bags of flour, a barrel of apples, nuts, sugar, and other supplies. He even purchased beds for them. As a final gesture, James gave his own overcoat to Brother McDearmon. Then, leaving Emma to help her parents through the winter, they returned to Dallas and the camp meeting.

Not more than two hundred people gathered at Plano, where camp meeting was held, many of whom traveled long distances over almost impossible roads. Twelve families had driven more than a hundred miles to reach the campground. But it was worth the effort, especially for one brother who said he had not heard a sermon for three years. Everyone who came was blessed. They especially enjoyed the sermons preached by James and Ellen White—six each.

Hoping to realize some profit from this trip and hearing that a mule costing $80 in Texas could be sold for $200 in Colorado, James White began to think of driving a herd to that State when the time came to leave Texas.[2] So he began purchasing mules and keeping them in a corral at Denison where they were staying.

275

One morning it was discovered that the mules had broken out of their corral and disappeared. Their loss would be a heavy financial blow to James. Involved in their recovery was a young man who was to become a long-term General Conference president. His name was Arthur G. Daniells. The Whites had been joined by Arthur and his wife, Mary, shortly after they arrived in Texas. Arthur was to serve as their secretary. After a few days the mules were found, and Daniells brought them home.[3]

The closing months of 1878 were pleasant in Texas but shortly before Christmas there was a dramatic change. The thermometer plunged. Ellen wrote, "The day before Christmas we went to town. . . . I never remember of its being much colder in Michigan." With the arrival of the New Year it became even colder with heavy falls of snow—heavy, at least, for Texas. There was enough to astonish the local citizens. On another occasion Ellen wrote, "It is all of nine o'clock before we can get the house warm enough to work, for we cannot handle pen and ink. This is the 'Sunny South,' hot enough to bake eggs in summer upon the ground, and so fearfully cold in winter."

Snow became so deep that James removed the wheels from his carriage and attached a pair of runners so he could get around. He wrote to Willie, appealing for warm clothing:

> Please send me a pair of new warm woolen socks by mail immediately. I walk so much that I stomp through a new pair each week. . . . Please send me a pair each week till the tenth of February. . . . Old Texans say this is the coldest weather that ever lay out down in Texas. In the morning we chop our teeth out of the solid ice before we can use them at the table.[4]

In spite of the cold the Whites managed to do a great deal of writing. James wrote for the *Health Reformer,* the *Signs of the Times,* but mostly for the *Review.* While in Texas they were joined by Miss Marian Davis, who was to remain one of Ellen's most valued literary assistants for more than twenty-five years.[5]

Fortunately the bitter weather did not last long. By January 23 James was writing to Willie, "The winter is past. It is cool and very pleasant."[6]

But even during the stormiest weather, James and Ellen continued with public meetings, often traveling from ten to fifteen miles to speak in crossroad country schoolhouses. In March they conducted a series of meetings in the city of Dallas.[7]

As the snow disappeared, black, gluey mud took its place. James wrote, "The rain gently falls. It is a fair morning. I walked to the depot, 1 1/2 miles and back in the sticky, slippery mud, and was completely bushed." [8]

In this newly developing country, James's fertile mind continued to discover new ways of earning money. He imported tubs of butter from Michigan as well as nuts, beans, and other commodities which sold well in the Southwest. At the same time he was buying buffalo skins and wildcat hides and shipping them northward to be sold. He wrote of earning four dollars in a single day selling brooms. For a short time he envisioned starting a broom factory in Texas, establishing an industry that would provide employment for needy Adventists. [9]

The money that James earned was not spent for self-gratification. That spring he and Ellen pledged $2,000 to help lift debts on the Dime Tabernacle and on the church in Oakland, California. [10] Times were hard and money scarce. "This state of things is by no means confined to Texas," James wrote. "We are entering the narrows. Economy! Retrenchment! is the battle." [11]

Meanwhile, James was concerned over the future prospects of the McDearmons. He suggested to Mr. McDearmon that his family would be better off in the higher, drier climate of Colorado. It was not difficult for James to persuade him that they should move. It was decided to organize an expedition that would leave as soon as there was sufficient grass for the animals. Several other Adventist families were eager to join the group, and planning began. [12]

At this point we discover a somewhat puzzling situation. Toward the end of March a telegram arrived at the Review office stating, "We will spend Sabbath, April 5 at Battle Creek." It was signed J. and E. G. White. [13] It is difficult to explain this telegram fully, for in early April their caravan was making final preparations to leave Denison. Nor is it clear by what means the men in Battle Creek came to the conclusion that "the state of Brother White's health did not permit of his being present," when it was learned that they were not coming. [14] Actually, his health was good. But, as we shall see, he feared another stroke.

The *Review* did announce that the Kansas camp meeting would begin at Emporia on May 15. It would continue for a week. The Whites planned to be there.

But the departure of the caravan was postponed because of sickness. Then they found the Red River in flood, so they had to wait for the water to subside. Finally they gave up and moved forty-five miles upriver where they found a ferry that landed them safely on the northern shore.

The wagon train with which the Whites traveled consisted of eight covered wagons besides James's two-seated spring carriage. Altogether the group numbered thirty-one men, women, and children. Responsibility for the safety and progress of the caravan rested largely on James. His wife and Marian Davis were burdensomely involved in providing food for part of the group. This was a laborious, time-consuming task.

Once across the river, the train started the long journey northward. Leaving Texas they passed into Indian territory, an area now part of Oklahoma. Here the wagons were formed into a circle every night with James's six mules in the middle along with the horses. Two men were assigned to guard the camp. The danger feared was not so much possible attack by Indians, but the schemes of white men who might employ Indians to stampede the livestock.[15]

The biggest problem was finding and preparing food, especially for a few sick among them. Ellen wrote, "No rest, not a bit of it for poor Marian; we have worked like slaves. We cook, repeatedly half the night. Marian the entire night. . . . Unpack, and pack, hurry, cook, set table, has been the order of the day."[16]

James and Ellen did all they could to witness as they passed along the trail from Texas to Kansas. Several times they passed meetinghouses on the open prairie. Word had gone ahead that there was a preacher with that particular wagon train, and the Whites were pressed into speaking. At one meeting some half-breed Indians were present, who listened with intense interest to the sermon. A Baptist minister present expressed the hope that the listeners would remember and obey the admonitions they had heard. James and his wife were urged to remain and conduct other meetings, but time for the Kansas camp meeting was approaching, so they had to press on their way.[17]

Many were the vicissitudes through which that wagon train passed on its slow way to Kansas and, ultimately, Colorado. There were cloudbursts that caused rivers to overflow their banks. Yet those rivers had to be negotiated. There were quicksands to avoid.

Wagons broke down. There were sickness and accidents and other delays. James finally concluded reluctantly that it would be impossible to reach Emporia, Kansas, in time for the camp meeting, and sent word ahead to that effect. Fast action followed. The next *Review* carried a notice that owing to high water, Elder and Mrs. White had been delayed and camp meeting would be postponed for one week. Unable to receive the church paper while on the road, the Whites were unaware of the change in time.

James rode horseback much of the time, galloping up and down alongside the other wagons, cheering the exhausted travelers. Concerned with food as she was during the entire trek, Ellen rose early many mornings, to pick wild strawberries and panfuls of greens. In spite of Ellen's best efforts, many meals were frugal. A small boy in the group never forgot how one morning he came upon Elder White sitting under a small tree, gnawing on an apple. He told the boy that all he had eaten for breakfast was a few dry crackers. At that stopping place there hadn't even been any water.[18]

With an eye on the calendar, James urged the drivers to move as fast as possible. When they camped near Coopersville, he sent a man on horseback to the post office, five miles away. It was there that he learned by telegraph of the changed date for the Kansas meeting. If they hurried, they would still be on time. When they reached the railway line, he and Ellen forsook the slow-moving caravan and took the "cars" for Emporia. Early next morning they arrived at their destination and found an omnibus waiting to take them to the campground. Pulled by "two span of splendid horses," the large carriage transported them to the campground "in style," Ellen wrote. Some Adventists had not heard of the changed date, and had come a week early. "We found about thirty who came two hundred miles in their wagons and did not receive the change of appointment. With the exception of two, all remain over another week," Ellen continued. Then she wrote, "I am worn and feel as though I was about one hundred years old. But enough of this. I cannot write much till I get rested. . . . This journey has nearly killed me. My ambition is gone; my strength is gone; but this will not last if we can have a fair chance. . . . I have not had even time to keep a diary or write a letter. . . . Marian astonishes us all. She is really forgetting herself and is efficient help. What I could have done unless she had taken the burden is more than I can tell. Poor child, she is tired, so tired. God bless dear Marian." [19]

After sleeping for weeks in rough wagon beds, it was with relief and anticipation of real comfort that the Whites lay down on soft beds in their tent that night. But their expectations were shattered. About 2:00 A.M. a violent thunderstorm struck the camp. Meanwhile, whoever had pitched their tent had failed to secure the flap. The wind got under this, causing it to expand and contract like a huge bellows. James shouted for help.

Unfortunately, all were busy tying down their own tents. At length two men came along. But they could do little more than prevent the tent from flying away. It was half an hour before sufficient help arrived to really fasten things down securely. The rain continued until dawn, leaving a bedraggled but cheerful group of campers to face a new day. [20]

Two days later the wagon train straggled into camp, and the weary travelers remained for most of the meetings. Then it was time to part. James and Ellen bade farewell to friends they had learned to know and love on the long trip. The caravan now turned westward toward Colorado. James promised to visit there before long and look them up. Then he and Ellen boarded the train, heading for their next appointment.

For the Whites the long trek was over, but not forgotten. James felt that he had never enjoyed better health, but the toilsome journey had certainly left its mark on his overworked wife. She had lost twelve pounds, and been sick on the trip. It was her hope, however, that "by the cheering light of the countenance of my Saviour, I shall have the springback power." [21]

---

[1] Ellen G. White letter 54 to Edson, Nov. 15, 1878.

[2] James White letter to W. C. White, Nov. 12, 1878.

[3] Ellen G. White letter 64 to Emma, Dec. 3, 1878.

[4] James White letter to W. C. White and MKW, Jan. 8, 1879.

[5] James White letter to W. C. White, Jan. 2, 1879.

[6] James White letter to W. C. White, Jan. 23, 1879.

[7] James White letter to J.E.W., March 11, 1879.

[8] James White letter to W. C. White, Jan. 17, 1879.

[9] James White letter to W. C. White, Jan. 21, 1879; Jan. 27, 1879.

[10] James White letter to Brethren in Battle Creek, Jan. 12, 1879.

[11] James White letter to W. C. White, Jan. 30, 1879.

[12] James White letter to W. C. White, Feb. 20, 1879.

[13] *Review and Herald*, April 3, 1879.

[14] *Ibid.*, April 24, 1879.

[15] Ellen G. White letter 20a to Willie and Mary, May 3, 1879.

[16] Ellen G. White letter 20 to Mary, May 20, 1879.
[17] Ellen G. White letter 36 to Dear Children, May 4, 1879.
[18] Document file, 967, Cornell Moore.
[19] Ellen G. White letter 20 to Mary, May 20, 1879.
[20] *Ibid.*
[21] *Ibid.*

Chapter Forty

CLOSING LABORS

THREE weeks after the Whites telegraphed word to the *Review* that they would "spend Sabbath, April 5, at Battle Creek," they set out on their long journey across the prairies, from Texas to Kansas. During that trip they virtually dropped out of sight so far as Battle Creek was concerned. In explanation James wrote,

Our nervous system has been shocked three times with paralysis, and three times the arm that traces these lines has fallen, for a time to be raised and moved only by the other. These dangerous attacks have usually occurred after severe mental strain, such as has ever been our portion at General Conference. We were reported absent from the late Conference in consequence of ill health. Thanks to that worthy body for the vote of sympathy. It is our duty, however, to state that our absence was through fear of another break down.[1]

This, doubtless, was a valid reason for the change in plan. But there was another reason. James's heart had gone out in sympathy to the poverty-stricken Adventists in Texas who wished to emigrate to Colorado and needed his help as organizer and expedition leader. From Kansas, James and Ellen, heading east, attended the Missouri camp meeting. Writing for the *Review* Dr. Kellogg reported: A glorious triumph for temperance was achieved. Brother and Sister White, although much worn with arduous labors, were ready to take hold of the work here, and did so with most excellent results.[2]

James and Ellen arrived in Battle Creek to have a joyful reunion with their children. But their stay was brief, for in a few days they started West once more to attend camp meetings, which would eventually take them to Colorado.

After attending the Wisconsin, Minnesota, and Iowa camp meetings, they headed for Sioux Falls, Dakota—this was before the States of North and South Dakota were formed—where camp meet-

An 1875 camp meeting conducted at Eagle Lake, Minnesota. Ellen White is fifth from the left, and James, seventh.

ing for believers in that State was to be held. Their last twenty-five miles to Sioux Falls were covered by stage coach. This was a small meeting, about two hundred being present. Eleven were baptized, and the Dakota Conference was organized. Among those present was a woman who had been one of James's students thirty-five years previously in Troy, Maine. Both teacher and pupil recalled with pleasure those long-ago experiences.[3]

From Sioux Falls, James and Ellen proceeded westward to Colorado and their beloved mountains. But, as at Battle Creek, they were not to stay long. The July 24 *Review* carried an announcement by Elder Butler of the dates for several camp meetings in the East in which he stated, "Brother and Sister White will most likely attend some of them."

The August 21 *Review* carried an announcement by James White in which he stated that he and Ellen had arranged to attend

283

several camp meetings in the East, but would be able to be at only one. The reason for the announcement stemmed from evangelistic meetings being held in Denver by J. O. Corliss. Arrangements made for Corliss to have help did not materialize, so James felt it was his duty to stay by the evangelist in that city of 35,000 people. He would attend the Massachusetts camp, but would return to Denver immediately afterward.[4] This announcement resulted in A. O. Burrill being sent to work with Corliss.[5] The Whites could now make their camp meeting itinerary.

At this time Elder White wrote informing the brethren that they might choose any date they wished for the next General Conference session, provided he and Ellen would not be expected to attend it. To conduct such a meeting minus the president would be difficult to imagine today.

In the *Review* James registered some complaints and suggestions regarding camp meetings. Meetings were not always held in the same place. Too often it was hard for attendants and visiting ministers to find them; proper directions were not given in the *Review*. This should be corrected. He stated, "The writer has paid his fare hundreds of miles out of the way during the past ten years, in trying to reach places of meetings, for want of definite directions."[6]

James was pleased with the camp at Waterville, Maine. He met some relatives there, and visited some others after camp closed. He promised to return the following summer and conduct some meetings in Maine. Also, he appreciated the help of G. I. Butler at the meetings. "Elder Butler was present, ready to lift at the wheel of every good work," he wrote.[7]

After Ellen and James had attended thirteen camps, they headed for Battle Creek, feeling worn out but in reasonably good health. James reported that he was enjoying better health than for several years past.[8]

Over the past year they had spent only two Sabbaths in Battle Creek, and were uncertain how long they would be there on this occasion. But, as General Conference president he had responsibilities there. The various departments and institutions needed his attention. A resolution by a committee set up to plan for the coming General Conference session urged them to stay at Battle Creek, so James decided to spend that winter fostering "those departments of the work where our labors are most needed." [9]

On November 7, 1879, the eighteenth session of the General Conference opened—a historic event, since for the first time the Adventist Church leaders were meeting in the Battle Creek Tabernacle. Thirty-nine delegates were present. For the tenth and last time, James White was re-elected president. Uriah Smith remained as secretary. There were fifty-two ordained ministers at the meeting.

When it closed, there were many matters to engage the attention of the General Conference president and to hold him in Battle Creek. When, on February 23, 1880, Ellen left the city with S. N. Haskell, and Willie and his wife for the Pacific Coast, James felt obligated to remain at headquarters. A number of matters relative to the functioning of various church agencies led him to call a special session of the General Conference for March 11-15.

The *Review* reported:

> Sabbath [March 13] was a day of unusual interest. Bro. White spoke on the position, privileges, and responsibilities of men as ambassadors for Christ. In the afternoon a portion of the time was spent in social meeting, and the remainder in examination of candidates for baptism. Four precious young men, two of them students . . . , came forward, desiring this ordinance, and at their special request Bro. White acted as administrator. The baptism passed off pleasantly and impressively, in presence of the large concourse of people who lined the banks of the river. In the stand these young men have taken, a triumph has been gained at which we all rejoice. [10]

The institutions at Battle Creek were now expanding, and new buildings and facilities were continually being added. The college was thriving. Sanitarium patronage was also on the upswing. Business in the publishing house was brisker than ever before. James reported: "The empty condition of our book-shelves at the publishing house, seems really fearful. Not less than twenty tons of publications have been sent out from this office . . . , during the past three months." [11]

James planned to attend several camp meetings—Iowa, Wisconsin, Minnesota—but did not get to any of them, no doubt because of the press of work in the office. He did visit a number of churches and held weekend meetings there. Whatever his duties may have been that summer of 1880, he wrote to Ellen that "this is the happiest summer of my life." [12]

James's weekend forays among the churches were occasionally
unplanned. He sometimes broke away from a closely structured
program and escaped the tyranny of timetables. This could not
happen often, but it did inspire C. F. Stevens to write to Willie
White, "I once heard Elder Andrews remark that if there was anything the Lord did not know, it was where Brother White would
be next Sabbath." [13]

Toward the end of July, James received a telegram from Ellen
informing him that she would arrive in Battle Creek on the night
of August 4—one day before the Michigan camp meeting was to
convene at Alma. James, of course, decided to wait for the arrival
of that train before going to Alma.

By catching a faster train, Ellen and Lucinda Hall, her traveling
companion, arrived at Battle Creek at one o'clock in the afternoon
instead of at night. They rushed, repacked for the camp meeting,
and with James caught a fast train for Jackson, where they stayed
overnight at the home of Dan Palmer. Next morning at seven they
took a train for Saginaw and reached the campground at Alma just
as the opening meeting was being announced, to be warmly welcomed by the believers gathered there. [14]

From Alma, James and Ellen traveled to Canada to participate
in the camp meeting at Magog, Quebec. During the meetings
James organized the Quebec Conference, with A. C. Bourdeau as
president. [15] After the Quebec meeting the Whites attended the
Maine and Vermont camp meetings.

Back in Battle Creek, James published in the *Review* an announcement that the annual General Conference session would
be held during a general camp meeting scheduled for Battle Creek,
September 28 to October 11.

The session—the nineteenth—convened in the Tabernacle on
October 6. During the session George I. Butler, who had been
president from 1871 to 1874, was elected president once again. [16]
And once again James's oft-repeated wish that he might be able to
shed some of the heavy load he had carried for years was fulfilled.
But, as is often the case when a leader is relieved of his responsibilities, he may have given them up with some reluctance.

Near the close of that year James purchased a large brick house
on the road to Goguac Lake, about a mile and a half from the center
of Battle Creek. This was by far the most imposing home he had

ever owned, and he took great satisfaction in being its owner. The estate contained thirty acres of land, ten acres in forest. The orchard consisted of more than two hundred fruit trees—apples, pears, peaches, and cherries. The total cost was six thousand dollars.[17]

To visitors, the Whites' new home seemed spacious and comfortable. James and Ellen, feeling secure and anchored after years of travel, enjoyed inviting guests to visit there. At least one marriage, that of D. M. Canright to his second wife, Lucy, was solemnized in the large parlor, with James performing the ceremony.

After the wedding, Lucy wrote a thank-you letter expressing the hope that sometime she and Dudley might entertain James and Ellen in their home, "although," she admitted, "it is not so grand and romantic as yours. Still we hope to make it a home in every sense of the word." [18]

James had his two sides. He could be crusty and forbidding, and he had a majestic air about him that awed some people. But beneath a somewhat stern exterior, there beat a sympathetic heart; and he enjoyed mingling with people. Lucy Canright wrote, "I used to be somewhat afraid of Brother White, but since our wedding and especially that ride, instead of feeling that way, you seem almost like my father. Indeed I shall love you for making our wedding go off so pleasantly." [19]

Wherever James White went, in whatever company he found himself, he made a vivid and lasting impression. In 1879 his plans for the future were simple but specific. To his children he said, "I shall take it easy, and grow old gracefully, and make you all love me half to death." [20]

The fulfillment of that hope was not granted to James White.

---

[1] James White, in *Review and Herald*, May 15, 1879.

[2] J. H. Kellogg, M.D., in *Review and Herald*, June 19, 1879.

[3] James White, in *Review and Herald*, July 24, 1879.

[4] ———, in *Review and Herald*, Aug. 21, 1879.

[5] J. O. Corliss, in *Review and Herald*, Sept. 18, 1879.

[6] James White, in *Review and Herald*, Aug. 21, 1879.

[7] ———, in *Review and Herald*, Sept. 25, 1879.

[8] ———, in *Review and Herald*, Oct. 9, 1879.

[9] ———, in *Review and Herald*, Oct. 16, 1879.

[10] *Review and Herald*, March 18, 1880.

[11] James White, in *Review and Herald*, March 4, 1880.

[12] James White letter to Ellen G. White, July 17, 1880.

[13] C. F. Stevens letter to W. C. White, July 31, 1934.
[14] James White letter to Willie and Mary, Aug. 9, 1880.
[15] *Review and Herald*, Aug. 26, 1880.
[16] *Ibid.*, Oct. 14, 1880.
[17] James White letter to W. C. White, Nov. 3, 1880.
[18] Lucy Canright letter to James White, May 17, 1881.
[19] *Ibid.*
[20] James White letter to "Dear Children," May 20, 1879.

Chapter Forty-one

A LITTLE LOWER THAN
THE ANGELS

T O SEARCH for perfection of action and judgment in the men and women chosen to lead out in God's work is to try to find that which is nonexistent. James White once said, "Show me the man who never makes a mistake, and I will show you a man who should be in heaven."

There were very human traits in the character of James White. No one was more acutely aware of his weaknesses than he himself. "I wish I were a better man" is a desire he expressed more than once.

After retiring from his many responsibilities in Battle Creek, it would have been well if James had moved to some other locality and found new areas of activity to occupy his mind. But home and hosts of friends were there, so he remained in a place where he would be tempted to scrutinize every error made by his successors in church leadership. Naturally, some decisions he regarded as mistakes were not such at all, as was proved by the test of time.

For thirty years Elder White had been the hub in the church around which everything seemed to revolve. It had been easy for other workers to permit this dynamic leader to shoulder heavy responsibilities, then sit back and criticize when his decisions occasionally misfired. In a letter to Willie, James put his finger on the difficulty:

I am continually blundering for two reasons. *First,* I undertake to do too much work. I shall not deny that I love to work, and am inclined to take too much on my hands, and my brethren at the same time are very willing that I should take cares and labor upon me.[1]

James White was a man who wanted to see action—things moving, everybody working. Because of this tendency he was sometimes abrasive in dealing with subordinates in the office and in the church. He did not hesitate to censure those who failed to do all he thought they should. As a result, for fear of incurring his displeasure, workers were inclined to sit back and let him do the job his own way.

While James was relaxing in Colorado in the summer of 1879, his feelings were hurt by someone who criticized his course. In a hasty mood he wrote:

"I am a sensitive man, and you can understand that apologies will have to be made or you will have to look for others to fill my place." [2]

When he took time for reflection, James realized that his letter had been hasty, and he reconsidered his demand for apologies. Keenly aware of his weaknesses, James analyzed his problem in a letter to Willie and his wife:

"I have in my discouragement wounded my own soul, and the precious members of my family. . . . Whatever may be the circumstances I hope never to wound your feelings again." [3]

In the same letter his wife put her finger squarely on the problem:

The large donations he (JW) has made from time to time, the sacrifices of means he has made upon the Pacific Coast to establish the Office and build meetinghouses there, have not been appreciated; but he should consider he did not do this for his Brethren, but for God. . . . His whole soul was ardent and full of zeal to push forward the work. . . . He has had to meet disaffection and murmurings on every side. These have been greatly magnified in his mind, and he has felt too keenly over them.

George I. Butler, who twice alternated with James in the presidential chair, explained the reasons for James's conflicts with his brethren:

It has been my fortune to labor in connection with him in this cause when our views were in harmony in reference to measures; also when they were not in harmony. Such things occur in every cause. Yet I feel sure he labored for what he thought was right, and honestly felt he must make efforts to carry out his convictions. With such force of character, such aggressive instincts and tenacity of purpose as he possessed, it was inevitable that he should come into conflicts with the men he found in his way in the carrying out of his plans. This is always so with men of earnest purpose who attempt the work of a reformer. [4]

In his later years, James found it increasingly difficult to accept opposition. Weakened by disease, he at times was irrational. Also, like many natural-born leaders, he felt his own ideas were wisest. Unless his brethren's plans coincided with his own, he often rejected them without giving sufficient explanation. This mood is reflected in a letter he wrote to Ellen:

When I return [from Otsego, Michigan], I shall go immediately to Colorado. . . . Never shall I consent to go here and there, and to do this and that by the direction of others. When I come to that point, it will be time for me to retire. A retreat is the most skillful part of military action, which you and I should be considering.[5]

He then went on to explain why he found it necessary to consider retiring:

The time was when it was my place to lead off, and where necessary to storm it through. Times changed, and organization came in. Then I had to hold the important offices from necessity. But the work became too large for any one man to stand at the head of all branches. And now the time has come for me to retire, and let younger men come to the front. I had a work to do, a place to fill. Now the work is too large for one of my age and temperament to preside over.[6]

But it was not easy for James to stand aside and watch blunders being made. He expressed his frustrations to his children at the time the Battle Creek institutions were plunged heavily into debt:

My brethren are all crazy, and left to themselves would soon put me in the grave. I am the only sane man in the crowd, and hope to remain so. I will save my money to buy help and try to save myself, and leave our institutions to the mercy of the go-in-debt men now at the helm.[7]

When he wrote this he was 58 and president of the General Conference. But he had been away from Battle Creek and more or less out of touch with his brethren for eight months. The institutions of which he wrote were becoming more or less autonomous.

As has previously been noted, during the early years of the work James found it necessary to employ various methods of earning money with which to advance God's work. Standing in the forefront of the work as they were, James and Ellen were obliged to set the example by giving to every new enterprise, helping those in special need, and heading the donation lists in the *Review*. In later years much of the necessity for this was removed by the adoption of systematic benevolence. But once James had caught the tremendous vision of a needy world field, his longing to help fill needs at home and abroad became greater as the years went by. It was unadulterated joy for him to be able to pour thousands of dollars into various projects—the Pacific Press, the mission of J. N. Andrews in Europe, Battle Creek College, the building of churches, and the purchasing of camp meeting tents. Looking back a few years after James's death, Ellen wrote:

> I do not begrudge a cent that I have put into the cause. And I have kept on until my husband and myself have about $30,000 invested in the cause of God. We did this a little at a time, and the Lord saw that He could trust these Daniels with His means and that we would not bestow it on ourselves. He kept pouring it in, and we kept letting it out.[8]

During his later years James added new methods to his ways of making money. A case in point was the winter he spent in Texas during which he dealt in butter, beans, buffalo robes, mules, and wildcat skins. At times too much of his interest and strength seemed to be consumed in carrying on these projects, yet this activity may have been a diversion as he battled to regain his health.

Ellen did not approve of many of her husband's business activities, especially those in Texas. The year they left there she wrote to Arthur and Mary Daniells about their experiences in the South, in which she expressed the hope that Mary and her young husband would not form a wrong impression of James, who had been ill and surfeited with business affairs.[9]

Half a century later, Mary Daniells wrote Willie White a letter that throws light on James's problem:

> I did the cooking for them (J.W. and E.G.W.), and they always had a crowd of people to feed, and it took a lot of food and he would sometimes scold me for its costing so much, but I always assured him that I did not waste a thing, and just cooked what he brought to me to use, et cetera.
>
> The spring before he passed away, I saw him at the Iowa camp meeting and in his last words to me he asked me to forgive him for being impatient, and wanted to give me some money, to give me more for my work. I would not take the money, but it has always been such a comfort to me that he asked me to forgive him, for he passed away in a few weeks after that. He was a good patient man, but he was not at all well.[10]

"He was not at all well." Here we have the explanation of many of the misunderstandings and deteriorating relationships James had with some of his brethren during the closing years of his life.

Feeling in desperate need of strength from above, James wrote to Ellen six months before his death:

> I pray much as the train is in motion that God will help us. This is my only hope, and I mean to get out of the way so that He can work. I will. I will. I will. I shall by the help of the Lord be where I can prevail with the Lord. I have long backslidden from God. I must return, and be like a child

before God. There is hope for us in God.[11]

To his children he unburdened his heart and confessed his weaknesses:

> I wish now to call your attention to a subject of graver importance. Probably, dear children, I may have erred in some of the sharp things I have written relative to the mistakes of younger heads. It is my nature to retaliate when pressed beyond measure. I wish I was a better man.[12]

As Elders Butler, Haskell, his own son, William, and others were involved in the operation of the General Conference and the interests of the church, they naturally did some things differently from how James would have them done. To the retired general, this appeared as a reflection on his record. In a moment of frustration he wrote to Ellen: "Now I propose to surrender the directing to Elder Haskell and Will, and the correcting and admonishing to yourself, and I will go about my work of feeding the sheep and lambs of the fold of Christ."[13]

It was characteristic of James that he would speak his mind, letting people know where he stood, regardless of the issue. In fact, his wife accused him of taking pleasure in a good "fuss" now and then.[14]

During the last year of his life, James was to strike out fiercely at those he felt had wronged him. At one time of emotional torment he felt that every man's hand was against him, including those of his sons. He could not have been well when he wrote to Willie:

> "And this wrong was done your father! The very man who established the Signs. Oh, my poor misled Willie! How could you be so cruel?"[15]

Focusing his attention on the General Conference president he wrote:

> Just at the time that I was trying to rise by faith and take responsibilities upon me as shown by my conversation at the lake the course and spirit of Brother Butler comes up to crush me in health, strength, and spirits.[16]

How did G. I. Butler react when he received critical letters from James full of censure and condemnation? His attitude was typical of most of the brethren. They remembered his accomplishments and what he had suffered. They bore in mind his dogged determination in time of illness to win through, and re-enter God's work. They never forgot his ardent zeal, and they made allowances for him. After his death, Elder Butler, in a personal letter to J. N. Andrews, placed the situation in kind perspective:

Our dear Brother White thought we were his enemies because we did
not see things as he did. I have never laid up anything against that man of
God, that noble pioneer who labored so hard for this Cause. I attributed it
all to disease and infirmity.[17]

Would that all James White's critics be as charitable to his
memory as Elder Butler!

Like all great leaders, Elder James White had his weaknesses.
But with all the power of his being he strove to run the race set before
him. As an overcomer, may he someday soon inherit all things!

[1] James White letter to W. C. White, May 4, 1880.
[2] James White letter to W. C. White, July 28, 1879.
[3] James White letter to Willie and and Mary, Nov. 17, 1880.
[4] George I. Butler, in *Review and Herald*, Aug. 16, 1881.
[5] James White letter to Ellen G. White, April 18, 1880.
[6] James White letter to "Dear Children," May 11, 1879.
[7] James White letter to "Dear Children," May 3, 1879.
[8] MS 3, Ellen G. White sermon, Oakland, Calif., Sept. 25, 1888.
[9] Ellen G. White letter 32 to Bro. and Sr. Daniells, July 17, 1879.
[10] Mary Daniells letter to W. C. White, April 21, 1936.
[11] James White letter to Ellen G. White, Feb. 11, 1881.
[12] James White letter to Willie and Mary, Feb. 27, 1879.
[13] James White letter to Ellen G. White, April 16, 1880.
[14] Ellen G. White letter 13 to James White, Sept. 2, 1871.
[15] James White letter to W. C. White, Jan. 7, 1881.
[16] James White undated fragment, James White letter file.
[17] George I. Butler letter to J. N. Andrews, May 25, 1883.

Chapter Forty-two

SUNSET

I N DECEMBER, 1880, when Elder and Mrs. White moved into their new home on the road to Goguac Lake, their two small nieces, Addie and May Walling, moved there with them. Because of family problems Mr. Walling had entrusted his children to the Whites the last time they left Colorado.

To the two little Walling girls the new, large house seemed very grand. They were happy to be living there with "Uncle White" and "Aunt Ellen." Each morning the little sisters walked a mile and a half to the Battle Creek school, and quiet descended on the big house. Ellen used the time in writing, and James was busy with his pen. All through the years it had been through the *Review* columns that he communicated with church members everywhere, and he was continuing this habit. What was he writing during that winter and spring of 1880-1881? The following are a sampling of the topics he covered—"The Mind of Christ," "The New Commandment," "The Glory of God," "The Christian Ministry," "That Precious Name," "The Water of Life," "Words of Comfort."

At the beginning of 1881 James resigned from all connection with the college and sanitarium. His resignation was accepted. He retained only the presidency of the Publishing Association and his cherished position as editor of the *Review.*

When spring came at last and roads were opened to wheeled traffic, Ellen and James began visiting the various churches not too far from Battle Creek. But they did not forget the work in their hometown. In May the husband-wife team held meetings for the Battle Creek College students, and rejoiced when revival resulted.

Between church appointments, James gave much attention to his home and farm. Ellen reported to the children in California:

Father has excellent health. He has worked hard on the place here; put in more than one acre of strawberries, some raspberries, more than an acre of potatoes, several acres of corn, fifty hard maples, many peach trees, pear trees, and two long rows of pie plant [rhubarb].[1]

James and Ellen had again vowed that they simply would not—could not—risk the strain of attending camp meetings that summer. But when it was time for the Iowa camp meeting, Ellen received a strong impression from the Lord, "Go to Iowa; I have a work for you to do." She told James of her conviction. He seemed startled, but promptly said, "We will go."[2]

They attended that meeting, had a blessed experience, and proceeded to another camp meeting, this time in Wisconsin. Never were these tried veterans more warmly received by ministers and laymen than at this meeting.[3]

Even though James's hand was no longer on the helm of the work as it had been, he still had a deep burden for the needs at Battle Creek. A few weeks before his death Ellen talked with him of the need of leaving the area altogether so that he could escape the burdens still placed upon him. With strong emotion he responded:

Where are the men to do this work? Where are those who will have an unselfish interest in our institutions? . . .

My life has been given to the upbuilding of these institutions. It seems like death to leave them. They are as my children, and I cannot separate my interest from them. . . . I would rather die than live to see these institutions mismanaged. . . .

In my relation to this cause I have been longest and most closely connected with the publishing work. Three times have I fallen, stricken with paralysis, through my devotion to this branch of the cause. Now that God has given me renewed physical and mental strength, I feel that I can serve His cause as I have never been able to serve it before. I must see the publishing work prosper. It is interwoven with my very existence. If I forget the interests of this work, let my right hand forget her cunning.[4]

James and Ellen had accepted an invitation to attend general weekend meetings in Charlotte, Michigan, to be held July 23 and 24. As they rode along in their carriage, they spoke of God's mercies and guidance. Later, Ellen was to write, "Little did I think, as we traveled on, that this was the last journey we would ever make together."[5]

The morning was hot and sultry, but a change occurred as the hours passed. The temperature dropped many degrees, and James became chilled.

On Sunday afternoon, James preached clear, powerful sermons

during the meetings. Ellen spoke on one of her favorite subjects, temperance. Appropriately the closing hymn was "Dare to Be a Daniel." Standing near her husband, Ellen was thrilled by the enthusiasm and vigor of his singing.[6]

On Monday they drove back to Battle Creek. During the journey James mentioned that he was not feeling well, and alluded to pains in his limbs during the week. He attended services at the Tabernacle on Sabbath, and offered the opening prayer for the preaching service.

On Monday, James suffered a severe chill; on Tuesday, Ellen also became very sick. On Wednesday Dr. Kellogg ordered them immediately to the sanitarium. "They were tenderly placed on a mattress in a hack, where they lay side by side for the last time." [7]

Edson and Emma were living in Battle Creek at the time. When Edson realized the gravity of his parents' condition, he wrote to Willie in California:

> I would advise you not to wait for anything as father and mother are both *very sick* with malarial fever. They are at the Sanitarium under good care, with good nurses in attendance. Mother was very sick last night, but is some better tonight.[8]

James slept heavily, almost in a stupor much of the time, which alarmed Dr. Kellogg. Ellen was taken to his room. Shocked by her husband's appearance, she immediately realized that he must be dying. Kneeling by his bed, she took his hand and prayed that if it was God's will He would spare his life.

"I asked him if Jesus was precious to him [Ellen wrote later]. He said, 'Yes, Oh, yes!' 'Have you no desire to live?' she inquired. He answered: 'No.' " [9]

On Friday evening, August 5, Elder Uriah Smith and other Battle Creek ministers knelt by his bedside, praying for his recovery. During the rest of the night they prayed in another room.

Although Elder White's condition seemed hopeless, Dr. Kellogg and his assistants labored over him all through the night. There were indications that he had suffered another stroke of brain paralysis. Dr. Kellogg expressed his opinion that even though the patient should live, his mind would be permanently enfeebled.[10]

Dr. Kellogg was personally involved in this struggle for life. It was James White, he remembered, who had encouraged and helped him financially when he was a young man starting out in

life. Ellen and James had been like second parents to him, and now he was battling for the life of a personal friend. As a doctor, Kellogg left a detailed record of Elder White's illness. He wrote:

> I first learned of the illness of Elder White about 4 o'clock P.M., Tuesday, August 2, when I received a message from him requesting me to visit him at his residence, which I immediately did. I found him suffering with a very high fever, the pulse being 112, and the temperature 103 3/4 F. . . . His head was greatly congested, and he complained of severe pain in the spine, extending into the lower limbs. . . . Treatment to relieve the fever and pain was immediately ordered, and administered by a bath attendant from the Sanitarium. After a short time copious perspiration appeared, and he was greatly relieved.

After reporting variations in fever and other details of Elder White's illness, Kellogg continued:

> At 7:30 P.M. [Thursday] several friends called upon him, but talked with him only a little, as he seemed inclined to sleep. . . .
>
> At 10:00 A.M. [Friday] he was able to converse a little in brief sentences, but . . . the symptoms of paralysis of certain portions of the brain, which had appeared in the night, continued.
>
> We felt strongly the conviction that, should he live, his mind would possess but a shadow of its former strength. The same conviction fastened itself upon Mrs. White, who had entertained but slight hopes of his recovery from the commencement of the attack the previous evening. Fearing a repetition of the preceding evening, we apprised the friends of the impending danger, and set a careful watch over him in order to detect the first symptoms of collapse.[11]

Through Friday night the patient was still conscious, but at 1:30 A.M. he fell into a coma from which he never emerged. Before the sun went down and Adventists bade farewell to the day that James White had loved to call "our dear friend the blessed Sabbath," he quietly and peacefully breathed his last. It was shortly after 5:00 P.M.[12] He was sixty years and two days old.

Dr. Kellogg sent a telegram to Willie in California. It read: "Died of pernicious malarial fever. Began sinking at one P.M. Died at five. Your mother says bring Mary. J. H. Kellogg."[13]

Willie and Mary immediately started on the long journey from Oakland to Battle Creek. In order to give them time to reach there, the funeral was delayed until the following Sabbath, August 13.

Citizens of Battle Creek were shocked by the news of the sudden death of one of its leading citizens. The *Review* of August 9 published the sad event. Thousands of Adventists who read it found the report almost impossible to believe, and even harder to grasp the

Elder James White as he appeared in 1878, three years before his death.

consequences to the church, of such a loss.

Dr. Kellogg described the feelings of many when he wrote:

No one, unless it be his bereaved family, can feel more keenly than we the loss of one who has been to us for years a father and a friend. To no one else have we been personally indebted for so many acts of kindness and so much wise counsel. We mourn not only for the irretrievable loss which the cause must sustain, but for a personal loss which cannot be repaired.[14]

The funeral was the largest ever held in Battle Creek. It was conducted in the Tabernacle, James White's own brain child. Although it was a regular business day in the town, many stores closed out of respect for the fallen Adventist leader.

Uriah Smith, who had been connected with Elder White in the publishing work for nearly thirty years, preached the funeral sermon. Eloquently he expressed his feelings that day:

Some have thought that he was deficient in social qualities, and sometimes rigid, harsh, and unjust, even toward his best friends. But these feelings, we are persuaded, come from a failure to comprehend one of the strongest traits in his character, which was his pre-eminent love for the cause in which he was engaged. To that he subordinated all else; for that he was willing to renounce home and friends. No man would have been more glad than he to enjoy continuously the pleasures of domestic and social life, and the intercourse of friends, had he not thought that integrity to the cause called him to take a different course. But . . . the voice of duty was first and all else was secondary. . . . The infirmities common to our nature he possessed in like manner as his fellow-men; and these he often saw and deplored. But who, in his circumstances, would have had less occasion for this than he? Utterly abhorrent to all the better sentiments of our nature would be that spirit which would suffer any feelings from this source to survive an occasion like this,—that spirit which would not bury them all, and bury them forever, in the grave which will close over him today. We turn, rather, to the thousands who have loved him as a brother, honored him as a father, and revered him as a counselor and guide, and who will cherish his memory sacredly, and never cease to regret the loss they have sustained in his death. . . . His influence will still be felt, the impress of his shaping hand will still be seen, and all the future workings of this cause will revive and keep alive his memory. His love for the work, especially the publishing department, continued to the last. But a few days before his final illness, holding up his right hand, he exclaimed, "Let my right hand forget its cunning if I forget the interests of this work."[15]

After Elder Smith's sermon, Ellen unexpectedly stood before the congregation. All eyes turned to the widow, just recovering from illness herself, and everyone listened intently as she spoke:

The White family burial plot, Battle Creek. James White's grave is indicated by the closer of the two foreground markers, engraved Father. Ellen's grave is beside his.

I want to say a few words to those present on this occasion. My dear Saviour has been my strength and support in this time of need. When taken from my sick-bed to be with my husband in his dying moments, at first the suddenness of the stroke seemed too heavy to bear, and I cried to God to spare him to me,—not to take him away, and leave me to labor alone. . . .

When my husband was breathing out his life so quietly, without a groan, without a struggle, I felt that it would be selfishness in me to wish to throw my arms of affection around him and detain him here. He was like a tired warrior lying down to rest. . . .

And now I take up my life-work alone. . . . I yield my precious treasure; I bid him farewell; I do not go to his grave to weep. . . . The morning of the resurrection is too bright. And then I look to that morning when the broken family links shall be re-united, and we shall see the King in His beauty, and behold His matchless charms, and cast our glittering crowns at His feet, and touch the golden harp and fill all Heaven with the strains of our music and songs to the Lamb. We will sing together there. We will triumph together around the great white throne.[16]

After Ellen White's remarks a hymn was sung, after which the mourners went to Oak Hill Cemetery. Besides the hundreds who walked there, a train of ninety-five carriages formed the long and mournful procession.

After describing the scene at the graveside, Uriah Smith wrote:

As we lay the dead away, a train of long years of the past, with all their associations, comes up before us. Memory brushes the dimness, accumulating through the lapse of time, from numberless deeds of kindness received at his hand. An overpowering sense of loss presses upon us. But duty still presents its claims, and we cannot linger. In the language of the beautiful hymn on the burial of one of the sainted Judsons, we can say,

"Now ye have buried him, up and depart
To life and to duty, with undismayed heart." [17]

Since the General Conference Committee members were scattered, it was not possible to draw up a joint resolution of grief at this sudden loss. Elder G. I. Butler, General Conference president, paid his personal tribute to the long-time torchbearer:

The leading man of this cause has fallen at his post. . . . For about thirty years I have known Elder White, and for ten years I have been acquainted with him intimately. He was a man of remarkable mind. In some respects, I never saw his equal. For force of character, for the grasp of the details necessary to the success of his plans, for foresight, and looking quickly and deeply into difficult and perplexing matters, and for preparing for emergencies when his plans were threatened, I think his mind was most remarkable. [18]

Newspapers across the land published news of Elder White's death, and many paid tribute to his achievements. Mr. George Willard, editor of the *Battle Creek Journal*, gave generous space to eulogies of this leading citizen:

He was a man of the patriarchal pattern, and his character was cast in the heroic mold. If the logical clearness to formulate a creed; if the power to infect others with one's own zeal, and impress them with one's own convictions; if the executive ability to establish a sect and to give it form and stability; if the genius to shape and direct the destiny of great communities, be a mark of true greatness, Elder White is certainly entitled to the appellation, for he possessed not one of these qualities only, but all of them in a marked degree. [19]

When Adventist believers heard the tragic news, the question naturally arose in many minds, Why did the Lord permit His servant to fall at his post, ten years short of the psalmist's three-score years and ten? Perhaps Elder Butler's reply to this question is the most satisfying solution. He wrote:

As I viewed him lying in the coffin so calm and peaceful, I almost envied him. The tears flowed freely. His Heavenly Father has in mercy to him, laid him away to sleep, secure from the strife and trials of this poor

life. His works remain to abundantly testify of his great efforts in the cause.
His influence remains among our people and they look up to him as to the
father of the cause, and always will. Had he lived he would, as he grew
older and felt more the shocks of the past and possibly of the future, inevitably [have] weakened that influence. Now his reputation is secure.[20]

Similar thoughts came to Bishop John White, the older brother
of James. John served the Methodist church as a minister near
Worthington, Ohio. Writing to Ellen a few months after the funeral
he said,

He was a man of wonderful energy, but not of philosophy enough to
have grown aged and feeble, and been supplanted by the younger, gracefully and happily.
So the Good Father saw, and when he began to fail from his long, protracted effort and care, He said, "I will call him home. He has done and
suffered enough. The rear ranks won't suit his zeal and I will take him
home from the front ranks." There are some men that can't retire and God
takes them.[21]

Bishop John traveled from Ohio to attend his brother's funeral.
Meditating on what he had seen and heard, he wrote:

I return from my brother's funeral a wiser, broader, and less selfish
man. . . . Let the Tabernacle be crowded; let one of eloquent lips, who
had found in the departed a father, speak words of eulogy. Let sympathetic
citizens fill ninety-five carriages and follow him to his grave. Let one hundred and ten persons, his companions and friends, draped in mourning,
lead the procession. Let the path be paved and arched as were the bottom
and sides of his grave with evergreens. Let loving hands weave rare and
costly flowers into an anchor for its foot, and for the head a cross; and let
him literally go down to his last rest amid the emblems of eternal life and
immortal beauty. And why? He lived and labored not for self, but for God
and humanity. To the people of Battle Creek I am grateful for this tribute of
respect to my brother.[22]

Upon Ellen's mind the drama of those days would be forever im-
printed. She remembered how, being too feeble to walk, she had
been carried in a chair to the house where her husband's coffin
rested, nearly buried in flowers.[23] She remembered the look of
peace and rest on her husband's face. She found it hard to believe
that he would not awaken shortly. But there was the casket and
above it a beautiful floral cross and crown woven of pure white double pinks and tuber roses, a gift of love from Dr. Kellogg.[24] And
she remembered how she had been sustained in her own weakness
through the ordeal of James's death and burial.

This house, on Lake Avenue, Battle Creek, was the last home in which James White lived.

For thirty-five long and hard, but intensely rewarding years, she had lived and labored with her husband. Contrary to the impression of many that she would not long survive him, she worked on for God another thirty-four years, part of that time serving in overseas countries—Europe and Australia. But after James was buried, she did not linger in Battle Creek. Nine days after the funeral she boarded the train for California, heading for her Healdsburg home. She left the imposing home that had pleased James so greatly, for now the light of that home was extinguished. Henceforth she would remember it in connection with one for whom it had been the fulfillment of a lifelong dream.

"It is grandly beautiful," she remarked, "but how can I ever regard it as I could if he had lived?" [25]

For her, Battle Creek would always hold poignant memories. There she had reared her family. James now lay near two of their sons in Oak Hill Cemetery. But she had no desire to live there. After James's death, with the exception of a few months following the 1888 General Conference when Willie served temporarily as president, Ellen had little to do with Battle Creek.

Twenty-two years later, in the spring of 1903, there was another sad and impressive funeral in Battle Creek. Uriah Smith, who had preached James's funeral sermon had fallen stricken by apoplexy. Elder Daniells, then president of the General Conference, was present and preached Elder Smith's funeral sermon. The day was beautiful, and as Elder Daniells entered the cemetery where Brother Smith would find his last earthly resting place, he passed by the White family plot. Of this experience he wrote:

> I felt very much impressed, as we passed this grave with the body of another grand, noble pioneer of this work. I said to myself, How many more men will fall before our Lord comes. And I felt to promise God anew to give my life, all there is of it, to the advancement of this cause.[26]

God's servant, Elder James White, and these other pioneers all sleep, awaiting the coming of the Life-giver. How much longer must it be before God's people, with lives committed as theirs were, will rise and, in the Holy Spirit, finish the work so nobly launched and for which these men of God gave their all?

[1] Ellen G. White letter 4a, to the children, 1881.

[2] Ellen G. White letter 5a, 1881.

[3] James White, in *Review and Herald*, June 28, 1881.

[4] *Testimonies*, vol. 1, pp. 106, 107.

[5] *Ibid.*, p. 108.

[6] Ellen G. White, in *In Memoriam, A Sketch of Last Sickness and Death of Elder J. White* (Battle Creek, Mich.: Review and Herald Press, 1881), p. 51.

[7] *Founders of the Message*, p. 194.

[8] J. E. White letter to W. C. White, Aug. 4, 1881.

[9] *Testimonies*, vol. 1, p. 109.

[10] J. H. Kellogg, M.D., in *In Memoriam*, p. 19.

[11] *Ibid.*, pp. 17-19.

[12] *Life Sketches* (1915), pp. 251, 252.

[13] Ellen G. White, Document File, 715-b.

[14] J. H. Kellogg, M.D., in *In Memoriam*, p. 20.

[15] Uriah Smith, in *In Memoriam*, pp. 34-36.

[16] Ellen G. White, in *In Memoriam*, pp. 40-43.

[17] *Ibid.*, p. 44.

[18] George I. Butler, in *Review and Herald*, Aug. 16, 1881.

[19] George Willard, editor of *Battle Creek Journal*, in *In Memoriam*, p. 10.

[20] G. I. Butler letter to W. C. White, Aug. 17, 1881.

[21] John White letter to Ellen G. White, May 13, 1882.

[22] John W. White, in *In Memoriam*, pp. 59, 60.

[23] Ellen G. White letter B-9, 1881, p. 3.

[24] *Ibid.*

[25] *Ibid.*, p. 4.

[26] A. G. Daniells letter to W. C. White, March 9, 1903.

Chapter Forty-three

PERSONAL GLIMPSES

PRIOR to the great disappointment in 1844, the believers in Christ's soon coming frequently met for earnest seasons of prayer. At such a meeting held one morning in the home of a Brother Jordan, an Elder H. led in prayer. James White became rather astonished and somewhat embarrassed as he listened to the following petition:

"O Lord, have mercy on Brother White. He is proud, and will be damned unless he gets rid of his pride. Have mercy upon him, O Lord, and save him from pride. . . . Break him down, Lord, and make him humble. Have mercy upon him. Have mercy." The prayer went on for quite a while.

When the prayer season finally ended, James asked Elder H. in what way he showed pride.

"Please look me over," he said. "Is it in my patched boots? my rusty coat? This nearly worn-out vest? or that old hat I wear?"

Elder H. said it was none of these things. Brother White's symbol of pride, he said, was the starched linen collar he was wearing. James quickly explained that his own shirt had been dirty and a good sister had offered to wash it for him. In the meantime she lent him one of her husband's shirts, which had a starched linen collar.

This explanation did not satisfy Elder H. He refused to be comforted and continued to lament over the coming fate of dear Brother White due to his pride.

Writing about the incident years later, James commented: "To see a coarse, hard-hearted man, possessing in his very nature but little more tenderness than a crocodile, and nearly as destitute of moral and religious training as a hyena, shedding hypocritical tears for effect, is enough to stir the mirthfulness of the gravest saint."—

Life Incidents (1868), pp. 115, 116.

On Sabbath morning, April 29, 1865, the Adventist meeting-house in Battle Creek was crowded as usual. James White was the preacher. He directed the attention of the audience to the fact that they were that day celebrating the creation of the world. One highly prized institution that had come direct from Eden was the Sabbath. But there was another institution that went back even further. Before giving the Sabbath to Adam and Eve, God had united them in marriage. James White then proposed to celebrate the observance of both institutions in the church that day. Inviting a young couple, Elder Isaac Van Horn and Miss Adelia P. Patten, to come to the rostrum, he performed their wedding ceremony. They solemnly repeated their vows and were pronounced husband and wife. They then returned to their places in the audience, and James White proceeded with the sermon he had planned.—See *Review and Herald*, May 2, 1865.

Times were hard during the winter of 1878/1879 when the Whites were in Texas. Late one night, as James was returning home from the east side of Denison, he met a poor man who had been trying to sell a load of stovewood all day. The man walked, tugging on a rope tied to the horns of his two oxen, which patiently pulled the loaded cart. In one hand the man held a whip, with which he occasionally belabored his tired, thin animals. James White's heart was moved with pity for the man and his beasts.

"How much for your load of wood?" asked the soft-hearted James.

"Six bits, sir."

"I'll buy it if you'll deliver it to my house a mile away on the west side of the city."

"I reckon it's so late I'll just take it home," said the Texan as he plodded on.

As James went on his way, he met another man with twice as much stovewood for sale, who likewise had been waiting all day to dispose of it.

"How much for your load of wood?" asked James.

"Six bits."

"Follow me," said James. He led off, with the man and his mules following. This man, past middle age, and his little boy seemed very happy as James gave the father a silver half and quarter.

At Hamilton, Missouri, the Whites were invited to speak at the Methodist church. James conducted a funeral on Friday afternoon, and Ellen spoke that evening to a crowded hall, though the people there had previously been very prejudiced. Many were turned away for lack of room.

The evening after the Sabbath Ellen spoke in the same hall. Her husband followed the next morning, speaking to a large audience. It was then announced that Ellen White would speak in the afternoon, on the subject of health. Long before the hour set for the meeting, the hall was so crowded that fears were expressed that the floor might collapse.

"Divide the preachers," someone called out. The idea was that James should speak in another nearby meetinghouse. James declined, saying with a possible twinkle in his eye that he feared he would not get his share of the audience. Men preachers were common enough, but a woman lecturer was a novelty in Missouri in those days.

Finally the problem was solved by the whole crowd walking or driving their teams to the other meetinghouse, which was larger. Even then extra chairs had to be brought in for the overflow audience, to whom Ellen White spoke for an hour and a half. (See Ellen G. White letter 17, 1870.)

In the spring of 1858 a conference was held in Battle Creek, attended by some four hundred brethren. At the evening meeting Brother Sperry introduced Sister White, who then spoke until nearly ten o'clock. After that, the meeting was opened for testimonies from individuals. Everyone was eager to speak, and after an hour of this type of participation the social meeting was still continuing. Five times Elder White tried to close the service. At length he said that if the congregation would allow him to make a few remarks he would promise to give opportunity to all to express their feelings. After those waiting to testify were seated, James requested all who were determined to press on toward Mount Zion to stand. The congregation rose en masse, after which James White proceeded to dismiss them, thus concluding a meeting which, it seemed to him, would have no end!—See *Review and Herald,* May 27, 1858.

At one early Wisconsin camp meeting the weather was very inclement. A steady rain fell nearly the whole time. Elder White was hovering over a few burning sticks when an elderly sister came along and in a high-pitched voice said, "Brother White, don't you think this is permitted [to come upon us] to test our faith?"

He replied forcefully, "No, no, no, a faith that will be tested by such a thing as this, ought to be thrown away and replaced by something stronger."

Though feeble and racked by illness, James and Ellen White felt it was their duty to attend a camp meeting in Ohio. They decided to follow their usual practice and step out by faith, trusting the Lord to give them physical healing and strength. The train took them from Battle Creek to Jackson, where they intended to spend the night.

They arrived in the evening to find the station in a state of pandemonium. Vast crowds had come to Jackson that day to attend the State fair and were now trying to return home. Five hundred people were all trying to board the train at once, making it impossible for anyone to get off.

Determined not to be carried on to Detroit, James picked Ellen up in his arms and headed for the platform.

"Make way for a sick woman!" he shouted. "Make way! Make way!"

Holding his wife as high as possible, James stormed down the aisle and finally reached the platform, where he put Ellen down, then turned to catch his satchels as they were tossed down to him. A friend came with his carriage and took them to their night's lodging. After a good rest that night, many of their aches and pains disappeared, and the next morning they traveled on to the Ohio campground.—See *Life Sketches* (1888), pp. 367, 368.

James's manner of labor is well illustrated by a trip he took to Iowa City in response to a request for his services. He made appointments all along the route to his destination.

Leaving Battle Creek at eleven o'clock on Thursday night, he rode the train all the rest of that night and all the next day, arriving at Crane's Grove Friday at 6:00 P.M. Sabbath morning he met with the church, and in the afternoon preached in a local schoolhouse.

Sunday he preached twice; Monday he rode in a lumber wagon to Brother Sanborn's in Wisconsin. Tuesday he rode in the same wagon back to Crane's Grove, and Wednesday he took the train for Iowa. Then he had to travel thirty miles in a Western stagecoach. Friday he rode a pony to Iowa City, swimming the river on the pony's back. Sabbath he preached twice in Iowa City, and again on Sunday.

Was he tired or broken down after such a strenuous week of meetings? Far from it. He wrote, "Now, thank the Lord, we are well, free and happy. Health is better than for twelve years."— James White in *Review and Herald*, Aug. 5, 1858.

A glimpse of James White's character is seen in this letter, written by Elder G. I. Butler, twice president of the General Conference.

"I am going to be very bold and very much out of my place. I am going to tell you what I think your duty is. . . . I think you ought both of you to go to the camp meetings. I don't believe it is your duty to settle right down in Battle Creek and for Brother White to run all the little minutia of the office, and take charge of every little thing, and wear himself out that way. . . . But I do believe He wants you to do just what He has told you to do, viz., go from State to State and give the people the benefit of your experience."—George I. Butler letter, to J. White, March 13, 1874.

In the summer of 1873, when the White family went to the Colorado mountains, Mr. Walling, with whom they were staying, suggested that they cross the range and camp at Grand Lake. They joyfully started out. Then, on the way, the axle on one of the wagons broke, and Mr. Walling turned back to get it repaired. A week later his hired man arrived with fresh supplies. Guided by this hired man, the Whites pushed on, finally setting up camp by the lake. When he left, they found themselves very much alone.

Aside from the Whites, the only other persons at that beautiful spot were two fishermen—and they were planning to return to civilization soon, with their fishing harvest. The days went by, and the campers' supply of provisions steadily diminished. One by one they burned up their candles. Each day they expected Mr. Walling, but he did not come.

Elder White had brought with him a copy of a pamphlet which he had promised to re-write and forward to the Review and Herald office in Battle Creek, for reprinting. As he often wrote in the evening, he was concerned about their candle shortage. And work on the pamphlet took longer than he had anticipated.

One morning Willie told his father that the fishermen would

be leaving the next day. Since there was still no sign of Walling, the only way James could get his revised pamphlet to the Review would be to send it with the fishermen for mailing. Unfortunately it was far from finished. He immediately went to work, but realized that he would need light that night—and the candles were all burned up.

Just then he remembered that on a walk with Willie he had seen a dead wolf in a trap not far from their camp. Handing a pan and a hunting knife to his son, James told him to return to the wolf and scrape off every bit of the fat he could find on its body. Willie also carried a double-barreled shotgun, for there were bears in the mountains.

Willie found the dead wolf, cut it open, scraped off all the fat he could, and took it back to camp. Elder White then twisted a rag, placed one end in the cup of melted fat, and lit the other end. With the light thus provided, he wrote on and on, finishing his work on the pamphlet shortly after midnight. The next morning he gave the finished product to the fishermen, who promised to mail it from the nearest post office.

Not long after this, Mr. Walling arrived with fresh provisions for the forsaken campers.

In the meantime, James White's ingenuity had saved the day, enabling him to keep his promise to the Review and Herald.— Arthur L. White, *Campfire Junior Stories* (1961), pp. 33-36.

QUOTES TO PONDER
From the Writings of James White

Seek for truth, search for it as for hid treasure. Be sanctified through the truth. This will enable you to stand. It will enable you to pass all the way through the perils of the last days, and be ready with the watching ones to exclaim, as Jesus comes down through the vaulted heavens, "Lo, this is our God, we have waited for him, and he will save us." We have waited to be changed to immortality. We step upon the sea of glass. We receive the crown, and palm. We walk the golden streets. We eat of the tree of life. We drink from the crystal fountain. We behold the face of Jesus Christ. We walk with the Redeemer. We associate with the angels. And this is the life we are to enjoy forever and ever. God help us to secure it.—*Review and Herald*, June 29, 1869.

The *Review* has never held that it was necessary to make a general chowder of truth and error in its limited columns, in order better to bring out truth. It has aimed to be a clean, straight-forward advocate of truth. Some oppose, and say, Let truth and error have the field together. Error has ever had the field, and, compared with truth, its batteries are a hundred to one. The teachers of error are many, firm, vigilant, and ever on the side of error. Should the one advocate of truth divide its strength under such circumstances, and with one hand help sustain the flag of error? Never! Never!—*Review and Herald*, June 2, 1863.

Why! oh, Why! will men and women who might be respectable, and good, and reach Heaven at last, sell themselves to the Devil so cheap, wound their bosom friends, disgrace their families, bring a reproach upon the cause, and go to hell at last? God have mercy.—*Review and Herald*, March 24, 1868.

Mother, my dear mother! When a few more battles for truth, and for God, are fought, and the storms of life cease, and the shades of the night pass before the glorious light of the morning, when the Coming One shall descend to gather all the just to their final rest and reward, then, mother, by the grace of God, we will meet again.—*Review and Herald,* Jan. 24, 1871.

God pity the world that it has so many putty-faced, dilly-dally, second and third-rate preachers. They may excel indeed in those "good long" afternoon visits, and be eloquent with the knife and fork at the tea table, but in the speaker's stand, as the Californians say, they "pan out" small.—*Review and Herald,* Oct. 7, 1875.

Re. Beards and Mustaches: As to its looks, and the plea that has been advanced, that to shave was to mar the divine beauty of the human visage as God designed it, we must remember that all have not the same ideas of beauty, and that in the eyes of many a projecting mustache and flowing beard, are as apt to make a man look like a rough goat as a venerable patriarch, and perhaps more so.—*Review and Herald,* June 25, 1857.

The *Review* cannot hold everything, and we hope it will ever be too small for spun out matters of local interest. Brethren, condense your resolutions as far as convenient, and be sure to give us stirring reports of what you, in the name of the Lord, *do.*—*Review and Herald,* June 3, 1862.

In view of all He has done for me, the language of my heart is "glory to God in the highest!" Whatever my lot may be—whatever I may be called to pass through, or do, or to bear, may the language of my heart ever be, Glory to God.

This earthly court is a heavenly place for us today. A full tide seems to be setting heavenward. My spirit is triumphant in God. I cannot taper off this subject but must leave it where the angels began it, Glory to God in the highest! Amen.—*Review and Herald,* Jan. 25, 1870.

Now friends, just place yourself in the position of right. Let the heavens gather blackness. Let all hell be astir. Let what will come, be men and women of God. There are ways leading in all directions out into the world. Here is a young theater in this city [Battle Creek]. Should any Seventh-day Adventist be found there, I should feel like putting on sackcloth. When you hear of any visiting that place, please buy a weed [sign of mourning] for my hat.

It is time we knew where we were. When we get into the right position, copious showers of God's blessing will come upon us, and we shall not be as dead as door nails.—*Review and Herald*, March 16, 1869.

The Bible presents one thrilling book called the Acts of the Apostles, but none entitled the Resolutions of the Apostles. It is good to resolve in the strength of the Lord, but better to perform.—*Review and Herald*, June 3, 1862.

Many make this [camp meeting] an occasion of feasting instead of fasting, which stupefies and makes many sick. If fasting is ever a Christian duty, it is at camp-meeting. Most of our tent companies set a table which is not equaled by one in ten of the hotels in our country. Good bread, a few vegetables, and one or two kinds of fruit or sauce, is sufficient for those in health.—*Review and Herald*, Aug. 31, 1869.

Brother Andrews is a man of God. He is a close Bible student. He walks with God, and shares largely of the Holy Spirit direct from the throne. Brother and Sister White, especially when groaning under responsibilities and trials, often find relief in counseling with Brother Andrews and listening to words of wisdom from his lips.—*Review and Herald*, Sept. 22; Oct. 13, 1868.

Everything I touch seems to prosper. And as long as I trust in God, and with a liberal, cheerful independence go forward in faith I expect He will prosper the work of my hands. . . . But we must all joyfully, and hopefully and trustingly press forward. God will help us if we work in Him.—James White letter to Willie and others, Aug. 1, 1875.

Now Smith, Brownsberger, Kellogg, and your parents have taken hold of matters. And we are bound to put them through. Things go very much as I say. I tell all hands that when they put me on a level with others, then they can get some young man to take my place and I will quit. I will try to fill my place, "A Counsellor to the Brethren." When they want my counsel, I will give it. I shall accept no offices. I shall be free. . . .

J. H. Kellogg is a popular surgeon. John is born to be smart. Poor fellow, he weighs only 103, and looks wan. God save the lad and make him a light on the health question.—James White letter to W.C.W., July 21, 1875.

It is said, "It is good for our preachers to labor some." Labor some! What is there but labor in the life of one of God's messengers, who travels through rain or snow, heat or cold, dust or mud, and then at the end of a long tedious day's journey, stands up and preaches two hours, and next day perhaps preaches three discourses, each near two hours long? He needs to labor some, does he? Needs a little exercise for his health, some think! Poor souls, they know nothing of the weary hours of body and mind, sleepless nights, aching heads and weary limbs of these messengers who are wearing out and living at least two years in one. When worn with travel and labor in the field, the Lord's messenger should go to his family, not to labor, but to rest. And if he had a few days to spare time, he should spend it in reading, writing, and teaching his children.— *Review and Herald,* Feb. 4, 1858.

Some of the sisterhood, not excepting old ladies, were decidedly gifted in talking about nothing in particular. When people will talk real sound common sense and religion, we may let them talk; but we confess our utter inability to enjoy hour after hour of common chatter, tinged with vulgar attempts at small wit. If there is anything that can be brought to a camp-meeting which God hates, it is this cheap, driveling nonsense.—*Review and Herald,* Sept. 7, 1876.

There is a period in the lifetime of every man who has trained himself to be a successful burden-bearer and care-taker, when he should seriously consider the fact that the time is not far distant when the feebleness of age will compel him to let those burdens he has well borne pass to the shoulders of others. Here comes in the careful study of every discreet man *when* to begin to lay off the burdens, and *how fast;* or, to learn to grow old gracefully.

The writer has been studying this matter several years. . . . Retired, with the blessing of God, we hope to restore that "lost art" in this fretting generation, of growing old gracefully.— *Review and Herald,* May 15, 1879.

3